Instructor's Manual to Accompany

Responding to Literature

Second Edition

Judith A. Stanford

Rivier College

Mayfield Publishing Company
Mountain View, California
London • Toronto

International Standard Book Number: 1-55934-539-X

Manufactured in the United States of America
10 9 8 7 6 5 4 3 2 1

Mayfield Publishing Company
1280 Villa Street
Mountain View, California 94041

PREFACE

Writing an instructor's guide presents one especially daunting problem: audience. Some instructors using this text are teaching an introductory literature course for the first time; others have taught the course for five, fifteen, twenty-five years or more. Some teach in small, two-year colleges, others in large universities. Some teach mainly traditional-age students from small rural communities; others teach classes filled with students of diverse ages from diverse backgrounds.

Never forgetting the complexity of this audience, yet trying to make writing this guide easier for myself, I tried to imagine common ground. As I wrote, I envisioned teachers of infinite variety who share a common goal: commitment to exploring various ways of teaching a course that introduces literature and also stresses the development of reading and writing skills. Keeping this audience in mind, I've written suggestions for those who are beginning to teach, discussed approaches for developing an interactive classroom, considered the development of goals and of methods of evaluation, provided sample syllabi, and discussed approaches for the first week of class. In addition, I've made specific teaching suggestions for the first four chapters as well as for the thematic sections. Please realize that I wrote each section of this guide to offer options. Intending to open possibilities—not to prescribe the only correct way or the only useful way or the only humane way to teach this course—I suggest processes and approaches that have worked for me and for my colleagues.

I would like very much to hear your responses—and your students' responses—both to the suggestions in this guide and to the text. Any teaching ideas you care to send will be considered for inclusion in the guide for the next edition of *Responding to Literature*.

CONTENTS

FOR BEGINNING TEACHERS: PREPARING TO TEACH
INTRODUCTORY LITERATURE/WRITING COURSES   1

DEVELOPING AN INTERACTIVE CLASSROOM   7

ESTABLISHING GOALS; MAKING EVALUATIONS   10

SAMPLE SYLLABI   13

INTRODUCTIONS   19

TEACHING CHAPTER 1: WHY READ LITERATURE?   27

TEACHING CHAPTER 2: JOINING THE CONVERSATION   35

TEACHING CHAPTER 3: CONTINUING THE CONVERSATION   39

TEACHING CHAPTER 4: WRITING ABOUT LITERATURE   44

CHAPTERS 5 TO 12: LITERARY THEMES   48

  CHAPTER 5: INNOCENCE AND EXPERIENCE   49

  CHAPTER 6: ROOTS, IDENTITY, AND CULTURE   73

  CHAPTER 7: WORK   91

  CHAPTER 8: MEN AND WOMEN   105

  CHAPTER 9: PARENTS AND CHILDREN   124

  CHAPTER 10: LEARNING AND TEACHING   140

  CHAPTER 11: WAR AND POWER   157

  CHAPTER 12: DEATH   175

CHAPTER 13: THREE AMERICAN POETS   194

CONNECTIONS: ART AND POETRY   206

FOR BEGINNING TEACHERS: PREPARING TO TEACH INTRODUCTORY LITERATURE/WRITING COURSES

What assumptions can be made about instructors who are teaching this course for the first time? Many will be graduate students; others will have just completed a graduate degree. Some instructors will have taken courses or participated in training seminars designed to help them as they begin teaching; others will have no such formal background. I'm going to make what may be an enormous leap of faith and assume that all new instructors share at least one thing with each other as well as with experienced instructors: love of literature. The question, then, becomes how to put this love to work in the classroom.

After talking to people whom I consider outstanding teachers of introductory literature and writing courses, and from constantly examining and evaluating my own teaching, I've come to believe that the teaching process is both incredibly fascinating and incredibly fluid. I don't believe it's possible ever to come to a point where one says, "Well, this it it. Now I know how to teach this class in the most effective way. This is how I'll teach it for the rest of my life." The options that I suggest in this manual are those that work right now for me or for instructors I know and respect. I offer these possibilities, knowing that within the next year—even within the next few months—I'll reread what I've written and see that I've changed my way of looking at a process or that I've discovered a new idea I wish I'd included.

To keep working on my own approaches to teaching, I've found the following processes essential:

LISTENING

I do a great deal of informal listening, both to colleagues and to students. If you're lucky enough to teach at a school where instructors readily share ideas and who are not afraid to discuss classroom disasters as well as successes, then you know what I mean. Listening carefully to what other instructors say about their teaching, learning what texts they are using, what writing assignments they are giving, how they are inspiring discussions, and how they view their students helps me to think about what I want to do—as well as what I do not want to do—in my own courses.

I listen, also, to what my students tell me. Most colleges and universities provide end-of-term evaluations, and students' suggestions have often provided me with easy ways to make the course more effective. The problem with end-of-term evaluations, of course, is that the students who make the suggestions fail to benefit from them. I've found it helpful to give questionnaires after four or five weeks of class, asking students to respond anonymously and drop their completed evaluations in campus mail to me. This process allows me to use a class-specific format (for instance, one class might need changes to facilitate discussion whereas another might have problems with group work). I don't jump to make a change in response to every student's criticism, but I've found that many times their observations have been astute and helpful.

Another kind of listening that encourages, inspires—and sometimes infuriates—me is the listening I do at conferences. Consider attending local and national conferences held by organizations such as the National Council of Teachers of English (NCTE) and the Modern Language Association (MLA). Keynote speakers as well as presenters in smaller sessions provide so much to think about that you need the long plane or car ride home to decompress your brain.

TALKING

The twin of listening is talking. I am forever grateful to the many friends, relatives, colleagues, and students who have allowed me to talk out my ideas about teaching. Putting thoughts into words, watching the expressions of others as they listen, and hearing their responses help me to understand how I am changing—and how I need to change—as a teacher. (Spontaneous conversations are great, but we are all incredibly busy. I find it essential to plan time—early breakfasts often work well—to talk with the people whose willingness to listen gives me a chance to grow.)

In addition to informal talking, consider speaking at local or national conferences. Putting thoughts together for a workshop or panel presentation forces me to rethink my ideas and to consider them in light of a broader audience than my own students and colleagues.

OBSERVING

I'm fortunate to have colleagues who welcome visitors to their classes. Watching different people—with different teaching styles—helps me to see classroom interaction from a new perspective. In addition to visiting classes taught by others, I pay close attention whenever I find myself in a student-like situation. For instance, when I attend a conference, I stay alert not only to the content of workshops, panel discussions, and addresses but also to the approaches the presenters use to reach their audience. As I monitor my own responses, in addition to the responses of others attending the session, I can easily identify the approaches that gain intrigued attention as well as the ones that cause yawns, restless squirming, and impatient glances at the clock.

Besides observing other teachers and their students, I observe my own students. Their expressions and gestures often show me who is bored, puzzled, irritated, amused, or amazed. Understanding their responses helps me to know when our work is going smoothly as well as to anticipate problems and to try to correct them.

READING

Of course I read the authors I will be teaching as well as biographies and critical books and articles relating to these authors and their works. Although it's impossible to research thoroughly each author I'll be teaching in an anthology, I pick two or three every semester and every summer as a focus for pleasure reading. Usually I choose at least one author who is new to me, someone a colleague may have mentioned or I may have read about in a review or seen listed in the table of contents of an anthology. I also read familiar authors, rereading one or two favorite poems or stories and then seeking out works by these authors that I have not read before. I've found reading new selections absolutely essential to help me keep in tune with what my students feel as they approach a complex work for the first time.

In addition to reading literature, biography, and criticism, reading works explaining the theory and practice of people I consider master teachers has become increasingly important to me. As I read what these teachers have to say, I never agree with everything they think and do. In fact, I usually find myself involved in a hot debate, resisting this idea or that observation. Later, when I read the notes I've scribbled in the margins and on the end papers I'm often astonished at how intensely I originally disagreed with a point I now find quite compatible. Observing these changes, I've come to realize that what sometimes seems unworkable or wrongheaded to me at first later "fits" with something I see in my own classroom and provides me with a new way to approach a problem or difficulty I've never before been able to solve.

Most college and department libraries subscribe to journals related to the teaching of literature and writing. Periodicals like *College English, College Composition and Communication, Teaching English in the Two-Year College, College Teaching,* and *Reader: Essays in Reader-Oriented Theory, Criticism, and Pedagogy* provide a broad range of possibilities.

There are dozens of fine books related to teaching literature and writing, but the five that have been most important to me are these:

Nancie Atwell, *In the Middle* (Portsmouth, NH: Boynton/Cook/Heinemann, 1987).

> I list Atwell's book with a bit of trepidation because she describes teaching literature and writing to eighth-grade students rather than to college freshmen and sophomores. However, her philosophy of teaching, her practical approaches to classroom management, and most of all, her engagement both with the reading/writing process and with her students make what she has to say useful and inspiring to teachers at all levels.

Mike Rose, *Lives on the Boundary* (New York: Penguin, 1989).

> Rose's account of his own struggles to be admitted to the "literary conversation" and his description of his students' struggles suggest new ways of looking not only at students but also at each instructor's progress through the academic world. Rose's refusal to write students off as culturally illiterate or as ignorant beings who are nearly impossible to educate provides new hope and encouragement for those teaching introductory courses.

Louise Rosenblatt, *Literature as Exploration*, 4th ed. (New York: MLA, 1976), and *The Reader, the Text, the Poem* (Carbondale: Southern Illinois UP, 1978).

> In these books, Rosenblatt sees reader and literary work as equally important. She provides a compelling, lucid, and sensible description of the literary experience (of both neophyte and experienced readers). In addition, she proposes a classroom where the instructor is not expected to provide an

accepted interpretation (or even several accepted interpretations) of a given work. Instead, instructor and students work together exploring the possibilities their reading opens. Rosenblatt has the admirable ability to combine theoretical explanation with practical examples from her own reading process as well as from classroom experiences and observations.

Robert Scholes, *Textual Power: Literary Theory and the Teaching of English* (New Haven, CT: Yale UP, 1985).

Scholes convincingly demonstrates that literary theory cannot be separated from the teaching of literature. My absolute favorite parts of the book are Chapters 2, 3, and 4, where Scholes invites the reader to explore a text—Hemingway's *In Our Time* —with him. I found myself digging out my dusty copy of these interconnected short stories, stopping to read the sections Scholes suggested, and then reading his discussion. The experience provides a glimpse of what it must be like to study texts in a classroom with Scholes. His approaches left my mind racing with possibilities for my own teaching.

WRITING

I have always written with my students. While I don't do every assignment, I try to complete at least one for each class I teach, and I often write outlines for others. Sometimes I use these as sample pieces to suggest possibilities to students. Sometimes the writing serves as an exercise that alerts me to the strengths and weaknesses of that assignment. When students write in class, I write along with them. I still feel a clutch of anxiety before I read aloud what I have written, and that reminds me how much more difficult it must be for many of the students when their turn comes.

In addition to writing with students, it seems to me a good thing for those of us who teach English to write something every year or two that we intend to submit for publication. (Of course, I realize many colleges and universities require faculty to publish far more.) It's been important for me to write about the books I teach and about my teaching process because, true to what we tell our students, writing is a way of thinking. When I write, I discover questions, possibilities, and ideas I never knew I had. In addition, waiting for responses from editors and reviewers—and then reading those students as they submit papers for me to judge. I find myself far less irritated with students who worry about grades when I stop to consider my own responses to the acceptance, rejection, criticism, or praise of something I have written.

DEVELOPING AN INTERACTIVE CLASSROOM

For teaching and for learning in the introductory literature and writing course, I believe an interactive structure works more effectively than does a traditional, lecture-dominated structure. In the interactive classroom, students and instructor work together. The instructor does much more than simply prepare a lecture and deliver information to students. Students do much more than read assignments, listen to lectures, and deliver unprocessed information back to the instructor through writing exams and papers.

In the interactive classroom students take responsibility for their own learning while the instructor provides whatever help and encouragement they need to accomplish this task. Some strategies that encourage interactive learning include the following:

1. **Build a sense of community and trust in the classroom.**

2. **Use warm-up writing sessions to initiate discussion.**

3. **Break a large class into small groups for discussion or for work on writing projects.** Often students who are uncomfortable speaking or asking questions in a large class situation are more at ease when they work in groups of three to five. In addition to the possible approaches to group work, consider the following issues:

    *   *Should students choose their own groups or should the instructor assign groups?* I like to vary my approach. Sometimes I ask students to form their own groups; at other times I assign groups to ensure a variety of voices in each group.

    *   *Should instructors participate with groups or stay away?* Opinion varies greatly among the proponents of group work. Most believe that instructors should interfere very little. Some believe that the instructor should leave the room entirely while groups meet. I usually sit by myself, reading or writing and not looking at students for the first few minutes. Then I move around from group to group, mostly listening, but occasionally responding to a question or making a comment.

- *Should groups always or nearly always work toward or reach consensus?* I think it's important to stress that the point of much group work is to discover multiple possibilities. Certainly students should be encouraged to think critically about one another's ideas, but it's not always necessary or desirable that a group arrive at a single, neatly planned response.

4.   **Be aware of the dynamics of full class discussions.**

- *Recognize that the arrangement of chairs can help or hinder free exchange of ideas.*

- *Understand that students often choose to sit in the same seats at each class and that "silent ghettos" can develop— areas of the classroom from which no voices are heard.* I find that I can sometimes break the silence barrier by choosing to sit or stand in that area of the classroom and by speaking directly to students who are sitting there. If anyone makes eye contact with me, I direct my next query or "long pause" toward him or her.

- *Recognize that some students may dominate discussion.* To allow time for students who may be shy, or who may think more cautiously than others, I sometimes watch the clock and half way through class announce that I appreciate the hard work and thoughtful observations made by those who have already commented. Then I encourage them to sit back and enjoy listening for the rest of the class period (or for the next ten or twenty minutes or whatever seems right) while those who have not yet spoken offer their ideas. Sometimes I have to wait many seconds before one of the quieter students volunteers, but once one has spoken, the floodgates open. (This strategy works best if the discussion has started with a warm-up writing. Then everyone has some thoughts committed to paper. Reluctant speakers may be willing to read what they have written as a way to begin their participation.)

- *Understand that gender issues can affect classroom participation.* Research suggests that, contrary to popular belief, men tend to dominate discussions and to interrupt more often than women do. In addition, discussion often follows "gender runs." If a man speaks first, then other men are likely to follow. When a woman does break into the conversation, others usually follow her. If I notice a gender run going on too long, I'll sometimes interrupt and direct the discussion to someone of the opposite sex. I watch students carefully and choose someone who looks as though he or she is waiting with something to say.

- *Understand that cultural differences may affect willingness to participate in class discussion.* For instance, some silent students may come from cultures where teachers do all the talking and where it is considered extremely rude to challenge or question a statement made by an authority figure. Be aware that students whose first language is not English may fear that others will laugh at or be impatient with their hesitant speech or less-than-perfect English.

5. **Require at least one office conference for each student.** Seeing students on a one-to-one basis, as early in the semester as possible, provides them with an opportunity to discuss any concerns they may have about the class. The early visit shows them the way to my office, lets them know that I am available, and encourages them to return with any questions or observations they may have about the assigned reading and writing.

ESTABLISHING GOALS;
MAKING EVALUATIONS

Establishing goals and making evaluations go together. I have to know what I (and my department) expect students to gain from the course before I can judge to what degree they have succeeded.

PLANNING GOALS

As I plan course goals, I keep in mind both short-term and long-term objectives. For example, a short-term objective might be for students to learn how to integrate quotations into their own writing. This skill enables them to do the kind of writing commonly encountered in academic settings. Another short-term goal might be learning how to write a well-planned, clearly organized response to a literary work. On the other hand, a long-term goal might be for students to develop pleasure in their own responses to literature and confidence in their own ability to evaluate what they read. Ideally, achieving this goal would lead them to regard reading as an integral, enjoyable part of their lives and not as a tedious, boring chore to be dreaded. I usually state goals on the syllabus in rather general terms to allow flexibility during the term. In addition, I encourage students to establish their own goals within the framework of the course requirements.

Establishing goals requires thinking about the direction the course will take. Will it emphasize reading literature or writing about literature? Or will both processes be equally valued? Will literary genres be stressed? Or will literary themes be emphasized? Or will students spend equal time studying genres and themes? How much will students be expected to write? What kinds of writing will they do? Primarily response? Primarily evaluative or analytic? A combination of both?

Establishing goals and considering the direction of the course also leads to thinking about ways of teaching. If I want students to learn to evaluate literature, how am I going to enable them to do that? If I expect them to be able to integrate quotations usefully and sensibly into their writing, how will I demonstrate that process?

For a sample of the goals I set for "Writing and Literature," the introductory course I teach, see the syllabi in the next section.

EVALUATING

While I'm setting goals, thinking about the direction of the course, and planning ways to teach, I consider how I will evaluate students as they work toward those goals. Short-term goals—goals that students can be expected to achieve during the time they are taking the course—are the only goals I can evaluate. Long-term goals must be evaluated by the students themselves. For example, I can assess students' ability to use evidence from a text to support an explanation of their response to that text (a short-term goal), but I cannot evaluate whether they have come to regard reading literature as an important and enjoyable part of their lives. While discussing the syllabus during the first week of classes, I point out the distinction between short-term and long-term goals so students will understand clearly the objectives I'll consider as I evaluate their progress and determine their grades.

To establish the evaluation process, I decide how many papers I will assign and how much weight I will give to each paper and to the midterm and final exams. In addition, I decide how much weight I will give to journals and to class discussion. For a sixteen-week course, I usually assign a journal, three papers, one in-class essay that serves as a midterm exam, and a final exam. I've found that students do best in my classes and develop the most positive responses toward literature and writing when I use an evaluation process that stresses growth and improvement. To accomplish this goal, I encourage students to revise their papers, and I consider both the original paper and the revision when writing my final comments and determining the grade. One evaluation system that has worked well is this:

Three short papers (3–5 pages)   *each paper, 20%*

> For each paper, I read and provide global comments for the *first draft*, but I do not grade it. I read and comment carefully on the *next submitted draft* and grade it.

> Students may choose to submit a *revision* for which I also provide comments and a grade. I arrive at the final grade for the paper by averaging the two grades. If students choose not to submit a revision, the original grade counts the full 20%.

Assignments for the papers vary. I want each student to write one response, one comparison, and one analytic or evaluative paper during the semester.

In-class essay (midterm exam)	10%

Journals (two entries per week totaling at least 250 words)   10%

I read and comment on journals, but I do not grade them. If students complete the requirement, they receive full credit.

Class participation   5%

I'm very lenient on this one. If a student attends class regularly (missing no more than three to five class hours) and makes a serious effort to participate at least in small groups, I give full credit even if he or she has spoken very little in the large class setting.

Final exam   15%

SAMPLE SYLLABI

FIFTEEN-WEEK SEMESTER:
EMPHASIS ON LITERARY THEMES

LITERATURE AND WRITING EN 220-E

Judith Stanford
Fall 199x

Office Location: Writing Center

Office Telephone: x581
Office Hours:
      Tues. 5:00–6 : 00 P.M.
      Thurs. 7:30–9:30 A.M.

Required Text: *Responding to Literature,* Stanford, 1992, Mayfield

Goals:

- To develop the following abilities by reading and responding to literature:

  Reading thoughtfully, critically, and creatively

  Understanding and practicing the writing process more fully

  Expanding vocabulary

  Developing oral communication skills

- To consider the connections among literature and other parts of life through exploring literary themes related to the human experience

- To enjoy reading literature, to trust your responses to what you read, and to develop confidence in your ability to evaluate what you read

Evaluation Criteria:

Three papers, 3–5 pages, each worth 20%; journals, 10%; midterm in-class essay, 10%; class participation, 5%; final exam, 15%

Attendance Policy:

I will make every effort to attend each class and to be well prepared; I expect you to do the same. If you must miss more than three class hours, please make an appointment with me, as excessive absence may prevent your successful completion of the course.

Week 1:   Introductions

Reading assignment: Chapter 1

Writing assignment: Make notes on poem of choice leading to an oral response

Week 2:   Reading assignment: Chapter 2

Writing assignment: Write four paragraphs; each should respond to one of the four works at the beginning of Chapter 2. For inspiration, see the suggestions for responding that follow each selection.

Week 3:   Reading assignment: Chapter 3

Week 4:   Reading assignment: Chapter 4

Writing assignment: Begin first paper, Writing a Response

Week 5:   INNOCENCE AND EXPERIENCE

Reading assignment: 2–4 short stories
1–3 poems
1 essay

Writing assignment: Submit draft of first paper

Week 6:   INNOCENCE AND EXPERIENCE

Reading assignment: 1 short story
1 drama
1–3 poems

Writing assignment: Review draft of response paper, returned with comments; work on revision with group

Week 7:   WORK

Reading assignment: 2–4 short stories
1–3 poems
1 essay

Writing assignment: Submit response paper

Week 8:   WORK

Reading assignment: 1 short story
1 drama
1–3 poems

Writing assignment: MIDTERM IN-CLASS ESSAY
(1 HOUR)

Review first paper, returned with comments
and grade

Begin comparison paper (reread and discuss comparison
section in Chapter 3)

Week 9:   MEN AND WOMEN

Reading assignment: 2–4 short stories
3–5 poems
1 drama
1 essay

Writing assignment: Submit draft of comparison paper

Week 10:   PARENTS AND CHILDREN

Reading assignment: 3–5 short stories
3–5 poems
1 essay

Writing assignment: Review draft of comparison paper,
returned with comments; work on revision with group

Submit final revision of response paper; include all
drafts with revision

Week 11:   PARENTS AND CHILDREN

Reading assignment: 1–2 short stories
1 drama
1–2 poems or 1 essay

Writing assignment: Submit comparison paper

Week 12:   WAR AND POWER

Reading assignment: 2–4 short stories (or drama and 1
                       short story)
                       1–3 poems
                       1 essay

Writing assignment: Review comparison papers, returned
    with comments and grades

Begin analysis or evaluation paper (Reread analysis
    section on pages 103–109 and evaluation section on
    pages 121–130 in Chapter 4)

Week 13:   LEARNING AND TEACHING

Reading assignment: 3–5 short stories
                       3–5 poems
                       1 essay

Writing assignment: Submit draft of analysis or evaluation
    paper

Week 14:   LEARNING AND TEACHING

Reading assignment: 1–2 short stories
                       drama
                       1–2 poems or 1 essay

Writing assignment: Review draft of analysis or evaluation
    paper, returned with comments; work on revision with
    group

Submit final revision of comparison paper; include all
    drafts with revision

Week 15:   DEATH

Reading assignment: 2–4 short stories
                       1–3 poems
                       1 essay

Writing assignment: Submit analysis or evaluation paper

EIGHT-WEEK QUARTER

Introductory material: same as for fifteen-week course except for **Evaluation Criteria.** Change to the following:

Two papers, 3–5 pages, 25% each; journals, 10%; midterm, in-class essay, 15%; class participation, 5%; final exam, 20%

Week 1:   Introductions

Reading assignment: Chapter 1
Chapter 4, Introduction and Section
on Writing a Response Essay

Writing assignment: Begin response paper

Week 2:   Reading assignment: Chapter 2
Complete Chapter 4

Writing assignment: Submit draft of response paper

Week 3:   Reading assignment: Chapter 3

Writing assignment: Review draft of response papers;
work on revision with group in class

Weeks 4–8: Reading assignments—3–5 literary themes (one to
two weeks on each theme):
2–4 short stories
(or 1 story; 1 drama)
1–3 poems
1 essay

Writing assignments:
Week 4:   Submit response paper; begin analytic or
evaluative paper

Midterm in-class writing (comparison):
one class hour

Week 5:   Submit draft of analytic or evaluative
paper; receive response paper

Week 6:   Review draft of analytic or evaluative
paper; work on revision with group

Week 7:   Submit analytic or evaluative paper

Week 8:   Submit revised response paper;
            receive analytic or evaluative paper

INTRODUCTIONS

Planning the first class meeting often requires ingenuity. Many students have not yet purchased their books. In addition, at most colleges and universities, instructors can expect several students not present at the first meeting to show up at the second.

Some instructors keep the first class short by simply calling the roll, distributing the syllabus, and dismissing students with an assignment for the next class. But with the limited hours each semester provides for class time, early dismissal seems to me a terrible waste. Other instructors prepare a lecture that introduces the study of literature and explains the syllabus and then spend time in their office going over the information with students who join the class late. My own favorite way of getting started conveys essential, practical information; begins to develop a community of readers and writers; and introduces the study of literature.

ADDRESSING PRACTICAL CONCERNS

I accomplish the first goal in the time-honored way of distributing the syllabus and mentioning practical items that are generally of great importance to students: for example, required texts, methods of evaluation, attendance policy, office hours, and, of course, the assignment for the next class. I then ask students to read the syllabus carefully and to bring any questions they have to the next class meeting. At the first class meeting, I try to limit time spent distributing and commenting on the syllabus to five minutes.

Delaying any detailed discussion of the syllabus and course requirements until the second class, and asking students to read the syllabus, often allows them to discover questions they might not have raised following a cursory skimming during the first class. This process also encourages students to spend time getting an overview of the course and to seek information actively rather than passively listen to my paraphrase of the syllabus. In addition, at the second class meeting, late arrivals to the course get a chance to hear their fellow students' questions and my responses, and then to ask their own questions. (If the class meets only once a week, I am forced by that time structure to pass out the syllabus during the first part of class, ask that students read it at break, and then discuss their questions during the second part of the class.)

BUILDING A COMMUNITY OF READERS AND WRITERS

For a course to thrive on sharing both written and oral responses to literature, trust among students as well as between students and instructor is essential. Obviously, I don't march into class the first day and announce, "This class will have trust!" But I do begin each new course by helping students to get to know me and to know each other.

If I am teaching in a room that permits moving furniture, I arrive early and move the desks into a circle or, if the class is large, into several nested semicircles. The point is to have a structure that encourages students to talk to each other and not to address every comment or observation primarily to the instructor (a practice that is hard to avoid with the traditional chairs-in-rows configuration). At the end of the first class meeting, I ask students to help return chairs to the original layout; I also ask that those who arrive early for the next and subsequent class meetings move the chairs to the circle structure.

On the day of the first class meeting, arriving at least twenty minutes early allows me time to get the chairs moved and to greet early arrivals. By asking their names as they arrive and writing them down with a quick note of description ("George Porter: dark-rimmed glasses"), I usually learn several names before the class even begins.

At the start of class, following the five-minute distribution of the syllabus, I introduce myself and then ask students to introduce themselves. The easiest way to do this is to go around the circle, with each person giving his or her name plus one or two introductory statements. I encourage students to tell something that will suggest their special interests or abilities because we are all developing a sense of audience. (And I point out that when I say "we," I really *mean* "we." *I* need to know my audience just as much as they need to know theirs.) We are all getting to know the people we will be writing and talking with for the weeks to follow. I also suggest that students try to learn the names of at least five other students during the introductions. I believe that when people call each other by name, they often begin to see each other as individuals and not just as "that kid in the back" or "that older guy" or "the one who wears black all the time."

Taking this approach provides a fine opportunity for reviewing (or introducing) the concept of audience—of writing with readers in mind and speaking with listeners in mind. Consider asking students to suggest some categories of things they would like to know about people who will be listening to what they say and reading what they write. If they jot down a few questions they would like to ask potential readers/listeners, they'll often more readily volunteer responses that you can write on the board.

Even when students have prepared a list, you can expect some reticence when you ask them to suggest questions they might want to ask. Try to wait out the silence if you don't get an immediate response. Research suggests that teachers typically wait less than three-tenths of a second before answering their own questions. Try waiting at least ten seconds (which seems like a very long time when there's utter silence) before prompting students further. This strategy is especially important at the first meeting because that class often sets patterns that students come to expect for the rest of the semester.

These are typical questions students say they would like to ask each other:

- What kind of paid work do you do or have you done?

- Do you do any kind of volunteer work?

- What activities do you enjoy?

- Where do you come from?

- What other states or countries have you visited? What was your reaction to those places?

- What made you decide to come to this school?

- After you graduate, what are your goals?

- What kinds of films do you like? Why?

- What was the most important decision you ever made?

- What were the results of that decision?

After students have suggested their questions, I usually give an example of my own desire to know my audience better. Because we will be reading together, I'd like to know what kind of reading they most enjoy. I'm curious to know whether they read a daily newspaper. What section do they turn to first? And why? Do they subscribe to or read certain magazines? Which ones? And, of course, what books do they read purely for pleasure? For information?

I ask students to keep the questions they have generated in mind, as well as questions I have suggested. Giving them a few minutes to jot down some observations about themselves and providing them with examples of previous students' comments makes the introductory exercise more varied and lively.

Here are some examples of introductory comments:

> I've changed my major three times because every time I take a new subject I get convinced that that's what I want to do.

> I work at a hospital as a nurse's aide and I don't know what I want to do when I grow up, but I do know I don't want to do anything that has to do with the medical profession.

> I made a decision not to go to college when I got out of high school. Now, ten years later, I feel like a different person, and that decision doesn't fit anymore. So I changed my mind and came back.

> My family has lived in England for the past five years. The thing that has surprised me most is how much most people there know about American history and American politics.

Although comments like these are not directly related to the study of literature, they serve as ways of helping both the instructor and the students to connect with each other's lives. I believe such connection is essential for developing a classroom atmosphere that promotes the risk-taking necessary for honest writing and open discussion.

For a fifty-five-minute class, I plan twenty to thirty minutes for these introductions. If your class meets for longer than fifty-five minutes, you may want to use a more elaborate version of this exercise. For example, after using the process described above to discover possible questions, you might ask pairs of students to interview each other for five to ten minutes. Students then introduce each other rather than themselves to the class. When I use this structure, I usually invite the person who is being introduced to add any comments he or she would like to make.

INTRODUCING LITERATURE

After distributing the syllabus and leading the introductory exercise (about thirty minutes), I ask students to sit back and relax, to put down pens and pencils, and to close notebooks. I tell them that I'm going to read them a story (or a poem or an essay) that I like. I talk about literature as having a strong oral tradition, explaining that long before most people could read or write, and even before written language existed, men, women, and children told stories and sang or recited poetry.

In modern times, once children can read to themselves they are seldom read to, but in the not-so-distant past, before the advent of radio and television, families and friends gathered to hear the latest installment of a serialized novel or to listen to the familiar rhythm of a well-known poem. I read aloud often in class, and I frequently ask students to read aloud because I believe that language becomes far more moving and powerful—and is often understood in more varied ways—when it is heard as well as read.

I tell students that when I finish reading, I'll be interested in hearing their response, but that they will not be quizzed or tested on what I read. I also tell them that they will not be asked to come up with a "correct meaning"; I'm simply interested in the thoughts and feelings the selection evokes.

In choosing a selection, I look for something quite short and highly accessible. I also read the selection several times before class so that while I am reading, I can look up at students most of the time, using eye contact to help keep them engaged in what they are hearing. Selections in this text that work well include the following:

Title and Author   **Text Page**

Fiction

"The Use of Force," William Carlos Williams   540

"The Storm," Kate Chopin   645

"The Lesson," Toni Cade Bambara   914

Poems

"My Papa's Waltz," Theodore Roethke   827

"Making the Jam Without You," Maxine Kumin   828

"The School Children," Louise Glück   947

"Ethics," Linda Pastan   949

"Mid-term Break," Seamus Heaney   203

Essays

"Salvation," Langston Hughes   329

"My People," Chief Seattle   528

After I finish reading, I ask students to sit and think about what they have heard for a minute or two. Then I ask them to write for five minutes, describing their response. Usually, I do not collect these responses, and I tell the students that I will not read them but that they will share what they have written during class discussion.

I provide the following examples of responses, assuring them that their own response need not conform to these patterns; they are offered only as possibilities.

- A description of the emotions (anger, amusement, indignation, pleasure) the selection evoked and an explanation of what specifically caused this response.

- A comment on an idea, character, description, and so forth, that seemed particularly intriguing, aggravating, strange, powerful, or . . .

- A comparison between some event, conflict, idea, character, or place in the selection and a similar event, conflict, idea, character, or place from the student's own experiences.

- A question about something that was puzzling, strange, complex, or hard to understand.

- An explanation of why the reader agreed or disagreed with the opinions, choices, or values suggested by the selection.

After students have written for five minutes, I ask them to stop. For a class that meets for fifty-five or seventy-five minutes, I ask them to save their responses to bring to the next class, thank them for their hard work and attention, repeat the assignment for the next class, and say good-bye.

For classes that meet for two to three hours at a time, I usually have students take a break at this point. When they return, I respond to their questions about the syllabus (which they have read during the break). Then I ask them to work in small groups of three or four, sharing with each other their responses to the story, poem, or essay I read during the first part of the class. (For classes that meet for fifty-five or seventy-five minutes, I do this same exercise at the second class meeting, following the extended discussion of the syllabus. I usually reread the selection so that it will be fresh in everyone's mind; this is especially important for those students who have just joined the course).

I ask students to use the following structure for the small group discussion:

1.   State their names and try to use names as they talk with each other.

2.   Choose one person to take notes during the discussion and to act as speaker for the group when the class reconvenes.

3.   Have *each* person read his or her response *before* any discussion of the responses.

4.   Discuss reactions to the responses.

While the small groups are working, I move around from group to group. Sometimes, I sit down and listen for a short while. I try not to comment although I do answer, briefly, questions that are addressed to me.

I usually allow from ten to fifteen minutes for the discussion, depending on the length of the class period and the engagement of students with the discussion. For instance, after five minutes, if they've all read their responses and are sitting there looking at each other or have segued onto topics totally unrelated to the task at hand, I'll reconvene the class and ask the speakers to describe what their group had to say. I ask speakers to address their comments to the whole group, and not just to me, and I invite students to take notes so they can remember their responses to what they hear and can use these thoughts in the discussion following the speakers' reports.

As each speaker talks, I take brief notes, and I work hard to refrain from commenting aloud. When all speakers have given their reports, I invite discussion. Usually, after a warm-up like this, several students will volunteer observations or questions. When a lull comes, I ask whether their responses changed at all after they heard what others had to say. After discussing this possibility, I like to reread the selection—or parts of the selection—sometimes stopping at crucial points to comment on observations that have come from the previous discussion.

To bring this class meeting to a close, I repeat the assignment for the next class. Then, using the notes I made as the speakers talked, I comment on the responses that came from the group discussions. Because I think it is essential to establish a positive tone at the beginning of a course, I work hard to acknowledge the strengths I saw. I might mention a particularly intriguing connection that had not previously occurred to me or a question that I'll think about the next time I read the selection or an observation that seemed to me especially aptly phrased. I praise at least one comment from each group, and, while I believe any class meeting is improved by gentle humor, I try my best not to say anything that will be interpreted as ridicule or sarcasm.

Because I have usually had a good time with this first class, I state my pleasure, thank students for their energy and effort, and tell them that I look forward to hearing more of their responses throughout the term.

TEACHING CHAPTER 1:
WHY READ LITERATURE?

This text will be used most frequently in required courses that are often taken somewhat reluctantly by students who have diverse backgrounds, varying interests, and dissimilar career goals. During the past twenty years, fewer and fewer of the students in introductory classes have been English or humanities majors. Many start their required literature and writing classes with a combination of resignation, resentment, and a desire to "get it over with." In addition, students come from high school English classes that range from superb to absolutely dreadful—with far too many in the middle ground of dull mediocrity. Many students view literature as difficult, puzzling, and boring; they see no reason for reading literature and many have vowed in their hearts never to read another literary selection after they complete their college requirements.

Through the years, I've heard over and over again fears and complaints from students similar to these:

- I like to have clear answers and to be able to see what answer is right. In literature classes that never happens.

- Literature has hidden meanings, and I can't ever seem to see them.

- Literature is so hard to read. Why can't they just say it in simple terms?

- Most literature is sad and depressing. I have enough troubles of my own; I don't want to read about other people's problems.

- Most literature is boring. I just can't get interested.

- I like to read literature, but I can't remember all the little details so I never get good grades on quizzes.

- I never have the same view as the teacher so I can't get a good grade.

- I don't see what reading literature has to do with being a nurse (or a computer analyst or a business executive or a technical writer or a lawyer, and so on).

Recognizing such complexities, instructors have every right to feel discouraged. Yet, I believe that many of these reluctant students can be convinced that reading literature does add an important and rewarding dimension to their lives. Because I've come to anticipate concerns such as those listed above, I try to make sure to address these issues (although not always directly) during the first week or two of class.

To prepare students for discussion, assign Chapter 1 as homework and ask students to come to class with brief written responses to each of the exercises. You may want to collect these written responses at the end of the class period to get an idea of your students' literary sophistication and writing ability. If you do plan to collect and read these paragraphs, consider these options:

- Ask students not to put their names on the papers; explain that you will read them to get to know the class as a whole, not to judge the abilities of individuals.

or

- Ask students to sign their papers. Explain that you will not grade or return the papers; you are reading them only to get to know the students better.

or

- Ask students to sign their papers. Explain that you will not grade them but that you will return them with a brief comment.

or

- Ask students to sign their papers. Explain that you will return them with a grade. [My own preference is to grade nothing so early in the term.]

Begin the discussion by asking students to read or explain their response to the ideas expressed by the sample paragraphs in the chapter. You might mention to them that many students see a sharp distinction between what they read for pleasure and what they read for school assignments. This is a great time to get them talking about what they read for relaxation. The discussion sometimes moves faster if you discuss your own pleasure reading, particularly if—like most of us—you sometimes enjoy a mystery, a science-fiction novel, a spy thriller, or even those thick tomes that trade publishers call "family sagas." Students seem to think that professors spend all their leisure time reading obscure epics in the original Greek. Letting them know that you, too, sometimes read strictly for entertainment helps to establish common ground.

Sometimes students are reluctant to describe what they read, but those who are self-confident enough to be honest often express variations of these responses:

> Stephen King! I could relate to the guy who
> reads King because I've read every novel he's
> written and to me he's great.

> I read Danielle Steele. Her stories have happy
> endings and they make me forget my own problems.

> The guy who writes about places and how they
> got started . . . yeah . . . Michener. The first
> hundred pages you really have to struggle with
> but then the story gets good.

> The *Clan of the Cave Bear* and her other stuff.
> I couldn't believe all the research, and she made that
> ancient history seem real.

Certainly these are not reading choices to gladden the heart of the literature instructor, yet they open the door of possibility. After listening to some examples of students' relaxation reading and after mentioning some of my own, I explain that in my own mind I see two distinct kinds of reading that I do for pleasure. The first kind of book I read strictly for entertainment. The example I usually use is the mystery novel with an academic setting—for instance, Amanda Cross's books. I tell students that I probably enjoy these mysteries so much because, in some ways, I can identify with their hero, English professor Kate Fansler. Yet, in many ways, Ms. Fansler's adventures—and Ms. Fansler, herself—also provide me with experiences that I will never have. She eats what she wants, yet remains thin and elegant as she solves one hair-raising murder case after another. As much as I enjoy reading these adventures, however, I have to admit that I don't remember much about them after I've finished reading. These books hold my interest, they are very easy to read, and they require almost nothing from me—perfect for evenings when I am exhausted or when I want to take my mind off my latest project. I read them without apology and regard them as one of the few pleasures in life that are reasonably inexpensive, nonfattening, and (as far as I know) noncarcinogenic.

Yet precisely because these books require little from me, they also give me very little to keep permanently as part of my life's experience. And that's where the other kind of reading comes in. The other kind of reading is, for me, quite often difficult. I may have to read and reread several lines or even a whole passage before I can make sense of it (or decide that "making sense of it" is not important). When I read a book, poem, play, or nonfiction selection of this kind, I gain more from the experience when I can share my responses and thoughts with someone else. Selections like this invite questions, elicit expressions of strong feelings, and quite often provoke friendly (or not-so-friendly) arguments. Sometimes I think this may be why I became an English professor—so I would have readily available groups of people with whom I could read works that require such energy and effort. Selections of this kind do not provide easy answers and often they do not end with happy—or even definite—conclusions. But what I love about reading books, stories, poems, or plays like this is that they stay with me. Years after I've finished an initial reading, I'll be moved to return to a familiar piece, wondering if I'll see it in the same way or if this older me will have a different reading.

For me, a complex, difficult work is often not entirely pleasurable— and almost never relaxing—the first time I read it. I can compare the experience to visiting a new country, or even a new city, for the first time. I have to spend a great deal of time and energy getting to know my way around. Each hour brings new challenges and surprises: some breathtakingly beautiful, some exciting, some infuriating or frustrating. I am watchful, somewhat on guard, hoping not to miss anything. Only after I know where I'm going, perhaps when I return for another visit, do I begin to feel relaxed and able to be more fully open to what the city or country has to offer. And, of course, when I'm home again, I replay the experiences of the visit in my head. Those images and memories become a permanent part of me. I think they make my life larger and fuller, just as I believe that reading challenging works of literature makes my life larger and fuller.

These are my own ways of thinking about why I read literature. You may have an entirely different way of looking at the demands and pleasures of reading literature. Whatever your beliefs, I am convinced that explaining to students how you read helps them to see that learning to read literature is a complex process that gives much, yet demands much. No one is born loving Shakespeare or Dickens or Dickinson or Baldwin. And very few readers fall in love with these writers at "first read." Yet those of us who have chosen this profession surely believe that giving challenging literature a fair chance is well worth the effort.

After discussing my own way of looking at reading (and of course admitting that many works do not fall clearly into either the category of pleasure reading or challenging reading), I ask students about their own experiences with a reading that they considered difficult when they first encountered it. I ask them to take a few minutes to make a list of such works and then to note what they remember about reading them.

Some students will come up with examples that show they have taken something they value from challenging reading; others will claim to remember little or nothing of reading that has been difficult for them in the past. I try to listen carefully to their experiences and to understand what they are telling me about both their frustrations and their positive experiences.

At some point in the discussion, I address any concerns students may have raised. These usually are similar to those described above. Because one of the main fears students often express is not having the "right" answer, it's helpful to ask for volunteers to read their responses to Frost's "The Road Not Taken." This poem is quite accessible and, in addition, many of the students will have read it before. By comparing your students' comments with the student comments in the text, you should be able to show that there are many different ways of looking at this poem and that the details of the poem support or back up many different readings.

For example, you might call attention to the section called "Commentary." The idea that a sigh may be interpreted in different ways might not have occurred to all students, but seeing these various possibilities opens new ways of looking at the poem. You may want to point out that because several people look at the poem differently, one person is not necessarily right and the other wrong; it simply suggests new possibilities.

ORAL RESPONSE

This chapter provides a transcript of a planned oral response to "The Road Not Taken." As part of the assignment for the next several classes, you may want to ask students to read a poem and to plan a response they will give orally. I ask that the response take no longer than three minutes, and I allow students to write out what they are going to say, although I encourage them to talk from notes rather than reading. I also note that the response I want in some way relates the poem to something they have experienced or observed in their own lives. Like the model in the text, their response should refer to the poem, but it does not have to "explain what the poem means." I like to have no more than ten students doing an oral response per class. Five per class is ideal. Keeping the number of responses short provides time for you or the student to read the poem aloud before giving the response and also permits discussion of the poems and the responses. I provide a list of suggested poems, and then ask students working on the same poem to give their responses on the same day. Poems that work well for this assignment include these:

Title and Author	Text Page
"Incident," Countee Cullen	192
"In the Orchard," Muriel Stuart	204
"Traveling through the Dark," William Stafford	1172
"We Wear the Mask," Paul Laurence Dunbar	412
"The Youngest Daughter," Cathy Song	418
"To Be of Use," Marge Piercy	596
"First Practice," Gary Gildner	950
"Patterns," Amy Lowell	689
"Lot's Wife," Kristine Batey	687
"Amniocentesis," Ellen Wolfe	832

JOURNALS

If you plan to have students keep journals during the semester, Chapter 1 describes journals and provides an opportunity for you to indicate what you expect. How many entries do you want students to write each week? Will you specify a length for each entry? Should the entries be carefully written, revised, and edited? Or are the journals to be a place where students can explore ideas, free from the restraints of formal writing?

For many years now, I've asked students to keep journals in all the courses I teach, from basic writing classes to graduate seminars. I find in journals the most important writing the students do during the semester, perhaps because I structure these writings to encourage and reward risk-taking. I urge students to look at the journals as a place to try out ideas and to explore responses both to the literature we read and to class discussions. At least one entry per week must be written on the works assigned for reading and discussion during that week. The other entry may explain new thoughts about works we've read earlier or comment on issues raised during class discussion. Each week, students write at least two entries which, together, must total approximately 250 words. As long as they fulfill these requirements, they earn full credit (I make the journals 10 percent of their grade).

Sometimes I use the journals as a way to get discussion started, either by inviting volunteers to read entries they may have written on a specific work or by asking students to work in small groups, reading what they have written to one another. (As always, one member of the group acts as recorder and later as speaker for the group.)

Journal entries provide a great place for students to explore possibilities for oral responses or for formal papers. Chapter 2 provides samples of student journal entries to introduce each section and in Chapter 4, several sample entries show how journal writing works as a way to discover and work through ideas for further development in formal papers.

Usually I encourage students to find their own journal topics, although I do provide a list of suggestions, which appears in the guidelines at the end of Chapter 1. I assure students that I will not correct or edit what they write in their journals. Instead, I will read carefully what they have to say and respond with my own comments and questions. As I read students' journals, I jot observations in the margins and usually write a sentence or two at the end of each entry. I try to keep these comments as affirming as possible. Obviously, I do not agree with or admire everything I read in the journals, and I often ask questions or suggest possibilities that I think might interest or encourage the student. For the most part, however, I try to praise an intriguing insight, a perceptive observation, or a moving personal connection.

The journals also provide a way to communicate with students each week in a private and safe setting. For instance, if I notice that a student seems uncomfortable during group work or during discussion, I make a note in the journal, asking if I can be of help and suggesting that the student see me during my office hours or talk with me after class. Just as I can communicate with students through the journals, so, too, have I found that they will often let me know about some aspect of the course that they either are troubled by or are finding particularly rewarding.

I collect journals once a week and return them no later than a week from the day they were submitted. To facilitate handling journals, I ask students to write on loose-leaf paper and to submit just one week's entries to me in a pocket-type folder. When I return the journals, students remove the entries on which I have commented and store them in a three-ring notebook. (Some students prefer to compose journal entries on a computer. In that case they can easily punch the paper with a three-hole punch after they have printed it out.) Then they place their new entries in the folders and hand them back to me. This process means that I carry home slim folders rather than heavy notebooks of varying sizes and shapes.

Some instructors do not collect journals but do ask students to bring them to class to use as a basis for discussion. Some instructors collect journals and return them with only a checkmark to indicate "accepted" or a minus sign to indicate "needs improvement before I can accept it."

Some instructors collect and grade journals, evaluating them in the same way an essay or research paper would be evaluated. My preference, as I suggest above, is to weight the journal 10 percent of the course grade. As long as students submit at least the required number of entries and write at least two hundred fifty words per week, they receive full credit. If a student misses entries and does not make them up, I deduct credit, 1 percent for each journal entry that is not completed. Usually students work hard on the journals because they are writing in a grade-free context that allows them a great deal of freedom. If, however, I feel that a student is putting in very little effort, I'll ask for an office conference to discuss the way the student sees the journal assignments and the way I see the journal assignments. We usually come up with a satisfactory solution.

The journal work has many helpful side effects. For example, because students have to write on the assigned readings, they come to class prepared and having thought about what they've read. Since I've been assigning journals, I've found quizzes neither necessary nor useful. Also, because students are doing so much writing, they begin to feel more at ease with the process. Journals convince them that writing *is* a way of thinking and many of them begin to be more comfortable with formal writing as well. Finally, journals provide a window into thoughts, hopes, and feelings that students might not readily express aloud in class. I have a chance to see what is really going on for them as they read the assigned selections, and often these insights help to shape future class plans.

TEACHING CHAPTER 2: JOINING THE CONVERSATION

As I suggested in my discussion of teaching Chapter 1, students often show some hostility or anxiety as they begin their required literature and writing courses. One of the concerns that I hear over and over again relates to literary vocabulary. Students often believe they cannot join the conversation because they don't know how to express and explore their responses. They know that a short story infuriates, bores, or confuses them; they read a poem that they like well enough to read a second time; they find a scene in a play puzzling, but intriguing. Yet when they try to explain or evaluate these responses, they feel shy and defensive.

This text differs from many in approaching the language of literature as a cohesive whole rather than as separate lists of terms that apply only to fiction, or to poetry, or to drama, or to nonfiction. Of course, each genre does have unique aspects that are addressed in Chapter 3. Chapter 2 provides four sample readings: Patricia Grace's short story "Butterflies," Langston Hughes's poem "Theme for English B," Wendy Wasserstein's play *The Man in a Case*, and E. B. White's essay "Education." Following each selection are topics inviting students to respond. As all of these selections are short, I assign them all to be read for one class. I also ask students to bring to class a short written response (perhaps a journal entry) for at least one of the selections. Suggestions for responding follow each of the works. These exercises and the explanations that accompany them introduce literary language in a natural, informal way.

At the beginning of the class, students might work in groups, with each group focusing on a different selection. If there are more than twenty-five students in the class, you'll probably want to have more than one group working on some of the selections, as groups of more than five or six become unmanageable. After students have shared their responses, have the class reconvene with the recorders from each group summarizing their discussion.

After the discussion, you might point out to students that many of the comments addressed certain aspects of the selections:

Actions and Events

People

Times and Places

Sounds and Images; Words and Patterns

Ideas

You might write these aspects on the board and then ask students to look at their own written responses to see if they addressed any of these points. Note, also, that many times a comment addresses more than one aspect. After students think about what they've written, ask for volunteers to read comments and to explain whether the comment fits into one of these categories, into several of these categories, or perhaps, into none of these categories (which, of course, is fine!).

This exercise leads to reading and discussing the rest of Chapter 2, which introduces students to ways of thinking, reading, and writing about literature. I recommend spending one class hour on "Actions and Events," "People," and "Times and Places," and another on "Sounds and Images; Words and Patterns" and "Ideas." In addition, you'll probably want students to read some selections from the thematic sections of the text to use as part of the class discussion.

Each section includes observations, evaluations, or questions written by students who read and responded to the selections that appear at the beginning of the chapter. Obviously, students are not expected to write responses exactly like these samples, which are included to suggest possibilities. In addition, these sample writings can serve as inspiration for journal entries.

Following the students' responses in Chapter 2, a commentary showing how these responses reflect the language of literature introduces literary terms. Each section ends with a list of terms related to the aspect of literature just discussed and with exercises designed to help students explore new ways of thinking, reading, and writing about literature. Frequently, an exercise asks students to apply the new terms to television programs or films. Because many students will have seen the same television programs and films, these examples provide common ground for exploring and thinking about literary terms. In addition, most students are comfortable with their knowledge of television and film and feel confident in expressing their ideas about these media.

Examples of comments relating to the television/film exercises include the following:

Events and Actions:

On an episode of *L.A. Law* one of the lawyers had a
brother who was seriously injured in a car accident and
was brain dead. The family had to decide whether to
remove him from life-support systems. There were

conflicts among the family members and between the family members and the medical professionals. You could see that it was not an easy decision and everybody seemed to have their good reasons for what they wanted to do.

People:

When I was watching *China Beach,* I was amazed at the changes in Colleen McMurphy. At first, she was really idealistic and then she got more and more cynical. After the war, she became an alcoholic. But it was easy to believe these changes because the program showed all the things these people went through. She was a nurse who saw people die all the time in horrible ways and then after the Vietnam vets and nurses came home, nobody cared. I think that's why she became so depressed. Nobody wanted to think or talk about what had happened there.

Times and Places:

If you take a program like *Star Trek,* it absolutely has to be happening in the future and also because it has the idea of going "where no one has gone before" it really has to take place either in a space ship or on a space station—something like that. So I would say that setting is very important. Even some of the characters, like complex androids or the blind person who has glasses to make him see, could exist only in the future. And every conflict I've seen on the program is related to a space-travel or future-related situation.

Ideas:

The film *Do the Right Thing* really made me think a lot because it seemed like no one was really a hero. No one was all right or all wrong. But the idea that seemed to come to me was that if people don't start looking at each other as humans and as individuals instead of "black" or "Italian" or "Korean" or whatever, this country is going to be completely torn apart.

Writing and discussing observations like these help students to see that they already understand varied ways of looking closely at literature.

In addition to the topics connecting the language of literature to films and television, the exercises that conclude each section of this chapter also provide opportunities for connecting the study of literary works with familiar aspects of students' lives. Consider using one or more of these exercises as the basis for a brief in-class writing. If you ask students to think about the topic before they come to class and then ask them to write for five or ten minutes when they first get to class, everyone will have something to offer in a discussion.

After an introductory warm-up writing like this, I often ask one student to volunteer to read his or her comment and then continue around the circle, asking each person to read or summarize what he or she has written. When I plan to ask each person to respond, I tell students before they begin to write so they are aware that they are writing for the whole class and not just for me or for themselves.

I don't usually collect the brief in-class writings that have been read and discussed in class, but sometimes I do use one or more of the exercise topics as the basis for a longer, more formal in-class essay, which I do collect and grade. Of course, if I am going to collect and grade anything the students write, I always tell them ahead of time. I also find that I get much stronger, more interesting formal in-class essays if I announce the topic (at least in a general way) at the class meeting before students are scheduled to write. I encourage them to think about topics ahead of time and to feel free to bring in a three-by-five card with an outline (to be signed and attached to the essay with a paper clip).

TEACHING CHAPTER 3:
CONTINUING THE CONVERSATION

Chapter 3 provides a chance to introduce students to two ways of increasing their repertoire of approaches to literature. The first part of the chapter reviews the major genres included in this text; the second part provides a brief overview to literary criticism.

AN INTRODUCTION TO SHORT FICTION

To begin the study of short fiction, I ask students to read the introduction and to bring to class a one- or two-paragraph response suggesting the ways they see early forms of fiction incorporated into modern films and television programs. For instance, one of my students pointed out that the *Star Wars* movies borrow heavily from allegory with a hero named "Skywalker" and a villain called "Darth Vader" (suggesting both Death and Invader). Other students argued that these films weren't truly allegorical because not all the characters had names that matched their personal qualities.

Someone always mentions the now-canceled series *Beauty and the Beast,* and there's usually some discussion as to whether this program was fairy tale or fable. Students are also quick to see the fairy tale qualities of films like *Ghost* with Whoopi Goldberg playing a hip fairy godmother who ultimately works magic and banishes the forces of evil.

After ten minutes or so of such discussion, I move to consider the relationship between fiction and truth, asking students to jot down— and then discuss—any instances they can remember when they read a fictional work that seemed particularly true to them. This exercise leads to exploring the complexities encountered in developing a definition of "truth" and in deciding what can be learned and valued as "truth" from the reading of fiction.

If time permits—or as an alternate exercise to introduce the pleasures and puzzles of short fiction—I ask students to meet in groups and to read aloud to each other from a story I select. Each person reads for a few minutes, stopping at any point he or she chooses. The next person then continues the reading, again stopping where he or she chooses to allow the next person to begin. The reading continues until everyone in the group has read, and then the first person begins the reading chain again until the instructor signals time to stop. (Five to eight minutes works well.) After the reading, students stop and write down their questions and responses, predicting possible outcomes as well as pondering issues that the reading raises.

I then ask students to read that story for the next class (or, in a two-and-a-half-hour class, I'll have them read silently in class; those who finish before others are asked to reread). When they are ready for further discussion, I ask them to jot down brief responses to these questions:

1. What differences, if any, did you notice in hearing the story read aloud, in reading aloud yourself, and in reading silently?

2. As you reread the story to yourself and as you finished the parts you had not heard read aloud, did you change your initial impressions? Were your predictions accurate? Did you find answers to your questions? Explain.

Stories that work well for this exercise include these:

Title and Author	Text Page
"The Red Convertible: Lyman Lamartine," Louise Erdrich	160
"Everyday Use," Alice Walker	371
"The Use of Force," William Carlos Williams	540
"The Conversion of the Jews," Philip Roth	770
"I'm Your Horse in the Night," Luisa Valenzuela	1009

To complete the introduction to short fiction, I call students' attention to the list of "Considerations," noting that these suggestions offer possible ways of reading, thinking, and writing about short stories.

TEACHING: AN INTRODUCTION TO POETRY

Students often tell me that they dread studying poetry. More than any other genre, poetry seems to them a form of literature that contains hidden meaning to which only the initiates (read teachers) hold the key. Few students have had the luxury of listening to poetry read aloud, immersing themselves in the sound before even beginning to think about the sense.

To start addressing this lack, my own favorite way to begin teaching poetry is to read aloud several favorite poems. I try to choose poems that are short, that are particularly appealing to the ear, and that offer reasonably accessible feelings/ideas/images. Students have been particularly surprised when I bring in a poem I've just discovered in *The New Yorker, The Atlantic Monthly,* or one of the small press magazines. They know that poetry is still being written, yet they tend to think of poems as old, dusty relics of the past. On the other hand, I also believe in the importance of reading an old favorite poem, perhaps several times with changes of voice that imply multiple possibilities, not one definite "right answer."

Poems that have worked well for me include these:

Title and Author	Text Page
"Incident," Countee Cullen	192
"The World is too much with us," William Wordsworth	411
"Telephone Conversation," Wole Soyinka	415
"Latin Women Pray," Judith Ortiz Cofer	422
"Waitresses," Ranice Henderson Crosby	602
"Let me not to the marriage of true minds," William Shakespeare	694
"My Son My Executioner," Donald Hall	836
"What Were They Like?," Denise Levertov	1062
"When a Woman Holds a Letter," Sandra Nelson	Art and Poetry Section

I introduce students to writing about poetry by asking for a response paper, emphasizing that I am looking for their own views, not for a preordained answer. I try to be especially open-minded as I respond to what they have written. Another assignment that works well in a small class is asking each student to choose a short poem (perhaps from anthologies placed on reserve at the library). Students bring a copy of the poem to class and read it aloud, later submitting both their poem and a short paper explaining why they chose it.

My goal with these assignments is not to train literary analysts, but instead to encourage students to read poems with energy, hope, and wonder rather than with a sense of doom and failure. Depending on the population of the course, I may move from these assignments to work that requires more literary sophistication.

TEACHING: AN INTRODUCTION TO DRAMA

I start discussion by asking students to jot down what comes into their minds when they hear the word "drama." The responses usually vary widely. In the one class I taught, several students said that they thought "drama" meant a film, television program, or play that was serious or sad. When I pursued the source of this impression, they cited the labels at videocassette rental stores ("Drama," "Comedy," "Adventure," and so on). I had never thought about this new definition of drama and these comments led to a lively exchange of opinions and ideas when other students contributed quite different definitions. Several, for instance, had attended live performances of plays and contended that these plays (whether comic or tragic) were "drama" whereas those same plays performed on television would be "programs." I asked how they would classify a Shakespearean play performed on screen. Some said it would still be a drama; others said it changed and became a movie. One person preferred the word "film" which she said indicated a screen performance that was serious and profound. Still another student said that if the Shakespearean play was a film of an actual performance it would be a drama but if it was adapted and changed it would be a movie or film.

While all of this may sound like quibbling, we worked hard at defining exactly what qualified a work to be called a drama. After reading the introductory section, and thinking about their own experiences, my students decided that to qualify as "drama," a selection should have the potential for being performed on a stage. It didn't matter whether the work was tragic, comic, tragi-comic, satiric, or romantic, but an essential dimension should be the dynamic between actors and audience. Most of them agreed—after some discussion—that a drama could be read silently, or viewed on television or screen. But they insisted that the "live audience" element had to be imagined and held in the reader's or viewer's head. One student compared the distinction to seeing a concert performed live and then hearing the same performance on tape or disk. The music might be the same, but the experience of the audience is very different. Another student noted that the difference was similar to watching a baseball game at a big league stadium, complete with hot dog vendors, "the wave," and cheering crowds as opposed to seeing the same game at home, watching television by yourself.

Because the live performance aspect also seems important to me, I always have students volunteer to prepare and read selected scenes from several of the plays. And, of course, when possible I arrange voluntary field trips to see plays being performed on campus or at nearby theaters.

TEACHING: AN INTRODUCTION TO NONFICTION

As I suggest in the text, I believe the key issue related to teaching nonfiction in a literature class is the question of definition. Even after reading the discussion in the text, some students (and instructors) will not be convinced that the selections in this section can legitimately be called literature. This controversy can lead to fruitful discussions about the nature of literature and of the literary experience for both the author and the reader.

TEACHING: CONSIDERING OTHER VOICES

This section in no way intends to be a full-fledged introduction to literary criticism. Instead, it offers chances for students to think about the way professional writers talk to their audiences about literature. While some literary criticism can be read and understood by only a few outstanding scholars whose field of expertise matches the writer's, there are also many essays, articles, reviews, and interviews that are accessible to the general educated public. I like students to feel that they have access to the conversation taking place in newspapers, magazines, and journals. These resources should not be viewed as locked vaults, available only to those with special keys, but rather as open doors ready to lead anyone willing to turn the knob into the "room" where thoughtful people discuss plays, poems, fiction, and nonfiction.

As an exercise to accompany the introduction to other voices, I often ask students to find a review of a film or television program with which they are familiar. Then I ask them to write a response to that review and to submit their response along with a photocopy of the review. This exercise can be done very informally—perhaps as a journal entry.

TEACHING CHAPTER 4:
WRITING ABOUT LITERATURE

Chapter 4 is long and covers a great deal of information. Students are asked to consider different ways of thinking and writing about literature and in addition are encouraged to review aspects of the writing process.

As I suggested earlier, students with varying interests, career goals, and academic preparation enroll in introductory literature courses. Nowhere are their diverse backgrounds more obvious than in their writing skills. When you begin discussing Chapter 4, consider asking students to jot down any memories they have of writing about literature in their previous English courses. For example, did they write papers? In or out of class? Essay exams? Did they write about their own responses? Did they write research papers? If so, what kind of research were they asked to do? What other kinds of writing did they do? Did they keep journals? What, if anything, seemed difficult about writing about literature? What, if anything, seemed rewarding?

Opening with this discussion offers students a chance to express their concerns and gives you the opportunity to discover some of the issues you may want to address during the term. As you listen to what students have to say, you'll be able to predict accurately that some will be fine writers who will further develop their abilities in this course. For example, some students, fresh from innovative classrooms with dedicated, energetic teachers, will have written response papers, including creative as well as evaluative and interpretive essays. Some students will have learned how to integrate details and examples from what they have read into the essays they write. Some will have learned how to use secondary sources in thoughtful, original ways. Many more will not.

For instance, at least half the students in every literature class I teach describe high school English courses where little or no writing about literature was required or encouraged. The short-answer or objective exam provided many of them with their only experience in writing about literature. Other students wrote responses to the questions at the end of the chapter in the textbook and then read them aloud in class while the teacher praised or corrected them. One student described a course where the teacher stopped frequently to consult the instructor's guide to see whether the "answers" were "right or wrong."

In addition to lacking the special skills required for writing about literature, many students still need instruction in the process of writing. Consider, for instance, the students whose first language is not English or those who took their freshman writing course ten or more years ago and have not used formal writing skills since that time. The introductory literature and writing course presents special problems for these students. In addition, although your college or university may have a fine introductory writing program, some students may have fulfilled their freshman writing requirement at a college or university that takes a less rigorous approach to the course. Still other students may have barely earned a passing grade in their freshman writing course. Whatever the circumstances, most students need to review the writing process and, in addition, learn specific ways to write about literature. This chapter provides that opportunity.

While the chapter is far too long to cover in detail during one class meeting, I would ask students to skim the whole chapter. You might mention to them that each section of the chapter provides a model of a student's process, demonstrating possible approaches to writing about literature in a variety of ways. To prepare for class discussion, students do not need to read the chapter thoroughly. Instead, ask them to scan the chapter quickly, but to read carefully the introduction as well as the first section, "Writing a Response."

During class discussion, you might point out the different parts of the student's process that are demonstrated in the "Writing a Response" section and remind students that each section provides the same (or similar) parts:

Invention/Discovery Strategies	Drafting
Audience Evaluation	Revising
Considering Voice	Editing
Planning to Write	Proofreading

Of course, each section provides different possibilities for these aspects of the writing process. Following this class discussion, students should be encouraged to read through the chapter to be sure they are aware of the many options open to them. In addition, as you assign papers during the course, you may want to ask students to read carefully and to discuss in class an appropriate section from Chapter 4.

POSSIBLE RESPONSES FOR EXERCISES, CHAPTER 4

*Exercise: Proofreading for apostrophes and quotation marks
(text page 117)*

1. The first stanza begins with the speaker's plea, addressed to old people.

2. The repetition of the word "rage" emphasizes the importance the speaker places on this fight against death.

3. They didn't speak like lightning.

4. This phrase shows the men's actions as lively and sparkling, like light on the water in a bay.

5. It represents power, energy, and life.

6. It's interesting to note that "grave" means serious, yet "grave" here could also maybe suggest the nearness to burial.

7. Now these lines are addressed directly to the speaker's father.

*Exercise: Editing—sentence combining; proofreading—
typographical errors and spelling (text pages 139–141)*

We Are All Poets

In *A Reader's Guide to Dylan Thomas,* William York Tindall describes the grave men in "Do Not Go Gentle" as poets (205). Whereas Clark Emery *believes* that the wild men are the poets (Murphy, 55), Michael Murphy does not identify any of the men as poets. He sees all the men mentioned in stanzas 2–4 as having a broader interpretation, suggesting "that life is always too brief and incomplete for everyone, regardless of how he has lived" (55). Even Murphy's interpretation, however, seems too narrow. Dylan Thomas's men, who are described as wise, good, wild, and grave, could share qualities with poets, yet *their* lives and *their* views of life also represent us all.

The wise men whose "words had forked no lightning" may be like poets who have not been heard. Of course they would not want to die because they would hope for a chance to have their words make a difference. Rather than representing only poets, however, the wise men might stand for any person who felt that he or she had not really had a chance to do anything in life that might make an *impact* on others. People who felt they had not yet done something significant or useful would almost certainly fight death.

The good men, too, could be poets, and the "frail deeds" might refer to writing poems. Line 8 says that those deeds "might have danced in a green bay," which could mean that the poems had the possibility to cause a beautiful *response*. They could have been bright, and they could have danced, but for some reason they didn't. Many people besides poets also see their work and their actions as not having caused the reaction they would have hoped for.

The wild men might be poets who spent most of their time "singing" (writing) about the sun, which represents beautiful things in life. Maybe they didn't really take the time to appreciate those beautiful things or to realize that nothing can last forever. Then, when beauty started to go, they *grieved*. These poets are certainly like many people who don't take the time to appreciate what they have. Yet at the end of their lives they want to live longer so that they can admire "the sun in flight." They finally understand what they *lose* when that sun (beauty) has gone from them.

Thomas describes the grave men as seeing "with blinding sight." We often think of poets as being able to see things that others cannot see, so the grave men, too, could be poets who are near death yet still have the ability to see special things. They want to live so they can continue to enlighten others. As the phrase "blind eyes could blaze like meteors" suggests, their knowledge could shine out still. So it's easy to see how the images in this stanza could apply *specifically* to poets, yet it's also easy to see how they could apply to most people. Most of us *believe* that we are unique beings who have special ways of seeing. Each of us sees the world in a slightly different way. When we are near death, our *physical* sight might be failing, yet we would probably still *believe* that we had a special way to "see" (understand) the world around us which would encourage us to fight against death.

It makes *sense* that Dylan Thomas, a poet, might have chosen examples of men who could be seen as poets. Horace Gregory suggests this possibility when he says that "Do Not Go Gentle" could be read "as Thomas's own epitaph" (129). On the other hand, a poet does not have to be somebody who stands *entirely* apart from the rest of humanity. The examples also suggest that those who fight against death could be any of us who look back and see our actions as *incomplete* or as unappreciated. Those who fight could be any of us who failed to stop to acknowledge fully the beauty in our lives or any of us who consider our view of the world to be unique and special. Perhaps, in a way, we are all poets. Thomas may be speaking to us all when he says, "Do not go gentle into that good night."

CHAPTERS 5 TO 12:
LITERARY THEMES

Each of the eight chapters in this section provides five or six fiction selections, ten to fifteen poems, one or two plays, and two nonfiction selections relating to a single theme. Each theme reflects some aspect of the human experience:

Innocence and Experience

Roots, Identity, and Culture

Work

Men and Women

Parents and Children

Learning and Teaching

War and Power

Death

Each section begins with a photograph, carefully chosen to provide inspiration for writing and discussion of that section's theme. Asking students to respond to the photograph works well as a way to get them thinking about the theme they'll be considering as they read the selections that follow.

Following most of the selections are "Considerations," suggestions for thinking, talking, and writing about the section's theme. At the end of each section are "Connections," suggestions for seeing relationships among the selections.

In this guide, each section's introduction offers possibilities for teaching that particular theme. Following the introduction is a list of additional selections related to the section's theme, but appearing elsewhere in the text. This supplementary list makes it possible to choose only two or three themes for a term's work. You might also use the supplementary list to provide works for students to explore and write about on their own in connection with the theme you are considering. At the end of each supplementary list, I provide possibilities for thinking, discussing, and writing about these selections.

CHAPTER 5
INNOCENCE AND EXPERIENCE

Most people can remember specific moments when a cherished idea was suddenly challenged or a much-admired friend or relative showed a particularly disillusioning weakness. You might begin this thematic section by asking students to write a brief reflection on such a moment in their lives. Consider suggesting that they focus on an event that is no longer deeply distressing for them. Even with this disclaimer, many may not be comfortable discussing such sharp and often intimate disappointments, yet others will provide examples demonstrating clearly the move from innocence to experience. Some may even have gained enough emotional distance to see humor in what was originally upsetting or even shocking.

Most of the selections in this section focus on the changes of young people: children or adolescents. Nonetheless, it would be worth discussing the nature of the move from innocence to experience. Does this passage occur primarily in childhood, adolescence, or young adulthood? Or does it keep happening throughout one's life? Even if there are no class members of nontraditional age, younger students should be able to provide generalizations based on observations of older friends and relatives or of older characters they have encountered in books and films.

"Salvation" and "Graduation in Stamps" combine humor and pathos to suggest both the beauty and the pain of innocence. Considering what the main characters gain—and what they lose— from the insights they achieve should provoke lively controversy and discussion. Providing a more somber look at the clash of illusion and reality are "Araby," "And the Soul Shall Dance," "Battle Royal," and *Hamlet.* All four of these works focus on the ways fantasies and expectations often clash with the realized experience.

To introduce the poems, ask students to consider the many parts of our lives that are touched by the move from innocence to experience. The poems offer a wide range of possibilities: the effects of racial bigotry in "Incident" ; the betrayal of love in "When I was one-and-twenty" and "In the Orchard"; encounters with sexual stereotyping in "The Centaur," "In the Counselor's Waiting Room," and "Snow White and the Seven Dwarfs"; and the contrast of life and death in "Richard Cory," "Spring and Fall," and "Mid-Term Break."

ADDITIONAL SELECTIONS FOR CONSIDERATION: INNOCENCE AND EXPERIENCE

Title and Author   **Text Page**

Fiction

"Sonny's Blues," James Baldwin   346

"Cathedral," Raymond Carver   379

"Rules of the Game," Amy Tan   402

"El Tonto del Barrio," José Armas   568

"Young Goodman Brown," Nathaniel Hawthorne   634

"The Conversion of the Jews," Philip Roth   770

"Through the Tunnel," Doris Lessing   782

"The Lesson," Toni Cade Bambara   914

"Guests of the Nation," Frank O'Connor   1013

"To Hell with Dying," Alice Walker   1142

Poetry

"Annabel Lee," Edgar Allan Poe   695

"My Papa's Waltz," Theodore Roethke   827

"Today," Margaret Atwood   834

"A Teacher Taught Me," Anna Lee Walters   948

"Ethics," Linda Pastan   949

"First Practice," Gary Gildner   950

"Dulce et Decorum Est," Wilfred Owen   1052

"What Were They Like?" Denise Levertov   1062

"To an Athlete Dying Young," A. E. Housman   1171

"Musée des Beaux Arts," W. H. Auden   Art and Poetry Section

"Home Burial," Robert Frost   1213

"Out, Out—," Robert Frost   1217

"First Death in Nova Scotia," Elizabeth Bishop   1225

"In the Waiting Room," Elizabeth Bishop   1227

Title and Author	Text Page
"Boy Breaking Glass," Gwendolyn Brooks	1236
"To the Young Who Want to Die," Gwendolyn Brooks	1237

Drama

Trifles, Susan Glaspell	608
A Doll House, Henrik Ibsen	697
Painting Churches, Tina Howe	839
Oleanna, David Mamet	955
Picnic on the Battlefield, Fernando Arrabal	1065

Essays

"Arrival at Manzanar," Jeanne Wakatsuki Houston and James D. Houston	531
"I Remember Papa," Harry Dolan	895
"Learning to Read and Write," Frederick Douglass	987
"War Cards, Purpose, and Blame," Donald Hall	1108

SUGGESTIONS FOR TEACHING ADDITIONAL SELECTIONS

1. Consider the connection between family relationships and the journey from innocence to experience. How do the parents in these works affect their children's development? What do you see as positive about the relationships? Negative?

	Text Page
"Sonny's Blues"	346
"Rules of the Game"	402
"The Conversion of the Jews"	770
"Through the Tunnel"	782
"The Lesson"	914
"To Hell with Dying"	1142
"Today"	834

	Text Page
"My Papa's Waltz"	827
"Home Burial"	1213
A Doll House	697
Painting Churches	839
Picnic on the Battlefield	1065
"Arrival at Manzanar"	531
"I Remember Papa"	895

2.   In the following works, the journey from innocence to experience is described with varying degrees of humor. After reading these works, compare the way the authors use humor to describe their characters' passage. Consider also episodes in your own life that moved you from innocence to experience. Did you consider any of them funny at the time they happened? Do you consider any of them funny now?

	Text Page
"Cathedral"	379
"Rules of the Game"	402
"The Conversion of the Jews"	770
"The Lesson"	914
"To Hell with Dying"	1142
"Arrival at Manzanar"	531
"War Cards, Purpose, and Blame"	1108

3.   In the following works, characters are affected because someone else sees them as different and, therefore, as inferior. Consider how individuals are moved from innocence to experience by the way others view them.

	Text Page
"Sonny's Blues"	346
"Cathedral"	379
"El Tonto del Barrio"	568

	Text Page
"The Lesson"	914
"A Teacher Taught Me"	948
"Boy Breaking Glass"	1236
Trifles	608
A Doll House	697
Oleanna	955
"Arrival at Manzanar"	531
"I Remember Papa"	895
"Learning to Read and Write"	987

4. Consider how an encounter with death, or contemplation of death, relates to the passage from innocence to experience.

	Text Page
"Sonny's Blues"	346
"Through the Tunnel"	782
"Guests of the Nation"	1013
"To Hell with Dying"	1142
"Annabel Lee"	695
"Dulce et Decorum Est"	1052
"What Were They Like?"	1062
"To an Athlete Dying Young"	1171
"Home Burial"	1213
"Out, Out—"	1217
"First Death in Nova Scotia"	1225
"To the Young Who Want to Die"	1237
Picnic on the Battlefield	1065
"I Remember Papa"	895
"War Cards, Purpose, and Blame"	1108

THEMATIC PHOTOGRAPH (p. 147)

Considerations

1. Describe the people in the picture. What do they look like? What are they doing? Do their expressions suggest particular emotions?

2. Describe the relationship between the woman and the boy.

3. Write a dialogue suggesting the conversation between the woman and boy that has been interrupted by the picture-taking.

4. Does one person in the picture suggest experience and the other innocence? Explain. As you respond, consider your definition of innocence and of experience.

READINGS

James Joyce, "Araby" (p. 148)

Readers who describe themselves as "enjoying a good plot" or "liking stories with lots of action" often have a hard time with "Araby." Many of my students have described their initial response to the story in two words: "Nothing happens." They are particularly disappointed with the ending which either makes no sense to them or seems vastly exaggerated. In addition, many first-time readers do not see that the person telling the story is much older than the person experiencing the throes of adolescent love.

To address these issues, I usually read several passages aloud. I start with the opening description, asking students to picture the world in which the narrator lives. Then I read a paragraph or two describing his reveries as he thinks of Mangan's sister. Students relate especially well to the fantasies he creates as he sits listening to the boring drone of his teacher. One student suggested that the external scenes seem like old sepia-print photographs while the daydreams are like paintings done with a full range of colors. The young narrator moves from the dreariness of his day-to-day life into dramatic, chivalric scenes with his own vision of Mangan's sister serving as the means of transportation: "Her image accompanied me even in places the most hostile to romance."

Students often initially think nothing happens in the story because most of the action takes place inside the narrator's head and heart. Addressing this point often leads to a lively discussion of whether they see their own journeys of the mind and spirit as equally significant as journeys of the body. Even those who are reluctant to offer personal experiences can usually relate to the idea of events, changes, and insights that have been extremely important to them, yet have seemed trivial to others who have not understood the emotional impact of these events, changes, and insights.

Another problem, especially with younger readers, is the lack of background knowledge to understand the details of the religious quest for the Grail. The narrator knows the story of King Arthur and his knights. He can relate both to the concept of courtly love and to the search for the chalice of faith. It's useful to recount briefly the details of this legend—and perhaps to ask students to see how this legend has become part of many of the films they watch. Also, discuss the implications of the name "Araby" with its connotations of the "Tales of Arabian Nights"—exotic sultans, mysterious tents, and magical happenings. Currently, many students have negative responses to things middle eastern and you'll need to remind them of the different responses adolescent boys in early twentieth-century Ireland might have had.

After students discuss the issues just mentioned, I close the class by reading the final passage and asking them to consider moments in their own lives when they may have felt themselves to be "creature[s] driven and derided by vanity." Most have no trouble doing so, and I've read many moving and powerful journal entries written in response to this request.

Wakako Yamauchi, "And the Soul Shall Dance" (p. 153)

The first paragraph of this story suggests its themes of loss and isolation. All the principal characters—save three—are dead and one of them, Mr. Oka, is described as an ugly, rather frightening alcoholic. His "bulging thyroid eyes," "the dark terrain of his face," and his appetite for viciously hot chilies as well as strong drink paint a picture of menace.

Mrs. Oka is repeatedly described as strange, different, and unusual. (paragraphs 3, 4, 8, 9). The young Masako seems to fasten on these adjectives as a way of accounting for Mrs. Oka's failure to conform to the narrator's view of conventional (and therefore safe) behavior. In fact, the details we are given suggest only very mild rebellion. Mrs. Oka fails to offer tea to her guests, she drinks too much saki, and some nights she leaves home for many hours. The narrator admits she knows other women in her community who are unusual, so she cannot account for her sense that Mrs. Oka is somehow unique in her strangeness. Masako does not seem sympathetic to Mrs. Oka; for example, she describes this neighbor's welts and bruises matter of factly, without speculation or apparent concern.

When Kioko-san arrives, Masako is surprised to find that she is more like a woman than a child. And very soon Kioko's behavior hints that she may, in fact, be fulfilling a woman's role in her new home. When she arrives at Masako's home, hysterical and not properly dressed against the November cold, Masako's mother puts Kioko to bed with her daughter, yet warns that she must return to her "people" in the morning. There is certainly a suggestion here that Kioko is being abused (possibly sexually) in her new home. While Masako does not elaborate on her feelings, her description of the visitor's icy cold feet and of the borrowed nightgown she leaves neatly folded show that the narrator was impressed by these events. Kioko lives through the winter, silently facing her difficult life. She appears often with red eyes and behaves in a depressed, withdrawn manner.

Masako's mother advises Kioko-san to "endure" because she "will be marrying and going away." In an odd and frightening way, I think that prediction comes true. It seems possible that Mr. Oka has taken Kioko as a lover. She now rides beside him, replacing the barren Mrs. Oka. She no longer appears with red, puffy eyes; apparently she has accepted her lot.

Mrs. Oka, on the other hand, refuses to accept her life. Her appearance in the spring, singing, dancing, and scattering flowers has, for me, strong connections to Ophelia's mad scene in *Hamlet*. In this scene, her spirit seems to be freed and her sensual nature finally allowed full and open play. Perhaps she remembers the "man of poor reputation" from her youth. Unlike Ophelia, she does not overtly commit suicide, but her experiences of loss and betrayal seem to lead her away from this life. This encounter is the climax of the narrator's relationship with Mrs. Oka. She seems astonished to see this side of her neighbor. Here are energy, joy, and sexuality where only depression and "strangeness" formerly appeared.

Just as the narrator puzzles over this story, trying to make sense of it, so, too, does the reader. Although there's no absolute evidence to prove my theory, I think it's possible that Mr. Oka created the story of an early marriage to Mrs. Oka's sister and of fathering Kioko. The truth may be that Kioko is Mrs. Oka's child from a liaison with the "man of poor reputation" (note that at the funeral, the minister expressed the irony of the "long separation Mother and Child"; the capitalization makes me think that this phrase is intended to move beyond literal statement and to suggest that Kioko and Mrs. Oka are more than aunt and niece). Mr. Oka then takes revenge on Mrs. Oka for his years of living with "damaged goods" by manipulating Kioko to take her place.

Louise Erdrich, "The Red Convertible: Lyman Lamartine" (p. 160)

Lyman Lamartine describes himself in the first section of the story as having a talent for making money. His pride in his precocious ownership of the Joliet Café is telling—he values his success because he was able to have "everyone of [his] relatives, and their relatives to dinner" and also because he was able to buy the red Oldsmobile convertible, which he shares with his brother Henry. Connection to family stands out as a primary value for Lyman, which makes the loss of his brother especially poignant. Before Henry left for Vietnam, he and Lyman were always open to new adventures and travels; small moments, like the incident with Susy and her long hair, seem to delight both of them, suggesting innocence yet not saccharine naivete.

When Lyman describes himself in third person (at the end of the first paragraph), he establishes himself as a storyteller. What follows will be a tale about himself, told through the filter of time. He becomes both a character and a narrator, giving the story a sense of immediacy yet also the perspective of distance.

The story jumps back and forth both in time and in geography. We follow the Lamartine brothers from Montana to Alaska and back to Montana. And, of course, Henry's tour in Vietnam is central to the story. In Section VI, Lyman's comments about his sister's picture of Henry provide foreshadowing for the ending. It's clear that something very bad has happened, and most readers will predict that by the time the story is told Henry is dead. The ritual of wrapping his picture and putting it away—in effect, burying the picture—confirms the reader's premonition.

While the narrator makes clear that he and his brother are Native Americans, the events and theme of the story do not seem limited to one culture. We can imagine nearly any young men loving a car, cherishing their travels, and being scarred by participation in a war like Vietnam. Note that Henry is not drafted, but rather enlists, and that Lyman does not seem particularly bitter about the war. He simply states that "the whole war was solved in the government's mind, but for [Henry] it would keep on going." His mother's fears about sending Henry to a "regular hospital" ("They don't fix them in those places . . . they just give them drugs") do not seem directly connected to the fact that Henry is Native American.

The red convertible symbolizes the freedom and pleasure Henry and Lyman experienced in their youth. Lyman believes that by beating up the car, he will give Henry a reason for living. He hopes that Henry will resurrect not only the car, but also himself. Once changed, however, the car cannot be put entirely right and neither can Henry. In the end, Lyman sends the car into the water to join Henry in death. This gesture shows the depth of Lyman's emotion and emphasizes his recognition that he has lost both his brother and a vital part of his younger self.

Ralph Ellison, "Battle Royal" (p. 169)

The action of "Battle Royal," which appears as the first chapter of Ellison's novel *The Invisible Man*, divides into six sections:

Section I: Main characters are introduced and hear grandfather's mysterious deathbed charge
Section II: Narrator arrives at the hotel, along with the other fighters
Section III: Blonde stripper dances
Section IV: Narrator and others fight battle royal
Section V: Narrator gives graduation speech
Section VI: Conclusion: the narrator dreams of his grandfather reacting to the award of the college scholarship

Through these scenes, the narrator traces his education about the racist world in which he lives. The grandfather's startling instructions suggest that a man who has appeared to be gentle and subservient all his life has, in fact, been inwardly angry and resistant to the injuries, slights, and condescensions of white people. The narrator arrives at the hotel full of hope, but as the blonde stripper dances, he becomes increasingly uncomfortable both with the way the white men watch the young black men for any signs of sexual arousal and with the parallel he sees between the woman and himself. Both are there for the entertainment of the whites; both are regarded as objects or possessions.

The power of the battle royal scene is enhanced by the narrator's being blindfolded. He is literally "in the dark" yet he "sees the light" with all his other senses and, particularly, with his mind. His physical pain and emotional confusion are expressed in language often achingly beautiful (see, for example, his description of the blood he has shed as "shaping itself into a butterfly"). In this section, the narrator recognizes that he has not been brought here because of the quality of his graduation speech but rather as an amusement to be displayed.

His growing understanding leads him to substitute, perhaps subconsciously, the phrase "social equality" for "social responsibility." Although he later recants, this dramatic moment marks a significant point in the narrator's life. He sees how truly "invisible" he is unless he is doing something to upset what white culture sees as the natural order. The scholarship to "the state college for Negroes" seems designed, as the ending dream indicates, to keep him running on the same treadmill for which his high school has trained him.

Jamaica Kincaid, "The Circling Hand" (p. 181)

Consider starting discussion of this story by asking students to think about topic 5 in the list that follows the story. Focusing on items significant to their lives leads them to see that each item in the mother's trunk represented an important moment in Annie's life. The mother's tender preservation of mementos representing the stepping-stones in her daughter's early life makes the rift described in the story all the more poignant.

As a child, Annie regards her mother as all-knowing and all-powerful. She knows how to keep her family healthy by cooking just the right foods in exactly the correct way. She sews magnificent, matching mother-daughter outfits. She keeps her laundry stainless with sun-bleaching. And with her baths, perfectly scented with fruits, herbs, and barks to defeat the evil eye of Annie's father's former mistress, the mother takes on the stature of a magical figure who will always keep the world safe.

As she enters adolescence, Annie finds her mother abruptly changing. Students will see different reasons for the change. Perhaps the mother simply recognizes that her daughter must become separate from her in order to mature and to become an individual. Some students have suggested that the mother now begins to see the daughter as a rival for the father's attention and that this motive accounts for the carelessness that forces Annie for the first time to recognize her mother and father as sexual beings.

And why does Annie keep a secret from her mother at the end of the story? Is she being vengeful? Might she fear that her mother would be jealous of Gwen? Does she want to know something that her mother does not to assert her autonomy?

A. E. Housman, "When I was one and twenty" (p. 191)

In just one year the speaker, originally filled with optimism, has moved to a pessimistic view of romantic love. In the first stanza, the wise man advises the speaker not to take any emotional risks. He seems to urge the speaker to avoid commitment to any one woman ("Keep your fancy free"). In the second stanza, the advice is retrospective. The wise man comments on what has already occurred, noting that whenever love is given fully there will be "sighs a plenty" and "endless rue."

Students readily debate whether the advice given is truly wise. Many argue that the speaker's misery simply reflects his recent experiences with romantic love and that he may well change, depending on what happens in the future. The "wise man," however, continues his view from one year to the next. He is apparently a confirmed cynic who will go through life avoiding connection with others because of the pain he may encounter.

Countee Cullen, "Incident" (p. 192)

Part of the poignancy of this poem comes from its sound; the regular cadence and rhyme bring to mind the Mother Goose rhymes read to children. These sounds emphasize the innocence of the speaker when he meets his first bigot and underline the ugly power of the disillusioning encounter. Most students can remember moments like this in their own lives and can write strong narrative essays describing their own struggles with physical or emotional bullies.

Edwin Arlington Robinson, "Richard Cory" (p. 193)

Why does Richard Cory commit suicide? It's far too easy to say simply that he committed suicide because "money can't buy happiness," but the poem does not indicate that being poor is necessarily better than being wealthy. The final stanza does, however, suggest that the speaker (and the people he represents) made the assumption that those who are handsome and wealthy would not have problems and difficulties as do the poor. They assumed that Cory was satisfied, since he seemed to have all that they longed for, and were ironically surprised to find they were wrong.

As an initial writing leading to discussion, consider asking students to respond to the following criticism of "Richard Cory":

> The poem builds up deliberately to a very cheap
> surprise ending; but all surprise endings are cheap in
> poetry . . . for poetry is written to be read not once but
> many times.
>
> Yvor Winters, *Edwin Arlington*
> *Robinson*, Norfolk, CT:
> New Directions, 1946, p. 52

Bettie Sellers, "In the Counselor's Waiting Room" (p. 194)

To what extent is—or was—the "terra cotta girl" innocent? She loves another girl (apparently a lesbian relationship). She no doubt knows that much of society will not approve of the relationship, yet until the mothers intervene, a kind of private innocence exists. The mothers of both these girls, who want their daughters to love in conventional ways so they will produce grandchildren, bring the girls to the counselor's office, thus suggesting that the relationship is wrong or problematic. The girls, then, are forced to see their relationship in a disapproving public light rather than a private context.

May Swenson, "The Centaur" (p. 195)

This young girl's wonderful tenth summer suggests her deep, intimate, and comfortable connection with her own wild spirit and body. Initially, she cuts a willow rod to use as her horse, but as she rides she mystically becomes one with Rob Roy, her imagined mount. As the speaker enters the kitchen, the spell is broken when her mother calls her attention to the knife that weights the pocket of her dress and tells her to tie back her hair. The mother, domesticated in the kitchen, seems to have no sense of her daughter's wonder as she rides through her tenth summer and into the complicated, taming fall of adolescence and maturity.

Anne Sexton, "Snow White and the Seven Dwarfs" (p. 197)

Admired primarily for her virginity and her doll-like appearance, Snow White may well find herself in later life following the path of her stepmother and dancing in red-hot shoes (note in the final two lines the ominous reference to Snow White's "referring to her mirror/as women do"). This poem suggests that age cannot be equated with wisdom. For women like Snow White and the Wicked Queen, trapped in the myth of beauty, the passage from innocence to experience brings disillusion rather than enlightenment.

William Blake, "The Lamb"/"The Tyger" (pp. 201–202)

Although both poems ask questions related to creation, "The Lamb" offers a fairly direct and commonly expected response that suggests an innocent worldview. "The Tyger" never provides an answer but continues to open up new questions. Whereas the lamb is depicted as a simple, easily understood creature, the tyger is mysterious, strange, and complex—a worthy symbol of experience.

Gerard Manley Hopkins, "Spring and Fall: To a Young Child" (p. 203)

The older narrator speaks to a child, Margaret, as she mourns the passing of the seasons. His tone suggests sympathy and consolation as he gently leads Margaret to see that she regrets more than the falling leaves: she also senses her own passage from innocent childhood to the responsibilities and knowledge of adult life. She sees that like the golden grove, she too is mortal.

Seamus Heaney, "Mid-Term Break" (p. 203)

The title to this poem proves a real shocker. Expecting a poem related to a vacation from the rigors of college study, the reader instead finds a wrenching description of a young man called home for his four-year-old brother's funeral. The break, of course, is the loss and separation the speaker feels from his brother. In addition, the title suggests the traditional metaphor for grief—heartbreak.

Muriel Stuart, "In the Orchard" (p. 204)

This narrative poem's story of desire and betrayal comes alive if two students will volunteer to prepare a reading. Identifying the two voices—where one speaker stops and the next begins—leads to asking why Stuart set the poem up as she did. Why not, for example, start a new line each time the speaker changes? One possibility: the intertwining of the voices suggests the pace of the speakers. They are nearly interrupting each other as each rushes to tell his or her side of the story.

Rita Dove, "Grape Sherbet" (p. 205)

The image of the children savoring grape sherbet while they "gallop" on the graves they are decorating for Memorial Day sharply contrasts the innocence of childhood with the knowledge of human frailty and mortality. The "diabetic grandmother," who must now refuse the pleasure of the secret-recipe dessert, and the dead who can no longer experience the small, powerful joys of human life symbolize the loss the innocent children cannot yet understand.

John Keats, "Ode on a Grecian Urn" (p. 206)

Considerations for Writing and Discussion

The "Ode on a Grecian Urn" raises more questions than it answers. You might ask your students to list several questions from the poem and, in addition, to list several lines that are not questions followed by the questions those lines raise in their minds.

Questions found in the poem include these:

> What leaf-fring'd legend haunts about thy shape / Of deities or mortal, or of both, / In Tempe or the dales of Arcady? (lines 5–7)

> What men or gods are these? What maidens loath? / What mad pursuit? What struggle to escape? / What pipes and timbrels? What wild ecstasy? (lines 8–10)

Lines inspiring questions from my students include these:

> Sylvan historian, who canst thus express / A flowery
> tale more sweetly than our rhyme (lines 3–4)

Why is the urn called "sylvan"/ Why is the urn a historian?

> Bold Lover, never, never canst thou kiss, / Though
> winning near the goal—yet do not grieve (lines 17–18)

Why should anyone or anything be happy to be constantly in the state of not achieving a desired goal?

> "Beauty is truth, truth beauty"—that is all / Ye know
> on earth, and all ye need to know. (lines 49–50)

Who says the words after the quoted sentence? The speaker or the urn? Is the speaker getting a message from the urn or giving a message to the readers?

William Shakespeare, *Hamlet* (p. 209)

Teaching *Hamlet* to an introductory class requires much thought and ingenuity. In recent years, I have been amazed by the number of students who have not read any Shakespeare in high school. In the past, I could confidently expect that, although many students professed a dislike for Shakespeare's plays, at least they had some acquaintance with his themes, his language, and the structure of tragedy. Since I can no longer make these assumptions, I have found myself faced with the dilemma of whether to spend two or three weeks on the play in order to achieve a fairly complete reading or to teach selectively with the goal of introducing—rather than fully teaching—the play.

After much soul-searching, I reaffirmed in my own mind that my primary aim in teaching an introductory course was to create a love— rather than a fear or dread—of literature. Therefore, my own approach to teaching any Shakespearean play has been to provide students with a brief scene-by-scene summary so that they are not struggling to understand what is happening and an introductory discussion of the play's themes, based on their reading of that summary. Next, I show them a film of the play. There are several good versions. I like the 1980 videotape with Derek Jacobi as Hamlet (available from Time-Life Video, Box 644, Paramus, NJ 07652).

After reading the summary and viewing the play, students seem more relaxed about approaching the text itself. I usually designate certain acts, scenes, and speeches for special attention and, in class, work through some of the more familiar (at least to instructors) parts by reading them aloud or asking students to read them aloud and then discussing the play's themes as reflected in those sections.

Should you find this approach compatible, I am including at the end of this discussion a brief summary that you may reproduce for your students' use.

Hamlet and the Theme of Innocence and Experience

Hamlet is included in this section because it seems to me that the play shows the painful transition of a number of young people from innocence to experience. For purposes of discussion and writing, I usually focus on Hamlet, a rather innocent character who begins the play facing the first challenge to assumptions he has made since childhood.

In Act I, Hamlet appears powerfully affected by the challenges to his belief in the sanctity of marriage, in loyalty, and in the honor of the crown. His failure to act once the ghost informs him of Claudius's treachery is often cited as the central problem of the play. It seems to me that when we remember that Hamlet is a very young man who has just faced his first major loss—the death of his father, complicated by his mother's hasty remarriage—the delay is highly understandable. He is not, after all, a world-weary and sophisticated court politician or a seasoned warrior. Only a few years away from adolescence, Hamlet still engages in angry shouting matches with his mother and resents his stepfather even before he is certain of Claudius's treachery.

It seems completely believable to me that Hamlet would wonder about the ghost's authenticity. He worries that the ghost might represent the devil rather than his dead father because the message the apparition brings is so frightening and the action it urges so extreme. Although angry at his mother and suspicious of his stepfather, Hamlet is not yet ready to give up entirely his naive (innocent) view that no action will really be necessary; he still hopes that somehow everything will come out all right and he will not have to take the responsibility of serious action. In addition to his doubts about the ghost, Hamlet also spends a great deal of time in subjective introspection. His thoughts—for example, contemplation of suicide in the "To be or not to be" soliloquy—underscore his youth and his desperate need to reassure himself that the disorder that now pervades his life will be resolved without his having to commit himself to violent action. Even the mousetrap scene, with Hamlet acting as theater director, underlines his youth and innocence. He seeks to play a trick on Claudius, to taunt him rather than confront him directly.

In his heated conversation with Gertrude in Act 3, scene 4, Hamlet acts because he loses his temper, not because he makes a reasoned decision to take action. He is prompted to murder Polonius by mistake, more by anger about his mother's remarriage than about his father's murder. No wonder that in this scene the ghost of the old king returns—the stern parent insisting that his son now throw off the protections and illusions of childhood and accept the demands of the complex adult world.

In Act 4, Hamlet finally faces his responsibility to himself, to his dead father, and to the state of Denmark. After going on the symbolic sea voyage where he successfully escapes the treachery of Claudius's envoys, Rosencrantz and Guildenstern, he returns to Denmark. He has gained experience through facing his own death and arrives at Elsinore determined to kill Claudius.

Continuing the theme of innocence and experience into the final act raises problems. Certainly, looking through the lens of present-day values, we would not see the bloodbath of Scene 2 as just punishment for Hamlet's inability to break loose soon enough from the innocence of his youth. You might point out to students that understanding the conventions of classical tragedy enables a fuller understanding of the play's conclusion. The sense of exaggeration gained from observing the fall of the great and powerful leads, of course, to the Aristotelian catharsis of pity and terror. In Act 5, we see Hamlet acknowledged as noble. Even Fortinbras calls him "most royal" and has his body treated with the honors due a heroic soldier. He has, indeed, moved from innocence to experience, most painfully and at a terrible cost. In the end, he urges Horatio to live and to "tell my story." He wants others to know what he has experienced, partly to clear his "wounded name" and partly to affirm the restoration of order that has resulted from his action and his sacrifice.

Sources for Further Study of *Hamlet*

Bradley, A. C. *Shakespearean Tragedy*. 1904. New York: St. Martin's, 1965.
Bradley's classic essay on *Hamlet* provides a solid, detailed discussion of character and motive.

Case Studies in Contemporary Criticism: Hamlet. Ed. Susanne L. Wofford. New York: Bedford-St. Martin's, 1994.
Provides biographical and historical contexts for the play as well as five essays representing various approaches to contemporary criticism: feminist, psychoanalytic, deconstruction, Marxist, and the New Historicism.

SUMMARY: HAMLET, PRINCE OF DENMARK

Act I

Scene 1: Night, outside Elsinore Castle

After relieving Francisco from guard duty, Bernardo meets Marcellus and Horatio and they see the ghostly apparition of the dead king who has been appearing regularly at this time of night. They discuss young Fortinbras's plan to recover the lands King Hamlet won from old Fortinbras. When the ghost reappears, Marcellus tries to hit it. The ghost fades from view, and the young men agree to tell Hamlet.

Scene 2: Inside the castle

After King Claudius dispatches Voltimand and Cornelius on a diplomatic mission to young Fortinbras's uncle, he and Queen Gertrude urge Hamlet to leave off grieving and to be more cheerful. Hamlet refuses and when Claudius and Gertrude leave, he expresses his distress at what he regards as his mother's hasty remarriage to his father's brother (less than two months after his father's death). Marcellus, Horatio, and Bernardo interrupt Hamlet as they arrive to tell him about seeing what they believe to be his father's ghost. Hamlet assures them that he will come at the appointed time to wait for the apparition that night. Following the period of mourning for King Hamlet, Laertes seeks and is given permission to return to Paris while King Claudius denies Hamlet's request to return to Wittenburg.

Scene 3: In Polonius's house

Before Laertes leaves for Paris, he warns his sister Ophelia to be cautious in her relationship with Hamlet because of his brooding melancholy. Annoyed with her brother's interference, she lectures him against pompous moralizing. Laertes's father, Polonius, makes a speech of advice to his son and then chastises his daughter, Ophelia, ordering her to stop seeing Hamlet. Reluctantly, she agrees.

Scene 4: Outside Elsinore Castle

Hamlet, Horatio, and Marcellus stand watch and the ghost appears. Hamlet follows the ghost's beckoning hand, although Horatio and Marcellus try to hold him back. When Hamlet breaks away to follow the ghost, they go after him.

Scene 5: Outside Elsinore, but away from the scene of the original appearance of the ghost

The ghost claims to be Hamlet's father and reveals the details of his murder at the hands of King Claudius. Overcome with grief, rage, and shock, Hamlet refuses to tell Horatio and Marcellus what he has heard. He makes them swear—and his vow is echoed by the ghost—never to tell what they have seen.

Act II

Scene 1: In Polonius's house

Polonius dispatches Reynaldo to Paris to check up on Laertes and to see whether he is leading a wanton life. Ophelia comes to speak to her father, telling him that Hamlet has visited her. She is upset because his clothes were in disarray, he stared at her, and then he left without saying a word. Polonius takes this behavior as evidence of Hamlet's excess of love for Ophelia and plans to describe Hamlet's actions to King Claudius.

Scene 2: In the castle

Assuming that Hamlet is mad, Claudius and Gertrude urge Rosencrantz and Guildenstern to distract him from what they see as his excess emotion. Ambassadors from Norway enter with Polonius; they explain that Fortinbras has been arrested and request Claudius to grant him safe passage through Denmark. After convincing the king and queen that Hamlet's love for Ophelia has brought on his madness, Polonius tricks Hamlet into meeting with him where he can be observed. In his conversation with Polonius, Hamlet seems to be speaking ambiguously; his words could be taken for madness but they also suggest ironic wisdom and comprehension of the circumstances he faces. When Rosencrantz and Guildenstern try to talk Hamlet out of his madness, he cleverly gets them to admit that they have been sent by Claudius and Gertrude. The actors for the play Hamlet has planned arrive. He welcomes them and gives them instructions for the play he has planned to trap King Claudius. In the soliloquy that closes this scene, Hamlet agonizes over his failure to act immediately to avenge his father's death.

Act III

Scene 1: In the castle

After Rosencrantz and Guildenstern report their encounter with Hamlet to Claudius, Gertrude, and Polonius, the queen leaves while the king and Polonius hide so that they can watch Hamlet and Ophelia meet. At this point, in an aside intended to be heard only by the audience, Claudius admits that his conscience is troubled by the crime he has committed. Hamlet enters and, believing himself alone, speaks aloud in a soliloquy questioning whether he should face his problems or avoid them by committing suicide. When Ophelia enters, he tells her he no longer loves her and rants against the inconstancy of women and the institution of marriage. Polonius sees this impassioned speech as evidence of Hamlet's lovesickness, but Claudius, perhaps because of his guilty conscience, begins to believe Hamlet's madness may have a different cause. After telling Polonius that he intends to send Hamlet to England, Claudius agrees that Polonius should hide and eavesdrop in Gertrude's room while Hamlet talks with her.

Scene 2: In the castle: the hall

Hamlet advises the actors on how to perform their roles and tells Horatio his purpose in directing the play. He asks Horatio to help him observe the King's reactions during the performance. Gertrude, Claudius, Polonius, and Ophelia arrive, and the play begins. In the opening action, the player King and Queen demonstrate their love for each other. Then another player pours poison in the player King's ear and immediately sets to wooing the player Queen with gifts.

At this point, Claudius orders the play to stop and leaves the hall, obviously upset. Rosencrantz and Guildenstern come to Hamlet after the play and tell him that Gertrude wants to see him. Hamlet talks mysteriously with them and later with Polonius, seeming to be mad. Yet in the closing soliloquy he reveals that his purpose is to trap his uncle: "to speak daggers, but use none."

Scene 3: In the castle

Claudius orders Rosencrantz and Guildenstern to accompany Hamlet to England, while Polonius goes to hide in Gertrude's rooms (as he and the king had previously agreed). After Polonius leaves, the King tries to pray, but finds he cannot ask God's pardon while he still holds the office he gained through murder. Hamlet enters and sees the King praying; while he recognizes the opportunity he has to kill Claudius, he decides not to do so, explaining that to kill him at prayer might mean the King's soul would be dispatched to Heaven. Hamlet vows to catch him, instead, at a time when he will be sent straight to Hell.

Scene 4: In the Queen's rooms

During his conversation with his mother, Hamlet alarms the Queen and she calls for help. Polonius, hiding behind a screen in her rooms, responds, and Hamlet, believing he has heard King Claudius, stabs and kills Polonius. As Hamlet tries to explain the evil of King Claudius to his mother, the ghost reappears. Only Hamlet sees the ghost, who urges his son to stay committed to his purpose: revenge. Shaken, Hamlet urges the Queen to ask heaven for forgiveness, to refuse to sleep with Claudius, and to tell him nothing about the murder of Polonius. Expressing his distrust of Rosencrantz and Guildenstern, Hamlet says good-bye to his mother and then takes Polonius's body into the adjoining room.

Act IV

Scene 1: In the Queen's rooms

After Gertrude tells Claudius that Hamlet has killed Polonius, the king expresses concern that Hamlet's action will be blamed on him because he did not restrain his nephew/stepson. He then summons Rosencrantz and Guildenstern to carry the body to the chapel, and goes to inform the court of Polonius's death.

Scene 2: In the castle

Rosencrantz and Guildenstern question Hamlet about the location of the corpse, but he refuses to cooperate. He accuses them of being toadies to the requests and favors of Claudius.

Scene 3: In the castle

Claudius expresses concern that he will not be able to punish Hamlet's murder of Polonius because the people of Denmark admire Hamlet so much. In a conversation that dashes from one point to another, Hamlet responds to the king's questions about the location of the corpse by saying that Polonius is in heaven; is at supper (actually, providing supper for worms); and that he is decaying and that Claudius will begin to smell him soon throughout the castle. After being ordered to England, Hamlet bids the king an ironic and bitter farewell. As he leaves, Claudius orders guards to follow him and then, in a soliloquy, reveals his plan to have Hamlet killed in England.

Scene 4: A battlefield in Denmark

As he is leaving, Hamlet encounters Fortinbras's army and learns from one of the officers that they are fighting for what the soldiers consider an insignificant plot of land. In a soliloquy, Hamlet reflects on the meaningless mission of these soldiers and compares their action for a cause of little importance with his lack of action for a cause of great importance. Recognizing the magnitude of his purpose, he vows to seek revenge through bloody action.

Scene 5: In the castle

  Singing lines from romantic ballads and behaving in a dazed manner, Ophelia tries to talk with Gertrude about her distress. After she leaves, Laertes angrily arrives with his supporters, insisting that he be told the name of his father's killer. Gertrude tries to quiet Laertes, but Claudius imperiously commands her to let him proceed. At this point, Ophelia enters again, still singing in a lost and distracted way. Her brother, Laertes, is heartsick to see his sister's grief and madness and he and the king leave to confer about Laertes's demands.

Scene 6: In the castle

  Horatio reads a letter from Hamlet explaining his capture by pirates and dropping oblique hints about the involvement of Rosenkrantz and Guildenstern in a plot against him.

Scene 7: In the castle

  Claudius seeks to calm Laertes by explaining that he could not punish Hamlet directly because of the people's love for him and because of his mother's pleas. The king implies, however, that Laertes will not need to seek revenge because Hamlet has been dispatched. This conversation is interrupted by a messenger bringing a letter from Hamlet informing Claudius that he will arrive back in Denmark shortly. Laertes heatedly expresses his desire for revenge, and Claudius decides to put Laertes's anger to use. He suggests a duel, knowing that Laertes is a skilled swordsman. Further, he intends to poison the tip of Laertes's sword. If both plans fail, the king will have a cup of poison which he plans to trick Hamlet into drinking. At this point the Queen enters and reveals that Ophelia has committed suicide by drowning herself.

Act V

Scene 1: The churchyard

  Two gravediggers make dark jokes about death as they prepare Ophelia's grave. Hamlet and Horatio enter, not knowing that the grave is for Ophelia. When the funeral procession arrives, the shortened ceremony tells Hamlet that the rites are for a suicide. He infers from Laertes's speech that the dead person is Ophelia. In his grief, Laertes leaps into the open grave, begging to be buried with his sister, and Hamlet follows him into the grave, proclaiming his love for Ophelia. Laertes and Hamlet fight, but are restrained and Hamlet leaves. Claudius then confirms with Laertes his plan for the duel.

Scene 2: In the castle: the hall

Hamlet explains to Horatio that he discovered the plot against him and tricked Rosencrantz and Guildenstern by substituting the letter they carried ordering his death with a letter ordering their deaths. He made the letter convincing by sealing it with his father's ring. A messenger arrives and delivers the challenge for the duel with Laertes. Hamlet agrees, but before the fencing begins, he pleads with Laertes to pardon him. Laertes refuses and the duel begins. Hamlet fences well and his mother toasts his performance, drinking from the cup of poison before Claudius can interfere.

At this point Laertes wounds Hamlet and, as they struggle, they both drop their swords and each picks up the sword belonging to the other. Hamlet then wounds Laertes, and Laertes (knowing the sword is poisoned) cries out that he is dying. Gertrude dies from drinking the poison, and in his grief and rage Hamlet finally carries out his promise for revenge and kills Claudius with the poisoned sword. As Laertes dies, he forgives Hamlet. In the final moments, Hamlet begs Horatio, who is threatening to kill himself, to remain alive to tell the true story of what has happened, to clear Hamlet's name, and to restore order to Denmark.

Envoys from England arrive announcing Rosencrantz's and Guildenstern's deaths and demanding their reward. Fortinbras enters, having won a victory, and claims the crown. It can be expected that Denmark will now have a new leader, just as Hamlet had earlier predicted. Fortinbras orders Hamlet's body to be carried off with the pomp and ceremony befitting an honored warrior.

Langston Hughes, "Salvation" (p. 329)

In Hughes's essay, *salvation* takes on at least two distinct meanings. To Auntie Reed, the minister, and the congregation of the church, *salvation* means achieving the state of grace that promises eternal life. In this view, the person who publicly testifies to his or her belief in Jesus is saved (attains *salvation*) from dying. To the speaker, however, *salvation* comes to mean being true to himself, literally saving himself from living a lie. Another possible definition of *salvation* might come from Westley, who takes a pragmatic approach and saves himself from enduring the pleas and prayers of the earnest church members.

The narrator cries, I think, because he recognizes that rather than being saved, he has, in fact, lost something. Not only has he lied, but worse, he has not been struck down by God, which suggests to him that God (as he has pictured Him) may not exist. He also sees his aunt differently, recognizing that her pleas were probably motivated not only by her concern for his immortal soul but also by her desire that her nephew behave in an accepted way at the church service where the focus seems to be on the outward form of religion rather than on inward and spiritual changes.

Maya Angelou, "Graduation in Stamps" (p. 332)

"The children in Stamps trembled visibly with anticipation." Beginning with this powerful opening sentence, Angelou describes in detail the preparations her community makes for the graduation. By stressing the importance of the ceremony, and its implications, Angelou develops in the reader the same sense of dread and anticipation she herself feels. In addition, the community's pride is sharply contrasted with the desultory attitude of the white speaker, Mr. Donleavy, who not only condescends to the graduates, but also fails to stay for the awarding of diplomas, giving the impression that he was now "off to something really important."

By assuming that the black graduates can hope only for menial work or, at best, to be star athletes on a high school or college team, Donleavy deflates the hopes of the graduates as well as their teachers, relatives, and friends. As Marguerite (Maya) goes forward to get her diploma, she has even been stripped of her sense of identity: "My name had lost its ring of familiarity and I had to be nudged to go and receive my diploma." Possibility and promise are restored to her— and to others—only by the unexpected and out-of-character action of the quiet, proper valedictorian who turns his back on the audience to sing with his fellow classmates the song they all know as "The Negro National Anthem." This single, inspired gesture brings the graduates together with their teachers, friends, and relatives in the audience who are now able to regain their pride and connection with one another and with their black identity.

Reading Hamlet's soliloquy aloud with a brief explanation of its context will provide an extra dimension to Henry Reed's speech and to Marguerite's response as she listens to it.

CHAPTER 6
ROOTS, IDENTITY, AND CULTURE

In another textbook, *Connections* (Mountain View, CA: Mayfield, 1993), I introduce the concept of "culture" as follows:

> Culture may be defined as the ideas, customs, values, skills, and arts of a specific group of people. Most of us belong not to one cultural group but to several. For instance, our age places us in a culture such as childhood, youth, or middle age. We may be called "baby boomers," or "children of the eighties,"and these phrases may trigger in the minds of those who hear or read them certain images or values. In addition, we are all either male or female, and the way various societies treat gender differences has traditionally created cultural distinctions between men and women. Another group we belong to relates to the country of our birth or to the country where our ancestors were born. We may be Norwegian, Japanese, Native American, Irish-American, African-American or we may come from a combination of ethnic roots.

The selections in this chapter all look at some aspect of the various cultures that make up the United States. As you introduce the theme of roots, identity, and culture, you may want to discuss with students the importance of cross-cultural study. For example, learning to read and to think critically in the context of different cultures are essential skills not only for reading this thematic chapter but also for fully appreciating many other college courses. In addition, these skills are necessary for working effectively in an increasingly diverse environment and for living, not just with tolerance, but also with real understanding for the many groups of people who make up the citizens of the United States—and of the world.

In many other courses—for example, history, sociology, psychology, business, science, literature, art, music, and religion—students will study aspects of other cultures. Similarly, in their future professional lives they will almost certainly work with people from different cultural groups who are making significant contributions to their chosen fields.

To encourage students to see themselves not as observers but rather as participants in cross-cultural study, you may want to use the following introductory exercises:

Exercise 1:

Ask students to list as many cultural groups as possible of which they see themselves as members. These cultural groups may relate to age, ethnic background, religious preference, political beliefs, current work status.

After the lists are completed, each student may choose one of the cultural groups to which he or she belongs and write a paragraph describing the ideas, customs, values, skills, and/or arts of that group.

Exercise 2:

Ask students to write a paragraph or two responding to one of the following topics:

A.   Describe an example of something you read or heard in another class that gave you a view of a cultural perspective other than your own. Explain what new ideas or possibilities were suggested by this perspective.

B.   Describe an incident from a television program or a film you have seen that showed you a cultural perspective different from your own. Explain what new ideas or possibilities were suggested by this perspective.

C.   Describe an event from your work that showed you a cultural perspective different from your own. Explain what new ideas or possibilities were suggested by this perspective.

The selections in this chapter focus on the relationship between culture and identity and suggest that defining "culture" or identifying one's relationship to "culture" is never simple. For example, "Sonny's Blues," "Everyday Use," "We Wear the Mask," "Telephone Conversation," "I Am a Black Woman," and *Fences* all look at individuals who are establishing their identity within the black culture. With the exception of the speaker in "Telephone Conversation," all come from the black culture of the United States. Yet the conflicts, values, and issues represented vary widely. Reading several of these selections should encourage students to view the topic of roots and culture as complex—not something that can be neatly packaged and easily explained.

"Cathedral" is an interesting piece because it looks at the culture of physical difference. One of the main characters is blind; his responses to the other characters and their responses to him challenge many stereotypical assumptions about the nature of physical, emotional, and spiritual blindness. The motif of blindness leads to the consideration of *Oedipus Rex*. In his search for identity and his misunderstanding of his roots, he is often blinded intellectually and emotionally, and this blindness is, of course, symbolically played out by his self-mutilation in the drama's conclusion.

Chief Seattle's speech and Jeanne Wakatsuki Houston's nonfiction piece explore the motif of exile as related to roots, identity, and culture. Both Seattle and Houston address the losses and injuries done to those who are torn from their homes—their roots—and forced to live as marginal people on the periphery of the dominant culture.

ADDITIONAL SELECTIONS FOR CONSIDERATION: ROOTS, IDENTITY, AND CULTURE

Title and Author	Text Page
Fiction	
"Araby," James Joyce	148
"And the Soul Shall Dance," Wakako Yamauchi	153
"The Red Convertible: Lyman Lamartine," Louise Erdrich	160
"Battle Royal," Ralph Ellison	169
"The Circling Hand," Jamaica Kincaid	181
"El Tonto del Barrio," José Armas	568
"Young Goodman Brown," Nathaniel Hawthorne	634
"Shiloh," Bobbie Ann Mason	665
"The Conversion of the Jews," Philip Roth	770
"The Lesson," Toni Cade Bambara	914
"The Loudest Voice," Grace Paley	921
"A Class of New Canadians," Clark Blaise	927

Text Page

"Famous All Over Town," Danny Santiago   935

"On the Other Side of the War: A Story," Elizabeth Gordon   1006

"Spoils of War," Janice Mirikitani   1038

"A Rose for Emily," William Faulkner   1132

Poetry

"Incident," Countee Cullen   192

"Grape Sherbet," Rita Dove   205

"The Unknown Citizen," W. H. Auden   604

"Lot's Wife," Kristine Batey   687

"My Papa's Waltz," Theodore Roethke   827

"Making the Jam without You," Maxine Kumin   828

"Digging," Seamus Heaney   837

"A Teacher Taught Me," Anna Lee Walters   948

"Raising My Hand," Antler   953

"What Were They Like?" Denise Levertov   1062

"Brueghel's Two Monkeys,"
    Wislawa Szymborska   Art and Poetry Section

"The Man with the Blue Guitar,"
    Wallace Stevens   Art and Poetry Section

"In the Waiting Room," Elizabeth Bishop   1227

"The Bean Eaters," Gwendolyn Brooks   1235

"Boy Breaking Glass," Gwendolyn Brooks   1236

"To the Young Who Want to Die," Gwendolyn Brooks   1237

Drama

A Doll House, Henrik Ibsen   697

Painting Churches, Tina Howe   839

Picnic on the Battlefield, Fernando Arrabal   1065

Title and Author	Text Page
Essays	
"Salvation," Langston Hughes	329
"Graduation in Stamps," Maya Angelou	332
"Where I Come From Is Like This," Paula Gunn Allen	758
"Being a Man," Paul Theroux	765
"I Remember Papa," Harry Dolan	895
"Learning to Read and Write," Frederick Douglass	987
"In Search of Our Mothers' Gardens," Alice Walker	992
"The American Way of Death," Jessica Mitford	1194

SUGGESTIONS FOR TEACHING ADDITIONAL SELECTIONS

1. How do relationships between parents and children relate to the connections between understanding one's roots and culture and developing a sense of personal identity? Consider the following works as you explore this topic:

	Text Page
"And the Soul Shall Dance"	153
"The Circling Hand"	181
"The Conversion of the Jews"	770
"The Loudest Voice"	921
"Grape Sherbet"	205
"Digging"	837
Painting Churches	839
"I Remember Papa"	895
"In Search of Our Mothers' Gardens"	992

2. How do gender considerations relate to the understanding of roots and culture and to the development of identity? Consider the following works as you explore this question:

	Text Page
"Young Goodman Brown"	634
"Shiloh"	665
"Lot's Wife"	687
A Doll House	697
Painting Churches	839
"Where I Come From Is Like This"	758
"Being a Man"	765
"In Search of Our Mothers' Gardens"	992

3. Characters and personae in some of the following works find themselves faced with a conflict related to the stereotyped assumptions about their culture group and their own hopes and dreams for discovering/building their own identity. As you think about this conflict, consider the following selections:

	Text Page
"Battle Royal"	169
"The Conversion of the Jews"	770
"The Loudest Voice"	921
"Incident"	192
"A Teacher Taught Me"	948
"Graduation in Stamps"	332
"Where I Come From Is Like This"	839
"Being a Man"	765
"I Remember Papa"	895
"Learning to Read and Write"	987
"In Search of Our Mothers' Gardens"	992

4. Choose any of the additional selections and compare the experiences of the characters or personae with your own experiences of the relationship between roots, identity, and culture.

THEMATIC PHOTOGRAPH (p. 345)

Considerations

1. Create a story that begins and ends with the arrival of one of the people depicted in this photo.

2. Write a journal entry relating to the "Roots and Memories" recalled by one of the depicted individuals.

3. Write an explanation of what you think any of the people shown here might have lost, as well as what you think he or she might have gained, through the arrival shown in the photo.

READINGS

James Baldwin, "Sonny's Blues" (p. 346)

The story begins with the narrator's distress over Sonny's arrest for selling and using drugs. Because the narrator's description is pain filled, yet also concerned, most readers feel strong sympathy for him. Yet the story is titled "Sonny's Blues" and, in fact, concerns Sonny as much as it does his brother. Sonny's story comes to us in fragments with recurring motifs, somewhat like jazz improvisation.

From the early years of his life, Sonny and his brother have heard their parents disagree about the possibilities that lie ahead. Sonny follows his father's view, leading a life that suggests the father's pronouncement that there "[a]in't no place safe for kids, nor nobody." The narrator, on the other hand, has adopted their mother's belief that they can escape the prisons of poverty and racial injustice. He has become a teacher and a committed husband and father.

No one in the family can understand Sonny's need to become a musician or the desperation he feels in trying to face down the dangers of the old neighborhood. The brothers grow apart, and yet when the narrator's young daughter dies from a painful illness, Sonny responds with sensitivity and kindness to the letter giving him the news. Recognizing Sonny's willingness to put the past behind him, the narrator—perhaps because of the pain he has experienced in his own life—becomes less judgmental and more forgiving.

In the final scene, the narrator listens to the notes of "Am I Blue" while Creole urges Sonny to create his own blues. The narrator knows the attraction heroin still holds for Sonny, yet he also sees the powerful attraction music holds for his brother. Sonny has managed to survive long enough to play his own song, and the narrator can now recognize the beauty in his brother's world as well as the danger.

Alice Walker, "Everyday Use: For Your Grandmama" (p. 371)

When you assign this story, you may want to talk with students about the Black Muslim movement and its influence, particularly in the 1960s. Many younger students who do not know about the Black Muslims will not understand why Dee and Hakim-a-barber have taken new names or why they don't eat pork.

Walker's subtitle refers specifically to the older generation of black people, and especially black women, who found the rush to adopt African culture bewildering and, in some cases, insulting. In a larger context, the subtitle may refer to all grandmamas who look at the younger generation and see a repudiation of their own way of life.

Walker's story shows the narrator's and Maggie's side of the story. Certainly the first four sections demonstrate the contrast between what Mama, Maggie, and the homeplace are and the way Dee/Wangero would like to romanticize them. For example, the first section shows Mama admiring her beautiful, carefully swept yard. Later in the story, Dee ignores the yard and instead takes pictures of the dilapidated house, intending no doubt to regale her friends with stories of her backward mother and sister who still live in quaint rural poverty.

While Dee definitely comes off as the villain of the piece, several students have pointed out that she is not entirely wrong. She sees her heritage from one narrow perspective, but Mama and Maggie are equally adamant in refusing to see the possibilities Dee's new awareness might bring them.

Raymond Carver, "Cathedral" (p. 379)

The discussion starts with energy and humor if students read aloud their descriptions of and responses to the narrator. Not since Archie Bunker has there been a bigot who makes such an easy target yet who also demands such careful attention. The narrator's view of blind people is incredibly prejudiced. He claims that his "idea of blindness came from the movies," yet his narrowness seems to move even beyond screen stereotypes. He is amazed that Robert wears a beard and cannot imagine that a blind man would drink alcohol or smoke.

His initial negative response to Robert's visit is compounded by his jealousy of his wife's former relationships. When she describes to him her final day at work with Robert, the narrator clearly interprets Robert's desire to "see" her face with his fingertips as a move that is primarily sexually motivated.

As the story progresses, however, Robert leads the unwitting narrator to grow and learn in spite of himself. As he sits drawing the cathedral, he thinks of Robert's question "[A]re you in any way religious?" The narrator begins to see that he has been spiritually blind and that Robert is the one who sees the world in its fullness and beauty. As the narrator sits with his eyes closed tracing the final lines of the cathedral, he feels truly free for the first time in his life. "I was in my house," he says. "But I didn't feel like I was inside anything."

Anna Lee Walters, "The Warriors" (p. 391)

Anna Lee Walters has stated that she sees the roots and culture of the Native American as alive, flourishing, and "by no means [the reflection] of a vanishing or defeated people." Uncle Ralph personifies this belief. Although he dies as what the dominant American culture might define as a "down and out" homeless man, neither Ralph himself nor his sister and nieces would have accepted or recognized this as a valid description of their brother/uncle.

Ralph sees himself as someone who looks at the world in an unconventional way. He accords the hobo culture a sense of dignity when he says: "You see . . . hobos are a different kind. They see things in a different way. Them hobos are kind of like us. We're not like other people in some ways and yet we are. It has to do with what you see and feel when you look at this old world." Like the hobos, Ralph refuses to be tied to material possessions, yet unlike the hobos the story depicts, he sees himself as strongly connected both to his birth family and to his tribal family. By choosing to view himself as a warrior, Ralph creates his identity as protector and provider. Although he bemoans the younger generation who "just want to go to the Moon," he has not given up on the possibility of transmitting the culture he knows. His lessons on Pawnee language, customs, music, dance, and legends create in his nieces a sense that they are special and that they have a connection with all other Native Americans. Note, for example, that when the two sisters meet the hobo who acknowledges that he is Indian, Sister insists that he does have people and tries to get him to return to his "folks [who are] probably looking for you and worrying 'bout you."

During Ralph's final visit with Pumpkin Blossom (the narrator), he asks her, "Do you know who you are?" When she hesitates, he goes on, "Do you know that you are a Pawnee?" It's clear that he regards his mission as a warrior as fulfilled; he has fought for and won an identity for his sister's children. They will not go through life "like all the others," but will, instead, remember what Ralph has taught them. They do not struggle simply for day-to-day survival, but rather look beyond. "Our battle is for beauty," Sister says in the concluding speech. Both sisters have learned the value of their heritage, the gifts it brings and the costs it exacts.

Amy Tan, "Rules of the Game" (p. 402)

Students who have read Tan's novel *The Joy Luck Club* (or seen the film) may recognize this story as part of the larger work examining the relationships among four Chinese immigrant mothers and their American-born daughters. In her determination to see her daughter succeed, Waverly's mother teaches her "the art of invisible strength." Although partly this invisible strength seems to relate to traditional female roles, part of it seems an adaptive strategy to survive in an unfamiliar circumstance. When Waverly whines for plums, the mother teaches her to "bite back your tongue," and Waverly finds herself rewarded when she follows this advice. On the other hand, when Waverly and her brothers are learning how to play chess, their mother warns them about "American rules." They need to learn these rules so that they will not find themselves at the mercy of people who understand how to succeed but who refuse to share this information with those who are new to the culture.

At first, Waverly's progress in chess can be attributed, in part, to her mother's advice. As she faces her opponents, she hears her mother's voice echoing, "Blow from the South. . . . The wind leaves no trail." She also keeps in mind the secrets Lau Po taught her. These strategies relate her talent to her roots in Chinese culture. As Waverly becomes more adept at chess, however, she begins to ignore tradition. She is no longer as polite with her opponents, and both she and her parents allow her to escape chores she would normally have done. As a result, she becomes disdainful of her brothers and, eventually, even forgets her role as dutiful daughter and goes so far as to act out against her mother.

While Waverly sees herself as different from her mother, believing that her mother is embarrassing, old-fashioned, and overly proud of her daughter, in fact, the two are very much alike. The final scene shows that they take competition equally seriously. Just as Waverly has been engaged in showing her power over her opponents, her mother (at least in Waverly's view) has been engaged in maintaining power over her daughter. The opponent in the final vision is clearly the mother—her eyes have been described previously as "angry black slits" and her earlier advice to Waverly is echoed here in her triumphant cry, "Strongest wind cannot be seen."

William Wordsworth, "The World is too much with us" (p. 411)

The speaker in "The World is too much with us" expresses his sorrow and concern that the modern world (this poem was written in 1807) has fallen out of touch with natural elements like the sea and earth. Rather than suggesting a literal return to the worship of gods and goddesses, the final lines indicate his yearning for a time when he believes human spirits were more connected with their roots in the elements of nature.

Paul Laurence Dunbar, "We Wear the Mask" (p. 412)

This poem provides a fine opportunity for students to respond visually to a poem. They might draw the masks they see confronting them in some situation in their lives or they might create one of their own masks.

T. S. Eliot, "Journey of the Magi" (p. 413)

The biblical gospels see the birth of Jesus in the Christian context. Every detail emphasizes the miraculous nature of the event. The speaker in Eliot's poem, on the other hand, does not understand the relation between Jesus's birth and his subsequent earthly death and so remains puzzled. The speaker was deeply moved by what he saw in Bethlehem and so questioned his old faith, culture, and identity. Yet as he has not made the leap to enlightenment, he feels weighted with doubt and disillusionment.

William Butler Yeats, "The Lake Isle of Innisfree" (p. 414)

Students admire different images of Yeats's Lake Isle retreat, but most agree that the qualities represented include simplicity, quiet, peace, solitude, self-sufficiency, and natural beauty. These are the qualities from which the speaker builds his identity; his roots are in the Lake Isle and wherever he may be, he is able to take strength, comfort, and renewal from what he finds there.

Wole Soyinka, "Telephone Conversation" (p. 415)

Students will notice immediately the expectations of the landlady. She wants a white tenant and when her hope is challenged, she tries to show her enlightenment by indicating that if the tenant is not "very dark" she may still consider him. She seems to believe that having a light color is a virtue and that even an African may be all right if he is light enough. The prospective tenant, in the meantime, amuses himself with ironic visions of his questioner, whom he envisions as having a "lipstick coated, long gold-rolled/Cigarette-holder" voice.

Mari Evans, "I Am a Black Woman" (p. 417)

The speaker envisions the black woman always watching the men in her life suffer and die: by leaping overboard to escape the slave ship; by lynching; and by dying in wars (Anzio Beach—World War II; Da Nang—Vietnam; Pork Chop Hill—Korea). She also suggests that she, too, has fought (perhaps in civil rights conflicts where tear gas was used to control protesters). She has endured these horrors and still survives.

While most students admire this prototype of the black woman, some find her description too strongly rooted in and dependent on male, rather than female, experience.

Cathy Song, "The Youngest Daughter" (p. 418)

The youngest daughter may plan an escape, but she will never be free even after her mother's death. The details of the poem suggest her close relationship with her mother and her ability to see her mother as a complex woman, not simply as an idealized parent or as a burden. Like the cranes that hang by the window, the daughter cannot leave, but she can "fly up in a sudden breeze" and surprise both her mother and herself by thinking new thoughts and imagining myriad possibilities.

One of my students provided an insight into the image of the cranes: it is a custom of some oriental cultures to cut or fold many tiny paper cranes and to hang them in a window as a symbol of luck and hope.

Wendy Rose, "I Expected My Skin and My Blood to Ripen" (p. 419)

In teaching this poem, you may want to explain the significance of Wounded Knee. While the story is complicated, most historians agree that U.S. troops fired on Native Americans because they refused to stop participating in the ghost dance, a ritual that the U.S. government saw as enforcing Native American resistance. Along with the ghost dancers, many of those killed were unarmed women, children, and elderly men. The dancers regarded their ritual as one way of maintaining their culture against the relentless assault from the U.S. government to undermine it.

The speaker in the poem rails against not only the original slaughter, but also against the insults of scientists and souvenir collectors who see the massacre only as an event from which to gather data and memorabilia.

Mei-Mei Berssenbrugge, "Chronicle" (p. 421)

The mother described in this poem definitely challenges her culture. By adopting the behavior that would normally be tolerated only by the "first son," she frees herself from the traditional responsibilities of wife, mother, daughter, sister. Students may find it interesting to discuss the costs and benefits of such challenges—What is gained? What is lost?

Judith Ortiz Cofer, "Latin Women Pray" (p. 422)

Students should really enjoy this poem, which challenges the images of traditional Judeo-Christian religion. The understated irony, particularly of the final two lines, indicates the contrast between the hopes the women have as they pray and the realities they have learned to face in their daily lives.

Sophocles, *Oedipus Rex* (p. 423)

Background

Sophocles wrote three plays depicting the lives and fortunes of King Oedipus and his children: *Oedipus Rex, Antigone,* and *Oedipus at Colonus.* Of course, the Greek audiences who viewed these plays would have known the original stories on which they are based. The pleasure the audience took in following the fateful steps of Oedipus and Antigone came not from a simple desire to know "how everything came out," but rather to see and contemplate once again the horrifying chain of events that leads to the tragic final scene of these plays. It is my belief that modern readers and theatergoers will increase their appreciation of Sophocles's works if they, like the ancient Greeks, understand what is going on before they see or read the play.

Before I teach the play, I spend some time acquainting students with Oedipus's story. Most listeners are hooked the minute the details of Oedipus's early life are revealed. Who could resist the tale of the helpless infant whom his mother, Jocasta, is forced to give up because his father, Laios, fears the Oracle's prediction that his son will grow up to murder Laios and marry Jocasta? The striking image of the baby with his ankles pierced and pinned together to prevent any possibility of escape helps students to understand the desperate lengths taken to ward off the Oracle's prophecy. Of course, the Greek audience would also have known that the Oracle was not so easily denied and that, after being discovered by a shepherd, Oedipus was adopted by King Polybus and Queen Merope of Corinth. As the tale progresses, Oedipus's discovery of the Oracle's pronouncement leads him to self-imposed exile from Corinth where he hopes to ward off his fate and the fate of Polybus and Merope, who he believes are his birth parents.

After learning of this background, students are also intrigued to learn of the immediate events that precede the play. Oedipus has saved Thebes from the Sphinx, a terrifying creature who has the head of a woman but the body of a lion. While Thebes was at the mercy of the Sphinx, anyone who encountered her was forced to guess the answer to the following riddle: What goes on four legs in the morning, two legs at noon, and three legs in the evening? Those who failed to find the correct answer became the Sphinx's next meal. Oedipus, however, gave the correct answer, "man," but shrewdly realized that the puzzle was also a metaphor: humans crawl on all fours in the morning (infancy); walk on two legs at noon (childhood, adolescence, and adulthood); and hobble on three legs—one "leg" being a cane—at night (old age). After giving the right answer, Oedipus kills the Sphinx, and the grateful city of Thebes awards him the crown and offers him the recently widowed Queen Jocasta as his bride.

Of course, the Athenian audience knew that, in fact, Jocasta was Oedipus's birth mother and that Oedipus himself had killed King Laios in an earlier encounter. Needless to say, none of the principals— the people of Thebes, Jocasta, and Oedipus— realizes that the man who killed the king is also, ironically, the savior of the city. The play reveals the intricate workings of this complex plot and shows Oedipus moving relentlessly toward the horrifying moment when he realizes that he has been unable to escape his fate. As the first scene opens, Thebes has experienced a series of catastrophic events, including a pandemic plague. A priest enters and begs that Oedipus, who has already once saved the city, again deliver the people from disaster.

Roots, Identity, and Culture

The theme of roots, identity, and culture dominates the play. Oedipus's mistaken understanding of his roots and identity and his failure to respect the beliefs of his culture (the power of the Oracle) lead directly to his downfall and to the tragic denouement. The conflict between the individual and the demands of his culture is embodied in Oedipus's relationship with Teiresias. If he were a completely free individual, Oedipus would no doubt choose to disregard the seer entirely, yet as king and as a part of the Greek state he cannot. Finally, he must admit that even though he rules Thebes, he is not omniscient. He needs Teiresias's wisdom and because he rejects the blind seer's warnings, he finds himself both without "vision" (in all senses of the word) and without a state.

Of course, there is enormous complexity in the way these themes play out. For example, many people, including Jocasta, the shepherd, and Teiresias, urge Oedipus to stop seeking Laios's murderer. Yet Oedipus refuses, perhaps because of stubborn pride, to pull back and admit that he may not be able to step forward once again as the savior of Thebes. On the other hand, his persistence also has an admirable side. He does seek the truth without fear for himself, and he does believe that this quest will serve the people of Thebes.

At the beginning of the play, Oedipus's identity is clearly connected to his sense of power and control, and even as he strives to protect his people, he does not forget his own welfare. In the play's Prologue, he states, "By avenging the murdered king, I protect myself."

Yet at the end of the play, in the Exodos, following Jocasta's death, Oedipus blinds himself and, in his anguish, recognizes that he must give over his power, exile himself, and show concern for the future of his children rather than himself.

August Wilson, *Fences* (p. 466)

Fences is the second play in a proposed series of ten that Wilson is writing to provide a complex, diverse picture of the black experience in America. To help students understand some of the history that creates the roots of this play, you might encourage students to pay special attention to the brief summary of events provided in the stage directions. Here, Wilson juxtaposes the experiences of white European immigrants—who, however poor or oppressed, arrived of their own free will—with those of blacks—who were brought to the United States as slaves in chains.

In the short, introductory history, the metaphor of baseball first appears. Later, in the backyard setting, a homemade rag-baseball hangs from a tree's branch while a bat rests against its trunk. The date of the setting, 1957, is the year the world series pennant was captured by the Milwaukee Braves, but "the hot winds of change that would make the sixties a turbulent, racing, dangerous, and provocative decade had not yet begun to blow . . ." Thus, Wilson deftly combines the roots of the black American with the image of the quintessentially American sport, baseball.

Throughout the play, baseball images dominate Troy's speech, actions, and thoughts. For example, he describes himself as having been born with "two strikes against" him, but as "coming home safe" when he settled down with Rose and began a family. At that point, he began to believe he would lead a straight life and would not "strike out no more." When Troy argues with Cory, he acts as much the umpire as the father, warning his son "All right. That's strike two. . . . Don't you strike out." Most important, Troy regards his failure to become a professional ball player as representing all the goals and possibilities that have slipped from his grasp.

In addition to the baseball metaphor, another typically American image—the back fence—plays a significant role. Throughout the play, the half-built fence suggests the family's interactions. As Cory and Troy work on the fence, Troy constantly criticizes his son. Their inability to build together compatibly reflects their alienation from each other. Rose longs for the fence to be finished, seeing it as protection for her family; yet ironically, Troy finally completes it only after Alberta dies. The fence, then, seems Troy's way of keeping out negative forces (see, for example, his demands that Death stay away), but it never preserved love and safety as Rose had hoped.

As students consider the characters' actions, decisions, and choices in this play, they may note that each character builds an identity related to his or her values. For example, Troy, through his various struggles—particularly his time in prison—has come to believe in the importance of hard work and of supporting one's family. In Act 1, Scene 3, he tells Cory, "A man got to take care of his family . . . Cause it's my duty to take care of you. I owe a responsibility to you." It's interesting to note, however, that in pursuing his relationship with Alberta, he seems to believe more in the importance of his own satisfaction than in loyalty to his wife. Even when he tells Rose about his affair, he does not express regret, nor does he indicate an intention to stop seeing Alberta.

Rose's values come from her strong religious belief and from her commitment to her family. She constantly works as a mediator to try to help Troy and Cory to understand each other. Her faith seems to be the force that brings her to overcome her anger at Troy's affair and to agree to help him raise the daughter Alberta has borne him just before her death in childbirth. Just as Troy sees the world in terms of baseball images, Rose (true to her name) thinks in images of the garden. Consider, for example, her deeply felt speech that ends Act 2, Scene 1. Here, she envisions herself as a gardener:

> Troy, I took all my feelings, my wants and needs, my
> dreams . . . and I buried them inside you. I planted a
> seed and watched and prayed over it. I planted myself
> inside you and waited to bloom. And it didn't take me
> no eighteen years to find out the soil was hard and
> rocky, and it wasn't never gonna bloom.

Whereas Troy sees life as a game of baseball where striking out equates with death and loss, Rose visualizes a garden where some plants flourish and others fail to blossom because they lack the proper nurturing.

Troy's brother Gabriel is a fascinating character who represents two powerful aspects of culture: war and religion. Because of a wound Gabriel suffered during his service in World War II, Troy believes his brother is the Archangel Gabriel. Throughout the play, he appears sometimes as an avenging agent of God, striking out against those who taunt and ridicule, and sometimes as a holy innocent, unaware of the complexity of the world around him. Gabriel presents the play's final image as he struggles to play on his horn the perfect note he has been creating in his spirit throughout the postwar years. As he recognizes his failure to find this note on the horn—the traditional symbol of the Christian messenger—he instinctively turns to a ritualistic dance that suggests the African roots of his own spirituality. With this gesture, he finally unleashes the power built up inside his own mind and life and also within his brother's life. As Gabe completes the final steps of his dance, "the gates of heaven stand open as wide as God's closet."

Chief Seattle, "My People" (p. 528)

Images relating to the natural world are interwoven throughout Chief Seattle's speech. He sees nature as responsive to his people; for example, the sky becomes a compassionate guardian who "has wept tears upon my people for centuries untold." In addition, he expresses his observations about white people and their proposals by using metaphors from nature. He says, for instance, that the country is now filled with white people who are so numerous that they are "like the grass that covers vast prairies."

His use of natural images suggests his conviction that his people and their lives are inextricably linked with the land on which they have lived. It's nearly impossible to read his words and fail to understand the pain that must have been experienced by the displacement of a people who believed that their essential selves—as well as the selves of tribal members who had died—were one with the fields, mountains, and prairies where they hunted, gathered food, and worshipped.

Seattle's speech is a masterpiece of diplomacy. While he indicates his appreciation of the offer to buy his land and even notes philosophically that the passing of his own tribe may simply be part of the cycle of nature, he also manages to remind the white men with whom he is dealing of their part in the demise of Native Americans. While he condemns the impetuous young men of his tribe, he also notes that "our paleface brothers" hastened the tribe's "untimely decay." In addition, he does not simply hand over the lands but instead shows keen understanding of what he and his people are losing. He makes the agreement primarily because the military strength now lies entirely with white people, and he reminds Governor Stevens that the treaty calls for the white military to protect Seattle's people against attacks from other tribes. Seattle ends his speech by insisting that his people be granted permission to visit their old lands whenever they want and by creating the powerful vision of those tribal members who have died as lingering spirits that will not go away. Instead, they will linger to remind white people where their lands came from and to act as a warning that no matter how great and powerful a people may seem, the time will come when they will be forced to give way to others who have become more powerful.

Jeanne Wakatsuki Houston and James D. Houston, "Arrival at Manzanar" (p. 531)

This section of the autobiography *Farewell to Manzanar* does a fine job of showing how prejudice develops in children. As a child, Jeanne Wakatsuki (whose father has kept her separated from other Japanese families and has threatened to "sell [her] to the Chinaman" if she doesn't behave) fears all Oriental faces that do not belong to her relatives. The people who decide to intern the Japanese seem guided by the same kind of unreasoning terror. Since Japanese nationals are fighting against the Allied forces, it is assumed that Japanese-Americans will also be a threat. Like the young Wakatsuki, these people do not see individuals; they simply see ethnic characteristics like the "very slanted eyes" Wakatsuki mentions in paragraph 3.

As the Wakatsukis prepare to be evacuated, they encounter an antique dealer who is clearly making a huge profit on their undeserved misfortunes as well as a bus driver who sternly performs his task, unable (or unwilling) even to return the smile of a small child. At the camp, conditions are primitive and, perhaps worse, humiliating; those who provide food have not even tried to find out what the Japanese families would normally eat. Assuming that the tastes and values of their own culture are universal, these officials serve rice with sweetened fruit. The Japanese, who eat rice only with salty or savory food, have lost not only their homes and their means of making a living but even the right to eat what they please.

You might point out the racist implications in the decision to intern only Japanese-Americans. Americans of German or Italian ancestry were not, as a group, considered dangerous to national security.

CHAPTER 7
WORK

To begin study of this theme, consider asking students to write their definition of work and to explain the ways in which they see work as a significant part of their lives.

To break the selections in this chapter into subthemes, you might ask students to think about the way work has often been traditionally divided into "men's work" and "women's work." Younger students may be surprised to learn that newspaper "Help Wanted" advertisements used to be divided into "Help Wanted—Male" and "Help Wanted—Female." Discussing whether these distinctions still exist in any way provides entry into the following works: "Tom's Husband," "The Revolt of 'Mother,'" "The Yellow Wallpaper," "Typists," "Ella, in a Square Apron along Highway 80," "Waitresses," "The Country Midwife," *Trifles*, and "Professions for Women."

"The Use of Force," "El Tonto del Barrio," "To Be of Use," "The Unknown Citizen," "The Country Midwife," and *Trifles* look at values and at moral choices related to the world of work. Ask students to list moral choices that might arise in the work they are currently doing or hope to do when they complete school. Writing some of these choices on the board facilitates discussion of this aspect of work.

Most students have held jobs and are eager and willing to explain their own experiences with worker-management or worker-customer relations. Sharing such anecdotes in class discussion encourages deeper appreciation of works that explore relationships between workers and those who have authority over them or those whom they must serve. Consider, for example, "Tom's Husband," "The Revolt of 'Mother,'" "El Tonto del Barrio," "Waiting Table," and "Willie."

ADDITIONAL SELECTIONS FOR CONSIDERATION: WORK

Title and Author   **Text Page**

Fiction

"Sonny's Blues," James Baldwin   346

"The Warriors," Anna Lee Walters   391

"Shiloh," Bobbie Ann Mason   665

"I Stand Here Ironing," Tillie Olsen   790

"The Lesson," Toni Cade Bambara   914

"A Clean, Well-Lighted Place," Ernest Hemingway   1162

Poetry

"Lot's Wife," Kristine Batey   687

"Making the Jam without You," Maxine Kumin   828

"Digging," Seamus Heaney   837

"A Midnight Diner by Edward Hopper,"
    David Ray   Art and Poetry Section

"Mending Wall," Robert Frost   1212

Drama

Fences, August Wilson   466

A Doll House, Henrik Ibsen   697

Painting Churches, Tina Howe   839

Oleanna, David Mamet   955

Essays

"I Remember Papa," Harry Dolan   895

"Being a Man," Paul Theroux   765

"In Search of Our Mothers' Gardens," Alice Walker   992

SUGGESTIONS FOR TEACHING ADDITIONAL SELECTIONS

1. What is the relationship between work and the creative arts? Can creating be considered work only when there is a visible product? Must the artist gain fame, acclaim, or monetary reward for his or her effort to be considered work? Do you consider activities such as making jam, building models, writing poetry, or gardening as art, work, recreation?

	Text Page
"Shiloh"	665
"Sonny's Blues"	346
"The Warriors"	391
"Making the Jam without You"	828
"Digging"	837
"Being a Man"	765
Painting Churches	839
"In Search of Our Mothers' Gardens"	992

2. How are workers affected by their employers or others on whom their continued employment depends (for instance, the guests a waitress serves or the audience for whom an actor performs)? When do workers have power over their own lives? When do they lack power? How do they respond to having or lacking power?

	Text Page
"Sonny's Blues"	346
"I Stand Here Ironing"	790
Fences	466
A Doll House	697
"I Remember Papa"	895
"In Search of Our Mothers' Gardens"	992

3. The following works suggest the relationship between work and family. How do family tensions and pressures affect the work

people choose and their attitude toward that work? To what extent do—or should—people consider the values, aspirations, and hopes of family members when they choose or reject their own work?

	Text Page
"Sonny's Blues"	346
"The Warriors"	391
"Shiloh"	665
"I Stand Here Ironing"	790
"Digging"	837
Fences	466
Painting Churches	839
"I Remember Papa"	895
"In Search of Our Mothers' Gardens"	992

4. In the following works, writers who are not part of the white American culture explore issues related to work. Use these works as a starting point for further research on questions and concerns unique to members of minority groups in their quest to find meaningful work.

	Text Page
"Sonny's Blues"	346
"The Warriors"	391
"The Lesson"	914
Fences	466
"I Remember Papa"	895
"In Search of Our Mothers' Gardens"	992

THEMATIC PHOTOGRAPH (p. 539)

Considerations

1. Describe the person visible through the window of the restaurant. What does he look like? Speculate on his feelings about his job, his dreams, his hopes for the future.

2. Imagine this restaurant in the morning. Describe the people who work there as well as those who come to eat. Write a dialogue between someone who works there and a customer or group of customers.

3. Write a detailed description of the restaurant as you see it through the window. What items seem especially significant to you? Explain.

4. If you have ever worked at a job that seems in some way similar to the one held by the man in the picture, describe one hour of that work that you consider typical or that you recall as particularly memorable (for either negative or positive reasons).

READINGS

William Carlos Williams, "The Use of Force" (p. 540)

Students are intrigued to learn that, in addition to writing prolifically, Williams worked full time as a pediatrician. You might also point out that in 1938, the year the story was first published, diphtheria was a disease that posed a terrifying threat to children's lives. Neither immunizing vaccines nor powerful drugs to fight the infection were available. Diphtheria, and a host of other diseases, struck the same note of fear in parents as does leukemia today.

Readers' responses usually shift back and forth as they read this story. Mathilda, a sick child, certainly rouses instant sympathy, yet her stubborn refusal to let the doctor examine her, including her physical attack on him, helps us to understand his growing impatience. Because the story is told from the doctor's point of view, his fears and concerns are clear and immediate in readers' minds. Nevertheless, by the end of the episode, the doctor is, as he admits, out of control. Blinded by fury, he experiences "a feeling of adult shame" and calls his final actions an "unreasoning assault."

Discussing the story usually raises more questions than it answers. For example, is the doctor's use of force in any way justified? Would

Mathilda, in fact, have been seriously threatened if he had failed to get the culture at that particular moment? Or might he have left and come back later when she had calmed down? Is force ever justifiable between a professional and a client? And what about the parents? What role do they play? What role should they play?

For an intriguing look at gender issues in the story, see R. F. Dietrich's "The Use of Force" in *Studies in Short Fiction* 3 (1966), pp. 446–50. Dietrich suggests that the doctor's behavior would have been different had the child been male instead of female. And, in fact, some of the doctor's comments suggest that he does look at her with the eyes of a man, not just the professional vision of a physician. He says, for instance, that she is "an unusually attractive little thing" and admits that he "had already fallen in love with the savage brat . . . "

Sarah Orne Jewett, "Tom's Husband" (p. 544)

This story was published in 1884, long before most women worked outside the home—and certainly long before nearly any man worked at keeping house. Considering Mary's and Tom's plight suggests the complexities related to finding meaningful work. You might begin discussion by asking who has more options within the framework of the story, Mary or Tom? While Tom certainly has the power to grant Mary her wish to manage the factory—and in the end to convince her to leave her work—he does not have the power to find within himself a vocation that will bring him peace and satisfaction.

Unlike Mary, Tom seems unable to get loose from the weight of public opinion. When the old woman who lives nearby innocently asks to borrow some yeast, Tom is driven into a rage. Later his stepmother's praise of his housekeeping, made "without any intentional slight to his feelings," leads him to insist that Mary take time off from the factory so they can spend the winter in Europe.

Early in the story Tom tells Mary that he "always rather liked" housekeeping; but after the departure of the female servants who have long kept the household running, Tom is unable to cope. Tom is not a person who truly longs to do work that has traditionally been done by the other sex; instead, he longs to work at hobbies—collecting coins and stamps. In other words, he wants to lead the life that men have traditionally believed women lead when they stay at home, a life that is filled with leisure and charged with few responsibilities. When he recognizes the reality of women's lives—and particularly when he sees how little the work of housekeeping is valued either by the outside world or by family members—he wants out. Unlike most women of his day who had few options, Tom can step back into the dominant male role and insist that his wife return to a more conventional family structure. Perhaps the most interesting question raised by the story is why Mary goes along with Tom's demand—and what this decision bodes for their future life.

Mary E. Wilkens Freeman, "The Revolt of 'Mother'" (p. 555)

Some readers object to Freeman's sympathetic portrait of Mrs. Penn, seeing her as a wife who acts in a devious way to assert power over her husband. Sarah Penn's defenders, however, point out the opening scene as evidence that she had exhausted all other means to achieve a reasonable standard of living for herself and her children. As the story begins, Sarah asks her husband, "What are them men diggin' over there in the field for?" Adoniram avoids her question and finally, when she persists, orders her back into the house. As he roughly saddles and bridles his horse, while keeping his back to Sarah, Adoniram shows that he understands very well what the battle is all about. He wants a new barn; Sarah wants better living conditions. Unwilling to face these differences or to discuss them with his wife, he rides off.

It's important to note that Sarah is not initially depicted as a particularly assertive woman. She has always meekly accepted her husband's will and is generally content to make do with what she has, taking care of her family as best she can. Now, however, she is faced with a dilemma. She wants a place where her daughter, Nanny, can meet her fiancé and, eventually, get married. After trying her best to convince Adoniram to build a new house, she gathers her courage and, for apparently the first time in her life, forces the issue.

While Sarah's move to the barn has its comic aspects, most modern readers sympathize with her and rejoice in her husband's ability to accept what she has done with humility and sorrow rather than anger and destruction. In the end, no one wins and no one loses. Adoniram recognizes the strength and justice of Sarah's feelings and she sees that, far from being the tyrant she had envisioned all these years, he "was like a fortress whose walls had no active resistance, and went down the instant the right besieging tools were used."

José Armas, "El Tonto del Barrio" (p. 568)

Everything is set up in this story to make Seferino, rather than Romero, look like "el tonto del barrio." It seems as though Romero is happy sweeping the streets and getting small services and gifts from the shopkeepers in return. Then, just before his freshman year at Harvard, Seferino convinces his father to pay Romero for his work. Predictably, the "college boy's" ideas turn out to be disastrous, and the other men in the neighborhood who are not so educated appear as the wise men who knew the truth.

Several students have pointed out to me, however, that Seferino is not calling primarily on his education when he asks for the 50 cents wage for Romero. Although Barelas "just knew that his son was putting something over on him," Seferino cites as his motivation his father's assertion that "Everyone should be able to keep his dignity, no matter how poor." While it is true that those who had observed Romero knew that he could not handle money and that if he "kept the sidewalks clean . . . the barrio [would] look after him," there's no evidence that Seferino was trying to attack that view. Instead, he genuinely believed that he would be helping Romero.

Romero's response is very interesting. He immediately begins demanding a higher wage—and he makes a good argument for his pay increase. At this point, Seferino seems less admirable. He's willing to pay a small amount, but not truly a living wage. The story ends on a comic note, and I believe readers are supposed to assume that the older members of the barrio knew best. Romero has returned to the traditional pattern and all's well with the world. But is it? Certainly Romero's arguments to Seferino suggest that he is not as slow at thinking as he has been assumed to be. Maybe his fight for higher wages came as the result of the first taste of dignity and possibility he had ever had. When he sees that he is going to be treated only as a token "dignified man," he chooses to return to the dependent sweeper role. But both the barrio merchants and the readers of this story have seen a glimpse of a different Romero, and the assumption that he is perfectly content with his broom and his free haircuts can no longer so easily be made.

Charlotte Perkins Gilman, "The Yellow Wallpaper" (p. 589)

"The Yellow Wallpaper" has appeared in anthologies of ghost stories indicating that the editor read the story quite literally, seeing the woman behind the wallpaper as a malicious spirit who haunts the narrator and drives her mad. Recent feminist criticism offers a far more complex version, with the figure in the wallpaper a projection of the narrator's self. As the narrator becomes more and more isolated from any hope of realizing a full life as a writer, the figure becomes more and more disturbed and eventually seems to break free of the restraining pattern that has held her captive. This final image is extremely troubling because the figure's freedom seems to require the narrator's breakdown into complete madness. For the narrator, and her double, to throw off their restraints, they must leave the world their society defines as sane.

Of course the narrator's husband, who is a medical doctor, believes his wife to be mad (or at least clinically depressed) at the beginning of the story. He is absolutely confident in his own professional opinions and in the opinions of those in the medical fraternity, including Weir Mitchell, the psychologist who has ordered a complete "rest cure" for the narrator. The narrator describes the room where she is confined as "a nursery first, and then playroom and gymnasium . . ." However, the details she cites, the barred windows and the rings in the walls, would also be consistent with the restraints used to keep the insane from harming themselves or others.

The narrator insists that "congenial work, with excitement and change, would do [her] good." She longs to be able to write and believes that writing would help her to become well. John, however, insists that she remain completely at rest and treats her like a child calling her "little girl," and condescendingly saying "she shall be as sick as she pleases." While no evidence shows that he plans to keep his wife from recovering, the central irony of the story is that she is denied the one thing that might have prevented her breakdown: congenial work with excitement and change.

Students will find confirmation of this reading by considering Gilman's commentary that immediately follows the story: "On Writing 'The Yellow Wallpaper.'"

Marge Piercy, "To Be of Use" (p. 596)

The speaker admires Greek amphoras as well as Hopi vases because, although they are now viewed as museum pieces, they originally had a practical use. Just as she admires art that has a function, she also values workers who put their full energy into what they are doing and who are not afraid to strain muscles or perform repetitive tasks to "do what has to be done." Although the images are all of physical labor, it's possible to see these images metaphorically and to read the poem as a hymn to unpretentious, committed work of all kinds. The speaker holds in contempt the "parlor generals and field deserters" of all occupations and professions.

P. K. Page, "Typists" (p. 597)

The typists in this poem are "without message." They type other people's words but have no time or energy to record their own thoughts. As they perform their rote task, ideas and questions form in their brains but never reach fruition. The final stanza suggests that typists working in a room together feel a sense of connection and recognize their own despair in their co-workers' plights. Page's tone is sympathetic yet also condescending. Students who have worked as typists may challenge her view of the job as mindless and boring.

Richard Wilbur, "The Writer" (p. 598)

The speaker—perhaps the poet himself—hears his daughter pause as she types a story. He listens to her efforts with the same astonishment and pain he felt when he watched a bird that had trapped itself in a bedroom trying to escape. He realizes that he can't go help his daughter because he might "affright" her (perhaps intimidate her or scare away her own ideas). Yet just as he felt joy when the bird found its own way out of the room, so too does he rejoice when his daughter resumes typing, indicating that she has found her own way further into her story. Why does he call that moment a matter of life and death? Perhaps because he values writing, sees it as important work, and does not trivialize his daughter's struggles to create meaning.

Judy Grahn, "Ella, in a square apron, along Highway 80" (p. 599)

Ella, the copperheaded waitress, may be an auburn-haired woman, but she also takes on the guise of a fierce pit viper who knows how to protect herself against a hostile world. She values herself and refuses to let those who do not respect her or her work treat her with contempt. She "flicks her ass / out of habit, to fend off the pass / that passes for affection" and "turns away the smaller tips, out of pride."

Kraft Rompf, "Waiting Table" (p. 600)

The key lines, 19–22, underline the speaker's attitude toward his work, his customers, and himself:

> But for a
> tip—for a tip, for a tip—
>
> I would work so very, very
> hard

The repetition stresses his concern with making money and his willingness to serve people he obviously holds in contempt. (Compare his attitude with Ella's.)

Ranice Henderson Crosby, "Waitresses" (p. 602)

Here is a third poem about waiting on tables that can be compared with "Ella, in a square apron" and "Waiting Table." Unlike Ella, who seems confident and well able to maintain her identity in spite of her encounters with the occasional "pass," the speaker in Crosby's poem seems to lose or hide herself in the uniform and the expected smile of her work. Students who have worked in jobs that require uniforms may provide insights for a discussion of the proposition in the first three lines.

Cherríe Moraga, "The Welder" (p. 602)

To explore the metaphors of work in this poem, students will need to understand the contrast between the welder who does regular daily work and the alchemist who envisions a magical power that allows instant transformations. The welder is a worker who knows how to combine various metals and elements but understands that it takes hard work. So, too, does the speaker in the poem recognize that creating connection between human beings requires hard work and cannot be achieved by a magical formula.

W. H. Auden, "The Unknown Citizen" (p. 604)

Although some students see the poem as ironic, noting the discrepancy between the speaker's voice and the impression of the citizen conveyed by the poem's images, others read the poem as praise of an ordinary person who led an ordinary life. The capitalization of certain phrases like "Greater Community," "Producers Research," and "High-Grade Living" may be pointed out as details that suggest a satiric tone. Certainly the comic name of the Citizen's employers, Fudge Motors, Inc., demonstrates that we cannot take the speaker's words entirely at face value. In relation to the work theme, consider especially the Citizen's attitude toward his work, toward his union, and toward those with whom he worked.

Ana Castillo, "Napa, California" (p. 605)

If you or one of your students can read Spanish, reading the poem aloud can be very moving. To hear the Spanish and English blending into one another gives a powerful sense of the divided world of the Hispanic migrant worker Castillo portrays.

This poem may lead to a discussion of the negative and positive aspects of hard physical labor. What kinds of hard physical labor do students see as earning respect in their own communities? What kinds lead to the sense of lost dignity described by the speaker in the poem?

Ai, "The Country Midwife: A Day" (p. 606)

This poem should elicit strong responses. The midwife faces "Old Grizzly," whom I interpret to be Death as he comes to claim yet another aborted fetus. At the end of the poem, the midwife apparently allows the patient to die. The question, of course, is why? Is it because she is disgusted with the woman who has had a third abortion? Or, perhaps, because she thinks the woman's life is so hard that it would be kinder to let her die? In any case, this selection should lead easily into a discussion of ethical decisions that are related to one's work.

Susan Glaspell, *Trifles* (p. 608)

This play considers the significance of the traditional division of labor between men and women. The men work at farming (Lewis Hale) and at professions related to the law (George Henderson and Henry Peters). The women, Mrs. Peters and Mrs. Hale and the absent Mrs. Wright, work at keeping house. In the list of characters, the men all have full names with their work designated. The women are known only by their husbands' surnames, preceded by "Mrs." Throughout the play, two of the men—the sheriff and the county attorney—are identified primarily by their professional titles.

Although the women, at first, defer to the men and pay respect to the work they are doing, the men sneer at what they consider the "trifles" of women's work. They have no sense of how hard it is to keep clean towels available or of the effort required to provide food for winter by canning on hot summer days. Students might be reminded that at the time the play was first published, 1916, farm women had no modern conveniences. Running hot water, air conditioning, and freezers were far in the future.

As the action of the play unfolds, we see the women putting together the details (the men would call them the "trifles") of Minnie Wright's life. When they discover the dead bird, they see her motive for the desperate murder. Not only do they find the evidence, but they also act as a "jury of her peers" seeing beyond the violent act and considering the circumstances. We might venture a guess that they allow Minnie to go free either by reason of temporary insanity or by reason of justifiable homicide. (You might mention to students that in 1916 women, who did not yet have the vote, could not serve as jurors.)

The grandly ironic final line of the play puns on the word "knot," suggesting that the view the men take both of the murder and of women's work in general is "not it" at all. In addition, when Mrs. Hale responds to the county attorney's condescending question by saying firmly, "We call it—knot it, Mr. Henderson," her words bring to mind Minnie Wright, desperately knotting the rope that would kill her husband and free her from her isolated, empty life.

Virginia Woolf, "Professions for Women" (p. 621)

Woolf builds her essay through a series of complex analogies that students sometimes find difficult to understand. In the first analogy, Woolf personifies her impulses to behave in what she understands as traditionally female patterns as "the Angel in the House." This designation comes from the poem by the same name written by

Victorian poet Coventry Patmore. Patmore's Angel epitomized the ideal of late nineteenth-century, upper-class womanhood. This Angel aimed to please others—particularly men—no matter what the cost to her own sense of self. Young women of Woolf's generation grew up with the Angel cast as a model for them to follow. No wonder, then, that as she sat down to write reviews of books written by men, Woolf found it very difficult to be honest. Some students may not understand the extended metaphor of the struggle with the Angel and you may need to make clear that there was only a symbolic and not an actual murder.

The second analogy comes in paragraph 5 where Woolf compares her experiences as a novelist with a girl who is fishing. She casts the line of her imagination and suddenly the bait is taken by a huge, unmanageable fish who represents images of sexuality. As the fish leaps and struggles, it stirs up "foam and confusion." No longer does the fisher control the fish; instead she, and her imagination, are "dashed . . . against something hard." She faces the dilemma of avoiding any mention of sexuality in her novels or of earning public disapproval because she has written of subjects thought unsuitable for women.

In the final paragraph of the essay, which was first delivered as a speech to an organization for professional women, Woolf asks her audience to consider her experiences as a writer and to think about similar issues related to their own work. She suggests that women envision the professional world as a house, previously occupied only by men. Now, however, women have earned access to some of the rooms in that house. Woolf challenges women to consider carefully what they will do now that they have "won rooms of [their] own in the house hitherto exclusively owned by men." Her questions can lead to thoughtful writing and discussion related to the changes (or lack of change) students discover in professions dominated by men in 1931, when Woolf wrote the essay, but now accessible to women.

Douglas Harper, "Willie" (p. 626)

This nonfiction excerpt is easy reading, yet some students describe it as "hard, because it's so long!" I've often had good luck showing them that they can read something they see as challenging simply by skimming, then dividing the piece into shorter sections and reading them separately. A final quick reading helps put all the pieces together. For example, "Willie" might be divided in this way:

> *Paragraphs 1–4:* Explore Willie's self-image in relation to his work and his family. We see that both his wife and children relate to him primarily in terms of the work skills they see him as having.

Paragraphs 5–9: Show Willie's self-image as it relates to community and particularly emphasize how Willie tends to "discount" (undervalue) what he does, mainly because he believes any good mechanic should be willing to do and able to do what he does.

Paragraphs 10–14: Emphasize the positive image Willie has of himself as a worker; these paragraphs show that "although Willie often discounts his skill, he also recognizes its quality."

Paragraphs 15–18: Examine Willie's attitude toward people who live on disability. His disdain indicates how much he values hard, competent work and how fully his identity is connected to these values.

Once students see what the excerpt is saying, you'll be able to pursue lively discussions about the pluses and minuses of basing one's whole identity on one's work. In addition, some students may disagree with Willie's comments on disability and may be willing to contribute anecdotes to counter those Willie tells.

CHAPTER 8
MEN AND WOMEN

Many of these selections look at love relationships between men and women. All selections focus on gender issues in our own as well as earlier times, in our own society as well as others.

Consider assigning Paul Theroux's "Being a Man" as the first selection. Theroux's definition of manhood and masculinity is certain to be controversial and should lead easily to discussion of womanhood and femininity. I ask students what they think it means to "be a man" or to "be a woman." Do males in the class define themselves as men or as boys? Do females call themselves girls or women? Pursuing these terms and defining them focuses students' attention on the gender-related questions this section raises.

"Young Goodman Brown" shows the struggle between a man's love for his wife and his need to explore forbidden dimensions. Kate Chopin's "The Storm" considers both physical and emotional connection between men and women. Bobbie Ann Mason's "Shiloh," on the other hand, shows a couple who are growing apart, while Moravia's "The Chase" and Ibsen's *A Doll House* look at men who believe women to be their possessions. Bombal's "New Islands" provides the image of woman as part of a mysterious, transcendent dimension and man as both longing for and fearing that dimension.

"To His Coy Mistress," "The Willing Mistress," "The Passionate Shepherd to His Love, " and "The Nymph's Reply to the Shepherd" all offer playful voices debating whether and when to make love. "For My Lover, Returning to His Wife" and "Annabel Lee" show very different images of the loss of love. "To Me He Seems Like a God" and "Let me not to the marriage" are tributes paid to the beloved. Kristine Batey in "Lot's Wife" examines and challenges the subservient roles women have often filled.

Paula Gunn Allen provides a view of male-female relationships in a culture quite different from that of mainstream America. The most intriguing points in this essay, however, may be not how the men and women from other cultures are different from the dominant culture but how they are the same.

ADDITIONAL SELECTIONS FOR CONSIDERATION: MEN AND WOMEN

Title and Author	Text Page

Fiction

"And the Soul Shall Dance," Wakako Yamauchi	153
"Cathedral," Raymond Carver	379
"Tom's Husband," Sarah Orne Jewett	544
"The Revolt of 'Mother,'" Mary Wilkens Freeman	555
"The Yellow Wallpaper," Charlotte Perkins Gilman	575
"I'm Your Horse in the Night," Luisa Valenzuela	1009
"The Jilting of Granny Weatherall," Katherine Ann Porter	1124

Poetry

"When I was one and twenty," A. E. Housman	191
"Snow White and the Seven Dwarfs," Anne Sexton	197
"In the Orchard," Muriel Stuart	204
"The Lady of Shalott," Alfred, Lord Tennyson	Art and Poetry Section
"When a Woman Holds a Letter," Sandra Nelson	Art and Poetry Section
"Home Burial," Robert Frost	1213
"The Bean Eaters," Gwendolyn Brooks	1235

Drama

The Man in a Case, Wendy Wasserstein	15
Hamlet, William Shakespeare	209
Fences, August Wilson	423
Trifles, Susan Glaspell	608
Oleanna, David Mamet	955
On Tidy Endings, Harvey Fierstein	1174

Title and Author	Text Page

Essays

"Professions for Women," Virginia Woolf	621
"In Search of Our Mothers' Gardens," Alice Walker	992

SUGGESTIONS FOR TEACHING ADDITIONAL SELECTIONS

1. How would you define a "good" marriage or a "bad" marriage? Consider the marriages depicted in the following works as you develop your definition.

	Text Page
"Tom's Husband"	544
"The Revolt of 'Mother'"	555
"The Yellow Wallpaper"	575
"The Jilting of Granny Weatherall"	1124
"Let me not to the marriage of true minds"	694
"Home Burial"	1213
Fences	423
Trifles	608
On Tidy Endings	1174

2. Suppose you were an anthropologist from another time—or even another world—and had only the following literary selections to assist with your assignment: to define typical images of women—and the roles they played or were assigned by nineteenth- and twentieth-century society.

	Text Page
"Tom's Husband"	544
"The Revolt of 'Mother' "	555
"The Yellow Wallpaper"	575
"The Jilting of Granny Weatherall"	1124

	Text Page
"Snow White and the Seven Dwarfs"	197
"In the Orchard"	204
"When a Woman Holds a Letter"	Art and Poetry Section
Fences	423
Trifles	608
Oleanna	955

3.   Recent research suggests that men and women sometimes speak a different "language." Consider the communication between men and women in any of the following works. How do they send messages to each other? With spoken words? Written words? Gestures? Actions? Do the men and women understand these words, gestures, and actions to mean the same things? How do their responses suggest their values?

	Text Page
"Tom's Husband"	544
"The Revolt of 'Mother'"	555
"The Yellow Wallpaper"	575
"I'm Your Horse in the Night"	1009
"In the Orchard"	204
"When a Woman Holds a Letter"	Art and Poetry Section
"Home Burial"	1213
The Man in a Case	15
Trifles	608
Fences	423
Oleanna	955

4.   Consider the issue of power as it relates to gender. In the following works, who holds power and who does not? As you address this topic, consider your definition of power.

	Text Page
"And the Soul Shall Dance"	153
"Tom's Husband"	544
"The Revolt of 'Mother'"	555
"The Yellow Wallpaper"	575
"The Jilting of Granny Weatherall"	1124
"Snow White and the Seven Dwarfs"	197
"In the Orchard"	204
"The Lady of Shalott"	Art and Poetry Section
"Home Burial"	1213
The Man in a Case	15
Hamlet	209
Fences	423
Trifles	608
Oleanna	955
On Tidy Endings	1174
"Professions for Women"	621

THEMATIC PHOTOGRAPH (p. 633)

Considerations

1. What differences or similarities can you imagine between the couple in the car and the couple on the screen?

2. Describe relationships between men and women as depicted in films and on television. Cite specific examples to support the observations you make.

3. Consider relationships between men and women as depicted in films made before 1960 (for example, *Gone with the Wind*, *Casablanca, The African Queen*) and films made in the past ten years. Describe the differences and explain your response to these changes.

READINGS

Nathaniel Hawthorne, "Young Goodman Brown" (p. 634)

While "Young Goodman Brown" focuses on the dark journey of its male title character, a female figure, Faith, plays a crucial role. As Goodman Brown allows himself to be drawn deeper and deeper into the forest of deception, hypocrisy, and evil, images of his honest, loving, innocent wife Faith beseech him to turn away from the disastrous path he is following. Certainly, there are both male and female characters in the story who represent negative forces, yet the primary contrast is between Goodman Brown who indulges himself in his search for the knowledge of evil and Faith who remains steadfastly by her home and the virtues represented by innocence and belief in human goodness.

Although this dichotomy may seem like a simple pitting of good against evil, the story is far more complex. Brown behaves in some ways like another female figure, Eve. In the traditional reading of Genesis, Eve gives in to her desire for knowledge that is forbidden to her. Goodman Brown pursues the same path. In Christian tradition, humans are saved by the sacrifice of Jesus Christ from the doom visited on them by Eve's actions. In Hawthorne's story, the roles are reversed; the male figure succumbs to temptation while the female figure represents the hope offered by f(F)aith. Yet Brown is not redeemed by faith. After his night in the forest, he passes his life believing that he has been betrayed by everyone he formerly admired and trusted. He lives the rest of his life in spiritual chaos, alienated from all the anchors that previously provided a center to his existence. At the end, "his dying hour was gloom"; he never recovers from his dark night of the soul.

As you consider this story, some students will no doubt theorize that Goodman Brown's visit to the forest was a dream rather than a reality. Certainly, there are details to support this point of view. For example, Goodman Brown sees Faith's pink ribbons in the forest; yet when he meets her later, she wears the same ribbons. The dream theory also provides a rational explanation for the supernatural elements such as the devil figure who tells Brown that he was in Boston just fifteen minutes earlier. Whether or not we are to believe that Brown actually makes the journey into the forest, its devastating consequences are the same.

For an excellent selection of alternative readings of this story, see *Nathaniel Hawthorne: Young Goodman Brown,* edited by Thomas E. Connolly (Columbus, Ohio: Merrill, 1968).

Kate Chopin, "The Storm" (p. 645)

Most students are surprised that "The Storm" was written in 1898. They are not surprised to hear that Chopin did not try to publish the story at that time or to learn about the scathing reviews of her novel *The Awakening*, which was published in 1899 and which, like "The Storm," presented a frank view of human sexuality (specifically, of female sexuality).

Perhaps the most shocking aspect of the story to many readers even in the 1990s is the lighthearted treatment of adultery. Alcée and Calixta meet accidentally, make love joyfully and apparently without guilt, and return to their daily lives where "everyone [is] happy."

This story is a sequel to another, "The 'Cadian Ball," in which Alcée urges Calixta to run away with him. However, he becomes entranced with Clarisse and leaves Calixta behind. The speech of the characters hints at the reason. Alcée's language—and Clarisse's language as reported from her letter—suggest upper-class, educated patterns. Both Calixta and Bobinôt, on the other hand, speak a patois, combining nonstandard English with French expressions. Quite possibly, Calixta and Alcée both chose mates who were deemed appropriate by their society but for whom they failed to feel the intense, intimate connection they sensed with each other.

Many students will condemn Alcée and Calixta. Calixta, especially, is often regarded as unsympathetic because in the opening and closing scenes both her husband and son are shown as loving and caring. Nevertheless, Chopin's description of the interlude in the storm creates a tone of tolerance. The lovers' passion is as brief, intense, and frighteningly beautiful as is the weather that allows them their isolated moment together.

María Luisa Bombal, "New Islands" (page 650)

A possible summary of the story's eleven sections:

Section 1:

Initially, Yolanda appears frail and perhaps sickly. She has trouble breathing as she sleeps, and her brother Federico worries about her. Federico informs Yolanda that a new island has emerged, making four so far. He wants to ride off to see it, and Yolanda thinks to herself that men are absurd in their unending desire to be in motion and "to take an interest in everything." Sylvester (apparently a houseguest) warns Juan Manuel not to touch Yolanda's flowers. They both hear the sound of scales being played on a piano. Later, Federico introduces Juan Manuel to Yolanda. Juan Manuel sees her as "uncoiling like a beautiful snake" and wonders at her tall thin beauty.

Section 2:

At dinner that evening, the men eat and drink heavily and Juan Manuel accompanies a drunken Sylvester back to the room they share. There Sylvester reveals that he was once engaged to Yolanda but she broke off the engagement. Juan Manuel is astonished because Sylvester is an old man and he had thought Yolanda a young woman. Juan Manuel listens to the sound of a distant train and finds himself fascinated with Yolanda. He wonders why, as he has seen her only once.

Section 3:

Yolanda dreams of a romantic meeting with Juan Manuel, but she struggles to resist his embraces and awakes, sobbing. As she weeps, she hears the noise of the train.

Section 4:

The men return to the island to hunt, but discover a foul-smelling atmosphere with strange vegetation and seagulls that fly in menacing circles. When the earth shakes and the sea boils, they are frightened and return to the mainland. As they arrive, Juan Manuel once again hears the sound of piano scales. As he walks into the garden, he meets Yolanda who greets him warmly and with a "sudden intimacy." She tells him of her dream, but then moves away, claiming she hears someone calling. Later, in the drawing room Yolanda is seated by the fireplace. Her mysterious beauty reminds Juan Manuel of something, and suddenly he tells her that she looks like a seagull. At this, Yolanda faints but Juan Manuel refuses to tell Federico what he said to her. When she regains consciousness, she sends everyone away, but Juan Manuel remains.

Section 5:

On the third morning when the hunters gather on the shore, they are shocked to see that the new islands have disappeared. Searching for the vanished islands, Juan Manuel finds only a small jellyfish that he captures and ties up in his handkerchief.

Section 6:

Yolanda arrives on horseback to meet the returning hunters. She reminds Juan Manuel of an Amazon. When he arrives in his room, a letter from his mother reminds him that she will take an orchid to his wife Elsa's grave to mark the fifth anniversary of her death. Juan Manuel guiltily remembers his beautiful wife who died of a terrible, disfiguring disease.

In Buenos Aires, Juan Manuel's mother takes orchids to the grave but cannot relinquish her hatred for her dead daughter-in-law. Even in death, Elsa has triumphed because the "strong dark little boy who continues their line," the grandson who has become [Juan Manuel's mother's] only reason for living, has the blue and candid eyes of Elsa.

Section 7:

Juan Manuel is drunk and rereading the letter from his mother. He becomes very disturbed by his young son's postscript, which defines the words "aerolite" (pieces of minerals that fall from outer space to the earth's surface), "hurricane," and "halo." He longs to see Yolanda, goes to her room, and forces the door open. She is moaning with fear, and after he wakes her, she thanks him for dispelling her nightmare of death. Juan Manuel expects her to order him to leave, but she does not. He embraces her and they struggle, but he overpowers her and throws her down. When she begins to cry, his passion subsides and when she asks him to go, he leaves without speaking.

Section 8:

On the fourth day, Juan Manuel goes hunting on the remaining islands and imagines Yolanda in various domestic scenes. He begins to think that she looks like a seagull, but stops himself before he completes the phrase.

Section 9:

On his return, Juan Manuel goes into the bathroom and sees Yolanda contemplating her right shoulder where a "light and flexible" wing has developed and covers part of her back.

Section 10:

Juan Manuel drives along the highway, trying to convince himself that he has seen a hallucination. He decides to return to Buenos Aires. He goes to his mother's house and demands to see his son, although it is eleven o'clock at night. He tells Billy he has brought him a jellyfish, but when they look for it, it has disappeared. Billy has a rational explanation: he knows it has melted because he has read that jellyfish are made of water. Juan Manuel goes into the hall and tries to call Yolanda, but when someone answers he slams down the receiver. He regrets not having confronted Yolanda about his response to learning her secret. He now thinks that he has confronted something more horrifying than death: "a suffering consisting of amazement and fear."

Section 11:

Anguished, Juan Manuel returns to his son's room where he reads passages from his geography book. As he reads about surreal ancient landscapes and animals, he feels a sense of connection with his feelings when he discovered Yolanda's secret. He knows, however, that he cannot explore such mysteries further. Most particularly, he "fears falling into some dark abyss that no amount of logic will lead him out of."

Bobbie Ann Mason, "Shiloh" (p. 665)

At the battle of Shiloh, Southern soldiers attacked the Union forces led by Ulysses S. Grant. Although the Southern troops were ultimately defeated in this battle, they were regarded by their compatriots as daring heroes and lauded for their astonishing first-strike raid against a much larger and more powerful enemy.

In Bobbie Ann Mason's story, Leroy, Norma Jean, and Mabel Beasley all seem to be fighting battles against enormous odds. Leroy, from whose point of view we see all the conflicts, struggles against the pain and disablement caused by his injured leg, and, most important, he tries desperately to understand where his life is going and what he can do to get his life under control. This quest, of course, means that he examines closely his relationship with Norma Jean in a way he never has before, working to address their old conflicts and to look squarely at their problems.

Norma Jean does physical exercises to develop her body, starts taking an English course, and begins to stand up to her domineering mother. Like the Southern soldiers at Shiloh, Norma Jean makes these daring raids against the boredom, inertia, and powerlessness of her life. As Norma Jean struggles to become independent, she moves in exactly the opposite direction of Leroy, who yearns for more connection and intimacy.

Mrs. Beasley, Norma's mother, battles against the changes of time. She would like to keep her daughter dependent and to see Norma and Leroy behave like her version of a nice, normal couple. Like Norma and Leroy, Mrs. Beasley seems never to have come to terms with the death of her infant grandson, Randy. She refuses to battle with that loss in a constructive way, yet continually reminds Norma Jean of the tragedy by her unthinking comments.

Some students have read the final paragraph as ominous, suggesting that Norma Jean jumps off the cliff and kills herself. Although I can find no textual evidence to contradict that view absolutely, my own feeling is that Norma Jean has the most hope for the future of any of the three characters. While Leroy is becoming more inward and dependent on a relationship that has never seemed to work, she strives to move away from her old life and toward emotional and intellectual growth.

Alberto Moravia, "The Chase" (p. 677)

The analogy established in the first few paragraphs of the story suggests the relationship the narrator sees between his wife and himself. In the hunting story, he is impressed by the bird who, he says, "is autonomous and unpredictable and does not depend on us." When his father presents him with the body of the dead bird, he grieves, apparently because that sense of freedom has been lost. Yet when he makes the comparison between the bird and his wife, it's easy to see that this freedom is only an illusion. Of course the bird *was* dependent on the hunters—dependent on them to decide whether it lived or died. Before the narrator was married, his future wife, like the bird, gave the illusion of wildness and vitality. Because of this illusion, the narrator pursued her. After the first years of their marriage, she became tamer, losing her "air of charming unpredictability, of independence in her way of living," and the narrator no longer found her fascinating.

The central incident in the story shows the narrator unexpectedly noticing his wife as she walks toward a bus stop. He sees in her once again the wildness he admired. When he discovers that her sense of energy and freedom is quite probably generated from her eagerness in meeting a lover, he faces a conflict. Should he confront her and thus assert his power over her or should he let her continue with her assignation and thus retain the autonomy he so admires?

Remembering the hunting incident and the dead bird, he decides not to interfere. He wants his wife to retain her wildness although he acknowledges that "this wildness was directed against" him. He has come to believe that "wildness, always and everywhere, is directed against everything and everybody."

Students may differ in their evaluation of the narrator. Does he truly value his wife's independence for his own sake? Or is he motivated primarily by the desire to continue seeing his wife in a way that fascinates and excites him? Is his decision to leave his wife alone with her lover based on respect for her innate qualities or on his need to see her in a particular way? Does he himself become wild and free through his choice? Or does the choice simply confirm his sense of control over the situation?

Andrew Marvell, "To His Coy Mistress" (p. 681)

Although images of time dominate the poem, the speaker's exaggerations ("I would love you ten years before the flood"; "An hundred years should go to praise / Thine eyes") all lead to his central argument. He tries to convince his mistress to give up her virginity because both he and she are mortal. They will not have long to enjoy physical passion.

Students have a good time evaluating the argument, with many agreeing that this same reasoning could be used to satisfy any desire. Why not steal a great car? After all, if you had enough time, you could work and earn the money to buy one. But because all of us are mortal, you might die before accumulating the funds you need. So why not just take the easier, more convenient, and direct route: take what you want with no real thought of consequences or moral implications?

Aphra Behn, "The Willing Mistress" (p. 683)

Aphra Behn, who lived during the seventeenth century and made her living writing plays, shows a view of women quite different from Marvel's in "To His Coy Mistress." While Marvel depicts his mistress as a shy virgin, reluctant to make love, Behn's speaker returns her lover's kisses eagerly. Just as the boughs in the opening stanza yield to "the winds that gently rise," so, too, does the speaker make it easy for her Amyntas "to prevail."

Alan Dugan, "Love Song: I and Thou" (p. 684)

The speaker apparently loves his wife, but the extended metaphor of the house, which seems to represent their relationship, suggests great complexity. During the early stages, nothing was ideal. The speaker "spat rage's nails / into the frame-up of [his] work." Then, for one brief moment everything seemed to be perfect: "It settled plumb, / level, solid, square and true." Now, however, the house is once more askew and presumably the relationship, too, has its problems. The final image (lines 27–31) suggests that the house (and thus the relationship) has become like a cross on which the speaker will be martyred. He accepts the sacrifice and calls on his wife to help him remain nailed to the "cross-piece" of their marriage.

Anne Sexton, "For My Lover, Returning to His Wife" (p. 685)

The first thirty lines include these representative images for the wife and for the mistress:

Wife	Mistress
melted carefully down for you	a luxury
cast up from your childhood	a bright red sloop in the harbor
Fireworks in February	littleneck clams out of season

Wife

real as a cast-iron pot

all harmony

the potter who produced his children

Images of the wife and mistress in lines 31–48 include these:

Wife	**Mistress**
a bomb with "a fuse inside her"	a watercolor
a drunken sailor	
the sum of [himself]	
like a monument . . . She is solid	

The early images of the wife show her as beautiful, familiar, and down-to-earth. She is the girl of the man's youth and the mother of his children. She is necessary to his existence. The mistress is strikingly exotic. She adds excitement to the man's life, but she is, in the end, not someone who will remain permanent. The wife is like a statue carved in lasting stone. The mistress appears, for a moment, beautifully evocative; yet, like a watercolor painting, she can be easily washed away and forgotten.

Kristine Batey, "Lot's Wife" (p. 687)

The Bible depicts Lot's wife as a disobedient, worldly woman who, against God's orders, turns to look at her native city of Sodom, burning as punishment for the sins of the people who live there. In retribution, she is turned into a pillar of salt. Students may want to compare the biblical account of this story, Genesis 19:1–26, with Batey's version where we are given a far more sympathetic view of Mrs. Lot who sees ambiguity and complexity even in "the city of sin."

Amy Lowell, "Patterns" (p. 689)

The formal garden provides a pattern as does the speaker's dress. She describes herself as "Just a plate of current fashion." As she weeps, the drops from the fountain provide a counterpoint pattern to her tears. She sees herself as caught in the patterns of manners and social graces that stifle members of her class in society (particularly women). She had dreamt that her fiancé, Lord Hartwell, would have provided an escape from those patterns, that with him she would have felt free enough even to make love in the garden sunlight (suggested by lines

87–89). Now Lord Hartwell himself has been destroyed by yet another "pattern called a war."

Sappho, "To Me He Seems Like a God" (p. 692)

The speaker uses extremely painful images to describe her reaction to the man who "seems like a god." She loses the ability to speak or to see light and her skin burns as if cracked by fire. The speaker's response seems to come from her sense of powerlessness. As a woman lacking in material wealth, she feels unable to meet the godlike man on his own terms.

Christopher Marlowe, "The Passionate Shepherd to His Love" (p. 692)
Sir Walter Raleigh, "The Nymph's Reply to the Shepherd" (p. 693)

Try asking two students to read this pair of poems aloud and then asking the class to evaluate the speakers in each poem and to explain who offers the more convincing argument. Responses vary, but my students usually favor the nymph. While the shepherd's pleas seem similar to those of hopeful suitors everywhere (and from every age), the nymph's answer shows that she is thoughtful and perceptive; she does not rely on clichés. Unconvinced by the promise of material gifts, the nymph thinks about philosophical concerns. While she does not deny the pleasure of passionate love relationships, she declines involvement in a fleeting moment of physical joy that is unrelated to more significant connection.

William Shakespeare, "Let me not to the marriage of true minds" (p. 694)

In reading this sonnet, I ask students to use the following process:

1. As you think about this sonnet, read the first sentence (which may be longer than the first line) to yourself. Then read it aloud. Next, jot down your predictions for the rest of the poem based on that line.

2. As you read the rest of the sonnet, note how each sentence (which, again, may be longer than a line) relates to the opening sentence and to your predictions.

3. Read the final two lines (the closing couplet) several times. What does this pair of lines contribute to your response and to your understanding of the poem?

Before using these considerations, I like to read the whole poem aloud. Then, I ask students to work in groups, considering the poem in sentences—rather than lines. When they find a place where meaning breaks down, I ask them whether the problem is vocabulary or word order. Often other students can suggest possibilities; if not, I usually offer several readings that make sense to me. After looking carefully at the poems, members of the groups reconvene as a class; we discuss responses and possibilities and close with an oral reading (preferably by a student volunteer) to leave the whole poem as the final impression.

This poem definitely requires students to use the dictionary. Many will not know what "impediments" means and most do not know the use of the word "bark" to mean "ship." Understanding the meaning of "bark" is necessary for seeing the speaker's claim that a true marriage acts for the husband and wife as does the North Star for a ship looking for direction (lines 7–8). Lines 9 and 10 refer to the image of time as the grim reaper, using his sickle to harvest all humans from their field of mortal life.

Edgar Allan Poe, "Annabel Lee" (p. 695)

Most students like this poem with its strong rhythm and its images of devoted love cut short by the early death of the beloved. Although the connection between life and literature is always tenuous at best, students are always interested to know that in 1836, Poe married his cousin Virginia who was fourteen years old on her wedding day. There is no evidence that I could find suggesting that her kinsmen—high-born or not—came "to bear her away"; however, she did die in 1847, leaving Poe devastated. In 1849, he wrote "Annabel Lee," some believe in honor of Virginia.

Henrik Ibsen, *A Doll House* (p. 697)

In his "Notes for *A Doll House*," Ibsen comments on the theme of his play:

> There are two kinds of spiritual law, two kinds of conscience, one in man and another, altogether different, in women. They do not understand each other; but in practical life the woman is judged by man's law, as though she were not a woman but a man.
> The wife in the play ends by having no idea of what is right or wrong; natural feeling on the one hand and belief in authority on the other have altogether bewildered her.

These observations might serve as a prompt for a brief, in-class writing or a journal entry to be used as a starting place for the discussion of this powerful and still timely drama.

There are widely varying readings of this play, with some seeing Nora as a manipulator who fully understands what she is doing throughout the play; my own reading is that in Act I both Nora and Torvald unthinkingly assume roles that their society has defined for them. Nora acts silly, empty-headed, and dependent. Torvald responds as a somewhat benevolent despot, both indulging Nora and scolding her as though she were a child or a pet. The names he calls her reinforce this image. At this point, I can be sympathetic to both characters, while admiring neither. As the play progresses and Nora's scheme to save Torvald's health is revealed, I begin to have more sympathy for her. It's still annoying to me to see how she refuses to confront him, yet his posturings and pronouncements, particularly about the role mothers (not fathers) play in the moral decay of their children, make her fear of honest discussion understandable.

Although Nora behaves in a devious and childish manner with Torvald, she is able to be reasonably honest with Dr. Rank. Even though she goes through the rather silly semi-seduction scene where she takes off her stockings in front of Rank, for the most part she tells him the truth and she is able to listen to the truth from him. Note that it is not only Nora who hides disturbing realities from Torvald; when Rank is dying, it is Nora in whom he confides and whom he summons to his bedside. He also, apparently, recognizes Torvald's resistance to facing difficult, ugly facts.

When Nora deals with Krogstad, she shows moments of courage, yet she also behaves as the supplicant. For example, she confronts him with her belief in what she has done, but she begs him not to reveal the truth to Torvald and even tries to coerce Mrs. Linde into helping her to prevent Krogstad's revenge.

As Nora moves through the play, she changes and those changes seem reasonably based on observing and hearing several things that make her question the way she has led her life. When she is reunited with her school friend, Mrs. Linde, she learns that although the way is hard, a woman can survive on her own. Mrs. Linde has managed financially, thus presenting a role model that is certainly not ideal yet does offer possibility. In addition, Nora's discussions with Krogstad lead her to understand the unfairness of the laws and customs that require women to have the approval of men before they can take what our society would consider normal adult actions. Most important, in her final confrontation with Torvald, she learns that she has based all her hopes for the relationship on a lie.

It is at this point in the play that I think Ibsen clearly shows us he is on Nora's side and that she is, although flawed, a character worthy of our sympathy and at least the beginnings of our admiration. Torvald has claimed throughout the play that he stands on high moral principles:

> He will not borrow money.
>
> He abhors people who (like Krogstad) cheat.
>
> He especially abhors people who cheat and who do not face up to their crime.
>
> He would never allow a lawbreaker to bring up children.
>
> He wishes Nora would be in jeopardy so he could protect her.

After having postured about these values and beliefs throughout the play, when Nora and he believe that she is in jeopardy, he shows his complete lack of moral fiber. First he says, "I'm ruined!" He thinks not at all of Nora. And he has no intention of taking the blame to protect her. When he learns that Krogstad will not reveal the truth, he encourages her to stay, saying that she should remain for the sake of the children. Seeing that he has gone against all his principles, Nora recognizes that "the greatest miracle," which I take to be true communication within the marriage, is never going to happen. When she leaves, she takes the only moral action she can, especially as she believes the children will be safe with the nursemaid who raised her and as she probably still accepts Torvald's view that she is in many ways not fit yet to be a mother.

Students may enjoy discussing the extra scene Ibsen was forced to write for the play when it was performed in conservative German theaters. Fearing that the theater directors would make their own changes, he created an additional scene in which Torvald drags Nora to the children's room. There, looking at the sleeping children, Nora declares, "Although it is a crime against myself, I cannot leave them"; then she falls to the floor in a faint.

Another consideration for students to ponder is this quotation from a speech Ibsen gave in 1898 to a Norwegian women's rights group who had honored him. Referring to *A Doll House*, he stated:

> I have been more of a poet and less of a social philosopher than most people have been inclined to think. I am grateful for your toast, but I can't claim the honor of ever having worked consciously for women's rights. I'm not even sure what women's rights are. To me it has seemed a matter of human rights.

Students may wish to consider the ways in which the conflicts, actions, and decisions related to Nora can be applied to both men and women.

Paula Gunn Allen, "Where I Come From Is Like This" (p. 758)

The opening paragraphs of Gunn Allen's essay suggest the importance of cultural definitions. How people see themselves relates directly to the expectations of the community in which they live. In the second paragraph, Gunn Allen emphasizes the diversity of roles Native Americans may play within their tribal structures, yet she also notes the differences between those tribal definitions and the definitions of "women in western industrial and post industrial cultures."

Gunn Allen describes the men and women in her culture as living in a balanced way; the women have as much power as the men. Some students may question Gunn Allen's interpretation of the scenarios she describes. For example, if menstruating women are banished because of a belief that their power will interfere with male power, what does that say about the balance she claims exists?

Gunn Allen's description of the double bind faced by Native American women also raises controversial questions. She describes, for instance, feeling powerless only when she is trying to get approval from those who are not Native American. Most people feel less comfortable and less powerful when they are away from their own culture, and perhaps the approval she gets within her tribal structure comes from her willingness to accept, rather than resist, the tribal definitions of women's roles.

Paul Theroux, "Being a Man" (p. 765)

Theroux's opening paragraph shocks many readers. Both the definition of the shoe fetishist and Theroux's statement, "I cannot read that sentence without thinking that it is just one more awful thing about being a man," are disturbing. Yet the discussion of fetishism also seems absurd and Theroux's reaction exaggerated, putting me immediately on the alert for irony.

As I read on, the details, examples, and diction continue to be hyperbolic and even downright unfair. Consider, for example, Theroux's statement that "there is no book hater like a Little League coach." Surely he realizes that many Little League coaches enjoy books as well as baseball. It seems that he intentionally sets out to insult many of his readers, perhaps to stir up their emotions and to engage them with his argument.

Most students will strongly disagree with Theroux's evaluation of high school sports, but many will agree with his premise (paragraph 3) that boys and girls are raised to see members of the opposite sex as adversarial or, at best, as the objects of sexual or matrimonial conquests. This essay lends itself very nicely to setting up debates, using small groups to prepare arguments for and against Theroux's assumptions and the conclusions he bases on these assumptions.

I find astonishing Theroux's contention that Americans expect male writers to be dismissive or apologetic about their profession. As prior to 1965 or so nearly all writers who were accepted as part of the traditional canon were male, his complaint is difficult to understand. Theroux bases this claim partly on his belief that male writers are taken seriously only when they demonstrate their masculinity. I think most men—whether they are business executives, doctors, plumbers, or bus drivers—are constantly under societal pressure to prove their male attributes. Is there really much evidence to suggest that male writers are particularly bedeviled by this expectation?

Comparing Theroux's view of gender issues as related to the profession of writing to Virginia Woolf's view in "Professions for Women" suggests that women who choose to be writers have had—and continue to have—more gender-related obstacles to face than do men. In addition, Woolf concentrates on issues related to her own writing process while Theroux seems concerned not so much with how being male affects how he writes but rather with how being a male writer affects the way people perceive him.

CHAPTER 9
PARENTS AND CHILDREN

The frustrations, rewards, pains, and pleasures of family life both absorb and renew enormous amounts of energy in almost everyone's life. The works in this section examine parent-child relationships from nearly every vantage point. You might introduce this theme by asking students to list the five most significant conflicts they believe arise between parents and children. In addition, ask them to list five important things they believe children can learn from their parents and five important things parents can learn from their children. (The items on this list may be specific rather than general; students might consider things they or their friends have learned from parents, for example.) These lists provide material for discussion, group work, or expanded journal entries and lead to consideration of the conflicts as well as the lessons learned and taught by parents and children in this thematic section.

In "My Papa's Waltz," "Digging," and "I Remember Papa," adult sons look at their connections with their fathers, focusing on remembered scenes from childhood; "My Father in the Navy" shows a daughter's memories of her father. "My Son, My Executioner" gives a father's view of his relationship to his child. Mothers contemplate their role in their children's lives in "I Stand Here Ironing," "Making the Jam without You," and "Today," while "Amniocentesis" and "Metaphors" suggest connections between mothers and unborn children.

Tina Howe's play *Painting Churches* shows parents and adult children struggling with questions of identity and changing family dynamics, whereas Harry Dolan's essay "I Remember Papa" raises the question: Do parents owe loyalty first to the welfare of their family or to the laws of the greater community in which they live?

Characters in "The Conversion of the Jews," "Through the Tunnel," "I Stand Here Ironing," "Making the Jam without You," "Today," and "A Parent's Journey Out of the Closet" face issues of growth and independence as the child develops a life apart from the parent.

"I Stand Here Ironing," "A Worn Path," and "I Remember Papa" provide rich opportunities for looking at the impact of economic circumstances and societal pressures on family relationships.

ADDITIONAL SELECTIONS FOR CONSIDERATION: PARENTS AND CHILDREN

Title and Author   **Text Page**

Fiction

"Butterflies," Patricia Grace   12

"And the Soul Shall Dance," Wakako Yamauchi   153

"The Circling Hand," Jamaica Kincaid   181

"Sonny's Blues," James Baldwin   346

"Everyday Use," Alice Walker   371

"Rules of the Game," Amy Tan   402

"The Use of Force," William Carlos Williams   540

"El Tonto del Barrio," José Armas   568

"The Loudest Voice," Grace Paley   921

"The Jilting of Granny Weatherall," Katherine Anne Porter   1124

"To Hell with Dying," Alice Walker   1142

Poetry

"Do Not Go Gentle into That Good Night," Dylan Thomas   80

"Slipping," Joan Aleshire   81

"In the Counselor's Waiting Room," Bettie Sellers   194

"The Centaur," May Swenson   195

"The Youngest Daughter," Cathy Song   418

"The School Children," Louise Glück   947

"Mother and Poet," Elizabeth Barrett Browning   1056

"Home Burial," Robert Frost   1213

"Out, Out—," Robert Frost   1217

"The Mother," Gwendolyn Brooks   1233

Drama

Hamlet, William Shakespeare   209

Fences, August Wilson   466

Title and Author	Text Page
Picnic on the Battlefield, Fernando Arrabal	1065
On Tidy Endings, Harvey Fierstein	1174

Essays

"Education," E. B. White	21
"Salvation," Langston Hughes	332
"Arrival at Manzanar," Jeanne Wakatsuki Houston and James D. Houston	531
"In Search of Our Mothers' Gardens," Alice Walker	992

SUGGESTIONS FOR TEACHING ADDITIONAL SELECTIONS

1. Can one generation understand another? Consider the following
   works to identify patterns of conflict between parents and
   children. In addition, note patterns of empathy and
   understanding. What aspects of life are most likely to evoke
   parental anger? Parental support? The anger of children? The
   support of children?

	Text Page
"The Circling Hand"	181
"Sonny's Blues"	346
"Everyday Use: For Your Grandmama"	371
"Rules of the Game"	402
"El Tonto del Barrio"	568
"In the Counselor's Waiting Room"	194
Hamlet	209
Fences	466
On Tidy Endings	1174
"Arrival at Manzanar"	531

2. Read any of the following works and consider how family traditions and rituals affect the lives of parents and children. Compare your observations about these works with observations about the role played by traditions and rituals in your own family or in other families you know well.

	Text Page
"The Circling Hand"	181
"The Loudest Voice"	921
"Everyday Use: For Your Grandmama"	371
"To Hell with Dying"	1142
"Mother and Poet"	1056
"The School Children"	947
Fences	466
"Salvation"	329
"Arrival at Manzanar"	531
"In Search of Our Mothers' Gardens"	992

3. The following selections focus on themes related to the lives of families who are not members of the dominant culture in their society. Use these selections as sources to discover complications, joys, and problems you consider unique to those families belonging to minority groups. Investigate your discoveries through further reading and research. As you work, consider both fictional and nonfictional sources as well as interviews and conversations.

	Text Page
"And the Soul Shall Dance"	153
"Sonny's Blues"	346
"Everyday Use: For Your Grandmama"	371
"Rules of the Game"	402
"El Tonto del Barrio"	568
"The Loudest Voice"	921

	Text Page
"To Hell with Dying"	1142
Fences	466
"Salvation"	329
"Arrival at Manzanar"	531
"In Search of Our Mothers' Gardens"	992

4. Read the following works to identify the roles played by mothers and fathers in their children's lives. How are they similar? Different? How do these fictional mothers and fathers, and the roles they play in their children's lives, compare to the parents you know? Do you think the roles played by mothers and fathers are changing? For the better? For the worse? Explain.

	Text Page
"The Circling Hand"	181
"Everyday Use: For Your Grandmama"	371
"Rules of the Game"	402
"El Tonto del Barrio"	568
"The Loudest Voice"	921
"The Youngest Daughter"	418
"Mother and Poet"	1056
Hamlet	209
Fences	466
Picnic on the Battlefield	1065
"Arrival at Manzanar"	531

THEMATIC PHOTOGRAPH (p. 769)

Considerations

1.   List the details you notice in this picture. Consider the four people as well as their surroundings. What inferences can you make based on your observations?

2.   Notice the expression on the woman's face. What emotions does the expression suggest? What might her relationship be to the man? To the babies? Explain all the possibilities you see.

3.   Write the dialogue that has taken place just before this picture was taken. As you create this scene, consider such points as what the four people are doing, what time of day the scene takes place, where the people are, and where they might be going (both literally and figuratively).

READINGS

Philip Roth, "The Conversion of the Jews" (p. 770)

Although the conflicts in this story go beyond those between Ozzie and his mother, they are epitomized by the parent-child tension. The Rabbi who teaches Ozzie represents a father figure, and his words and actions closely reflect those of Ozzie's mother. Both of them insist on a narrow view of religion and of God and both find themselves so frustrated by Ozzie's persistent and deeply thoughtful questions that they strike out at him.

For students not familiar with Judaism, you might want to explain that Jews do not believe that the messiah has yet come and thus do not recognize Jesus as God. This point may seem obvious, but I've found that many students are completely unaware of this basic Jewish belief. In addition, you might also explain that Ozzie and his friends are attending classes in preparation for becoming bar mitzvah. For Jewish boys, the bar mitzvah ceremony marks the moment at which their religious community considers them to be men. Ozzie's critical view both of his mother and of the Rabbi shows that he is paying more than lip service to the process of passing into adulthood. Notice particularly in section 3, as Ozzie climbs to the roof, he asks over and over again, "Is it me?" As he acts out against parental authority, he seeks to find himself.

Although Ozzie is the most sympathetic character, there are certainly moments when his mother seems appealing. For example, when she lights the candles for the Sabbath, she reacts emotionally, showing that connection with tradition is more for her than simply looking for Jewish names on lists of airplane crash victims. She obviously loves Ozzie and is willing to humble herself in front of everyone in order to prevent his carrying out the threat of jumping off the roof.

Most students will enjoy this story. The irony and humor that run throughout let readers know the story will come to a happy resolution. We are never for a minute worried that Ozzie will jump. The only tension comes from wondering how his dramatic stand will be resolved. Certainly, when he comes down off the roof, he will be regarded by his fellow students as a hero. And his relationship with the Rabbi and with his mother will be markedly changed. It might be interesting to have students write brief dialogues showing post-roof meetings between Ozzie and his mother and Ozzie and the Rabbi.

As for the question regarding the story's possible anti-Semitic bias, you might ask students to consider the view of critic Peter Shaw who says in *Contemporary Authors* that what Roth advises is that Jews "transcend being Jewish." Do students agree with this point? If so, how would they feel about stories that urged readers to transcend being Catholic, Protestant, or Buddhist? What is gained or lost through transcending one's religious identity? For another look at this topic, see "The Loudest Voice" by Grace Paley.

Doris Lessing, "Through the Tunnel" (p. 782)

Lessing offers a moving view of a boy working to achieve independence from his mother and to develop a sense of self. The opening paragraphs show that both mother and son care deeply for one another. The mother is not a stereotyped overprotective guardian. She recognizes that her son is old enough to go off on his own, yet that doesn't stop her from worrying about him. She acknowledges her anxiety as she courageously encourages him to explore the rocks he has pointed out to her. Jerry, sensitive to his mother's emotions, feels contrite when he contemplates going off without her. But his chivalry does not paralyze him, and he is able to let her walk down the beach in one direction while he goes in the other.

As the story progresses, Jerry continues to be torn between growing up and remaining a child. He admires the older boys, yet tries to attract their attention by showing off. After watching the boys swim through the tunnel, he longs to do the same, but he begs his mother for the necessary swim goggles by nagging and pestering her just as a young child would do. As he works on his plan for swimming the tunnel, Jerry grows increasingly independent of his mother, to the point that he does not ask her permission to go the beach. He also waits carefully to develop his ability to hold his breath, demonstrating a "most unchildlike persistence, a controlled impatience."

When Jerry finally swims through the tunnel, the details build suspense even though the outcome seems clear. He will not drown, but will make it through the metaphoric birth canal to be reborn as a fledgling adult—someone who can give in to his mother's request not to "swim any more today" because he now knows that he can face dangerous and difficult tasks on his own. He no longer needs to resist his mother's simple request or to challenge her because he has successfully met his challenge to himself.

Students may enjoy comparing Jerry's relationship with his mother—and his challenge to her authority—with the relationship and challenge depicted in "The Conversion of the Jews."

Tillie Olsen, "I Stand Here Ironing" (p. 790)

Someone from Emily's school, a teacher or counselor, has called her mother. The meditation at the ironing board represents the mother's imagined response both to that call and to the voices of authorities who, over the years, have tried to tell her how to raise her children and have then criticized her for what has resulted from following their advice. Consider, for instance, her describing Emily's feeding patterns. When her first daughter was an infant, child care authorities strongly urged parents to feed babies on a strict schedule. The mother followed this rule, although Emily often cried for hours as she waited out the four-hour stretch from feeding to feeding. Now the mother fears (and modern child care authorities would agree) that following such a rigid pattern may not have been the best process for her child. When Emily was sick with red measles, the mother was urged to put her in a convalescent home where disdainful social workers believed she would receive better care than she would at home. The mother's description of the conditions at the convalescent home suggest that, in fact, Emily was virtually imprisoned in a cold, rigid, draconian institution.

Both the feeding episode and the convalescent home episode show the mother following the advice of experts yet later questioning the results achieved by her obedience. Certainly she was free not to adhere to the course of actions she was advised to take, and some students will see the mother as responsible for Emily's problems because she made the wrong choices.

One of the most intriguing questions posed by the mother's meditation is the degree to which parents are responsible for the way their children grow up. Students differ widely on the way they view the mother. Usually older students are at least somewhat sympathetic with the mother whereas younger students tend to condemn her for not being able to overcome her early economic problems. (You may want to call students' attention to paragraph 9, which notes that Emily's father deserted the family during the Great Depression of the early 1930s, a "pre-relief, pre-WPA world" when the welfare options of today were unheard of.)

Eudora Welty, "A Worn Path" (p. 797)

In her discussion of "A Worn Path" in her book *The Eye of the Storm*, Welty says:

> A story writer is more than happy to be read by students; the fact that these serious readers think and feel something in response to his work, he finds life-giving. At the same time, he may not always be able to reply to their specific questions in kind.

Welty explains that the question she most often receives from students and their instructors who write to her after lively classroom discussion is this: Is Phoenix Jackson's grandson really *dead*? While assuring readers that they do not have to have the same responses to the story as does the writer, she explains that in writing the story she identified as fully as possible with Phoenix and in this capacity she, like Phoenix, believes the grandson to be alive.

The important focus in the story is the journey itself. Whether the grandchild is alive may be intriguing, but it is not essential. What makes a difference is Phoenix's belief in her own power to keep going year after year on this essential errand. Like the bird whose name she bears, she cannot be destroyed by her own infirmities, by grinding poverty, or by the condescending observations of others. When, at the end of her visit to the doctor's office, we learn that "Phoenix rose carefully" we are reminded both of her endurance and of her commitment to life and to her parental role in her grandson's life. Just as she makes his life possible, he gives meaning and structure to hers.

Flannery O'Connor, "A Good Man Is Hard to Find" (p. 805)

Somehow O'Connor manages to make this quintessentially dysfunctional family into an intriguing group of characters. Bailey, the grandmother's only son, has never become an independent person. He argues with her or ignores her as though he were a child and then gives in to her whims without considering the consequences. It's no wonder that June Star and Wesley are equally whiney and manipulative with their parents, as they are living with the model of their father and grandmother. Throughout the trip, the mood of the family is quarrelsome and petty; they never show any ability to rise above their own small-minded concerns.

The title indicates that good men are hard to find and, indeed, they seem nonexistent in this story. Bailey has never reached the maturity of manhood while The Misfit, Hiram, and Bobby Lee are classically amoral individuals who seem to have no pattern or plan to their lives. They are desensitized to any true emotion as well as to normal responses. Right after shooting the grandmother, The Misfit says, "Shut up, Bobby Lee. . . . It's no real pleasure in life," thus defining his barren and meaningless existence.

The central irony in the story is the connection between The Misfit and the grandmother. When he tells her that he behaves the way he does because he has nothing to believe in, she sees a reflection of herself. As she reaches out to him crying, "Why you're one of my babies," he recoils in horror and shoots her. Even The Misfit shrinks from any sense of relationship with this self-centered, emotionally bankrupt woman.

Theodore Roethke, "My Papa's Waltz" (p. 827)

For years I read this poem as a loving, yet not sentimental, picture of a bedtime romp shared by father and son. About ten years ago, students began pointing out to me how dark the images really are. Of course, I had always noted the frowning mother, but she had seemed to me perhaps only mildly disapproving. Possibly she didn't want the boy excited when he should be getting ready for sleep or maybe she resented the way the father invited his son to celebrate yet left her out.

How could I have ignored phrases like "I hung on like death" and "At every step you missed / My right ear scraped a buckle"? At the very least, these images suggest that the waltz is in some ways frightening and painful for the child. Many of my students go further, believing that the poem shows the terror of a family trapped and menaced by the father's alcoholism.

Maxine Kumin, "Making the Jam without You" (p. 828)

I read this poem as a gift from a middle-aged mother to her nineteen-year-old daughter. The mother remembers the sensual pleasures she shared with her daughter as they went through the summer ritual of making blackberry jam. But rather than wishing for bygone days when the daughter was with her, this mother fantasizes for her daughter a delightful encounter with a wonderful young man. She sees the two picking berries together and making jam while their "two heads / touch over the kettle." At the end of the poem, the wise, generous mother slips out of the fantasy, leaving us with the final image of the daughter and the young man with their "two mouths open/ for the sweet stain of purple." For me, this image indicates a sexual experience, but many students disagree, arguing instead that the encounter is innocent and childlike, as suggested by the fairy tale imagery of the castle and the thicket of brambles. (Suggesting the sexual nature of fairy tales has, so far, earned me only groans and exasperated sighs.)

Judith Ortiz Cofer, "My Father in the Navy: A Childhood Memory" (p. 830)

The father becomes a figure altogether separated from the world of his family. His navy cap sits on his head "like a halo," his uniform is a "flash of white . . . like an angel." These images show the father as a holy figure, revered by the speaker, her mother, and her brother who keep a "vigil" until he arrives. But the father is also an "apparition on leave from a shadow-world"; he works beneath the sea in the "bellies of iron whales." These images suggest that the father might inspire fear as well as reverence. The speaker also sees the family as sirens, the lures who bring the father back from the sea and his ship where he really feels most at home.

Robert Mezey, "My Mother" (p. 831)

Almost every reader will agree that this mother is downright irritating. She tries to run her son's life first by manipulation (lines 4–13), then by example (lines 13–25), and then, in the final twenty lines of the poem, through appeal to authority (the "great writer" Sholem Aleichem) and direct pleas ("try to put some money away").

Still, although every line reveals the mother's intrusiveness, the son seems to view her with good-natured humor rather than with anger and resentment. The fourth line may be read ironically, yet the mother's breathless appeal to her son also seems to flow from a genuinely caring heart.

Ellen Wolfe, "Amniocentesis" (p. 832)

Most students know someone who has undergone amniocentesis. This prenatal test for birth defects seems to be performed more and more frequently in this age of older mothers and technology-conscious doctors. The speaker in this poem addresses her unborn child as she thinks about the medical professionals who will look for problems as they perform the test. The final line of the poem is her prayer for the child and for herself.

Anonymous, "Lord Randal" (p. 833)

The relationship between the mother and son in this poem is puzzling. She knows almost as soon as the son returns that he has been poisoned (stanzas 3–7). Yet instead of mourning or placing blame, she immediately asks him what he has left to her and to the rest of the family. The final stanza suggests that Lord Randal has finally lost his patience. He will not leave anything to the woman whom he and his mother both know has poisoned him. The repeated final line of each stanza, traditional ballad form, enforces the growing distress Lord Randal feels as his mother relentlessly questions him rather than leading him to the rest for which he longs.

Margaret Atwood, "Today" (p. 834)

The innocent young daughter (probably two or three years old) is led to the bluegreen water of a pond or lake by the soft, white allure of the ducks. The sun shines on the water, making it look like gold. The mother sees the danger (the daughter may drown) and knows she must pull her daughter back. But she also recognizes the loss that comes with experience. From now on, her daughter will begin to view her world with wary questioning, always looking for the possibility of danger, never simply plunging forward and joining with beauty for its own sake and with no conscious thought of consequences.

Sylvia Plath, "Metaphors" (p. 836)

I'm always surprised that so few students solve the riddle easily. Perhaps because I had already given birth when I first read the poem, the melon strolling about on vinelike legs gave me a mental picture that left no doubt about what was going on. And of course the opening line, "I'm a riddle in nine syllables" immediately brought to mind the nine long months of pregnancy. The red fruit and ivory timber are a bit more difficult to envision; I think they refer to the fetus whose body and bones are the fruit and timber. (A future engineer in one of my classes pointed out to me that each of the poem's nine lines has nine syllables, reinforcing the metaphor in the first line.)

Donald Hall, "My Son, My Executioner" (p. 836)

Many students find the title rather grim, but of course the poem simply acknowledges the powerful experience of becoming parents. As the young mother and father (25 and 22) look at their son, they realize that he is their way of passing on both their genes and their values. Yet his birth also forces them to face the inevitable march of generations; as their son grows to maturity, they will pass into old age and death.

James Masao Mitsui, "Allowance" (p. 837)

I think this would be a great poem to pair with Donald Hall's "My Son, My Executioner." Here the speaker listens to his mother's stories while he pulls out her white hairs. Apparently, she is paying her son in a vain attempt to ward off the effects of aging.

Seamus Heaney, "Digging" (p. 837)

As he describes the hard physical labor done by his father and grandfather, the speaker discovers connections between them and himself. He shows pride in his father's and grandfather's ability to "handle a spade," the first while harvesting potatoes, the second while digging fuel from peat bogs. Unlike either of his forebears, the speaker will not carry on the tradition of physical labor. Nevertheless, like them, he will bring energy and effort to his own work. Rather than using a spade to dig for potatoes or peat, he will use a pen to discover and reveal words, images, and ideas.

Tina Howe, *Painting Churches* (p. 839)

Most readers readily identify with the complicated mixture of love, doubt, longing, and conflict that holds the Church family together. One student suggested that the description of light in the opening stage directions reflects Mags's relationship with her parents and her parents' relationship with each other. At times the light is "hard edged and brilliant" while at other moments it is "dappled and yielding." The central childhood incident in the first act of the play—Mags's creation of the crayon masterpiece—can be imagined in light that is "hard edged and brilliant." On the other hand, the key remembered moment in the second act—the mystical night swim Mags shared with her father—suggests light that is dappled and yielding.

Mags creates the crayon sculpture at great personal cost, both physical and emotional. She is banned from the family table because she persists in squirting her chewed up food onto her plate. While her father, looking back, describes these streams of food as "colorful, actually; decorative almost," her mother was horrified. Mags's explanation that she feared she would not be able to swallow her food suggests that, in fact, she may not have been able "to swallow" her mother's attempts to control her life and to mold her daughter into the same proper Bostonian mold the mother has filled all her life. During the six months Maggie was condemned to spend the dinner hour in her room, she worked on a fantastic crayon sculpture. For Mags, the crayon-covered radiator became a brilliant monument to her own creative powers. Unable to feed her body, she assigned each new color an exotic, mystical flavor with which she fed her spirit.

When her parents discovered Mags's creation, the light became even stronger and harsher. As he did at every significant crisis in his daughter's life, Gardner turned away or fainted, refusing to face any hint of real pain or conflict, while Fanny completely misunderstood what Mags had been doing and destroyed the crayon sculpture. As she retells the story, Mags realizes that her mother could not really have used a blow torch, but her childhood memory retains the image of her mother viciously attacking the artwork that had become her means of survival for six months.

In Act II, Mags's searching examination of her past focuses on a magical moment with her father. As a young woman, home from art school, Mags accompanied Gardner for a spontaneous nighttime swim. The phosphorus in the ocean caught the moonlight and, as they moved through the water, father and daughter seemed bathed in magical sparks. Mags remembers grabbing Gardner's foot, wishing she could hold onto that moment and never let it end. She felt she was experiencing perfect beauty, wished she could preserve it forever, yet knew that part of the mystery of beauty was its transience. As Mags describes this incident, her mother cannot remember it at all. Fanny seems to have been present mainly during the painful and difficult times of Mags's childhood and young adulthood, while Gardner was there for the moments of joy and pleasure.

While Howe herself has warned that she sees "terrible dangers in insisting on tidy parallels and meaningful departures" because "it drains away all the mystery," it's tempting to see at least one important parallel and an equally significant departure between the two acts. In each act, Mags recalls a powerful incident from her past that relates to her connection with her parents. It seems significant that the crayon incident, which is filled with anguish, is described in Act I whereas the swimming incident, which is filled with joy and wonder, comes in Act II. The play moves from the harsher, shadow-filled memories to the lighter memories that suggest reconciliation. Had Howe chosen to reverse the order of these memories, the drama would feel like a tragedy leading to the death of a relationship rather than a comedy leading to insight, acceptance, and understanding.

In the end, Mags creates a portrait that pleases both her parents, yet—most important—first pleases herself. Fanny and Gardner seem determined throughout the play to approach life differently. Gardner rigorously practices denial and withdrawal when any crisis arises. He begins the play ensconced in his study while Fanny struggles to make the decisions related to moving. And when they discuss what to take to their new residence, they cannot agree even on the worth of the Paul Revere spoons as compared to the Robert Frost first editions. Nevertheless, when they see the portrait their daughter has created, they are able to understand both her and themselves more fully. Both are clearly in accord when Gardner delivers his final line: "The whole thing is absolutely extraordinary!"

Agnes G. Herman, "A Parent's Journey Out of the Closet" (p. 888)

In nearly any class, there will be students who are gay and/or students who have family members or close friends who are gay. In addition, there will almost certainly be students who hold deep religious or social beliefs against homosexuality. To establish a somewhat comfortable discussion atmosphere, I usually ask that everyone consider the diverse makeup of our society and, therefore, potentially, of our class as they contribute to the discussion of any work relating to gay issues. If someone, nonetheless, feels called upon to state something like, "God hates homosexuality" or "the Bible says homosexuality is wrong," I point out that within nearly every established religion there is varied opinion, even among clergy. This essay is particularly interesting in this regard because the writer is a religious Jew and her husband is a rabbi.

I found this essay both moving and annoying—moving because Herman's deep love for Jeff comes across in every sentence and because she clearly believes that her "coming out of the closet" in some way will improve her relationship with her son; annoying because the early part of the essay, particularly, reinforces stereotypes without any examination or refutation. As Herman tells about her concerns that Jeff was "too good" and his father's concerns that Jeff preferred a rolling pin to a baseball bat, she seems to indicate that these were early predictors of his homosexuality. Why should kind, gentle, neat behavior in males be looked on as cause for concern? Whether a "good" boy who likes to cook grows up to be gay or straight, should those qualities be viewed as worrisome? I have not taught this essay yet, so I do not know how students will react. I would hope they would challenge these assumptions.

Much of the focus of this essay is on the mother's feelings: her guilt, her fear, her sense of responsibility. It would be interesting to know how Jeff really felt after she published her article in the national Jewish magazine *The Reconstructionist*. Herman reports that she and her husband received an outpouring of support, yet Jeff's life was no doubt also changed by the publication of the article. I would like to know if it changed for the better.

Harry Dolan, "I Remember Papa" (p. 895)

Dolan's father advises him that "the pitfall sometimes seems to be the easiest way out" and urges him to "beware of the future" because he must be the one to fulfill his father's dreams and ambitions. Considering the episodes described in the rest of the story, it's clear that Dolan believes he, too, may be faced with choices as desperate as those that finally closed the door on his father's hopes and aspirations, although his decisions may be made under different circumstances. As suggested by the opening narrative, his choices will concern not finding a way to make a living for his family but rather deciding how he will defend his own honor as a black man faced with racist actions and attitudes.

Dolan's view of his mother is primarily admiring. Although she is sick (apparently with tuberculosis), she tries hard to keep the family together and to comfort her husband through every difficulty he faces. The essay shows the mother mainly in relation to Dolan's father rather than as a separate individual.

In contrast to the direct tribute Dolan pays to his mother, his picture of his father is far more complex. For years after his father's imprisonment for stealing five loaves of bread and twelve dollars, Dolan does not see him. When he finally visits his father in prison, Dolan at first feels resentment. However, his bitterness against his father turns to a reevaluation as he thinks about the wasted energy and ability now locked behind bars. The episodes described in the rest of the essay suggest how difficult life was for Dolan's father and certainly demonstrate that he does not fit the stereotype of the lazy black man Dolan describes in the essay's introduction. By explaining his father's life, and particularly by ending with the stunning episode of the kitten, Dolan urges readers to examine, and perhaps reconsider, their own views of families like his own and, particularly, of the choices made by the men who are the fathers of those families.

CHAPTER 10
LEARNING AND TEACHING

"The Lesson," "Famous All Over Town," "The Loudest Voice," "A Class of New Canadians," "A Teacher Taught Me," "Learning to Read and Write," and "In Search of Our Mothers' Gardens" all look at aspects of education related to students who are not part of the dominant culture. Bambara's short story, Harper's poem, and Douglass's essay suggest the power of learning as a means of gaining opportunity and show the historic background that often denied education to oppressed people. "A Teacher Taught Me" shows that even when schooling is mandated for all, educational institutions can be coopted to maintain oppression rather than to fight it. "The Loudest Voice," "A Class of New Canadians," and "Famous All Over Town" address the question of assimilation, asking what is lost and what is gained when students are educated by teachers and institutions (however well meaning) that do not share their culture and values.

Some selections criticize formal education. For example, "The Scholars" suggests that professors have their heads and hearts buried in dusty research tasks, the teacher in Anna Lee Walters's poem patronizes and condescends to her Native American student, and the professor in Mamet's *Oleanna* is condescending and self-centered. Other selections, however, offer a contrasting view. For example, Sugar and Sylvia in Toni Cade Bambara's "The Lesson" challenge Miss Moore's every word and action, but this persistent teacher, remaining calm and determined, pursues the neighborhood children beyond the classroom to make certain they learn for themselves the lesson of economic inequality, and the speaker in Tom Romano's "The Teacher" shows a compassionate and appreciative view of his students.

Many of the selections in this section invite a look at the power structures in the teaching-learning relationship. If I were introducing this idea, I'd consider assigning "A Class of New Canadians," "Famous All Over Town," *Oleanna,* "The School Children," "A Teacher Taught Me," and "Ethics."

ADDITIONAL SELECTIONS FOR CONSIDERATION: LEARNING AND TEACHING

Title and Author	Text Page
### Fiction	
"Butterflies," Patricia Grace	12
"Battle Royal," Ralph Ellison	169
"Cathedral," Raymond Carver	379
"The Conversion of the Jews," Philip Roth	770
### Poetry	
"Theme for English B," Langston Hughes	13
"When I was one and twenty," A. E. Housman	191
"Spring and Fall," Gerard Manley Hopkins	203
"Digging," Seamus Heaney	837
"Dulce et Decorum Est," Wilfred Owen	1052
"What Were They Like?" Denise Levertov	1062
"Elegy for Jane," Theodore Roethke	1172
### Drama	
Fences, August Wilson	466
### Essays	
"Education," E. B. White	21
"Graduation in Stamps," Maya Angelou	332

SUGGESTIONS FOR TEACHING ADDITIONAL SELECTIONS

1. Read the following selections to see how a speaker tells a story or uses anecdotes as a way of teaching or convincing others, either directly or indirectly. Then compose a story or an anecdote of your own that you believe will teach your audience something new (perhaps showing a new way of looking at a familiar idea, belief, person, or place). Your story may be as

fanciful as you like; remember that the lesson you teach may be subtle and indirect.

	Text Page
"Cathedral"	379
"Theme for English B"	13
"What Were They Like?"	1062
Fences	466

2. Consider the relationship between power and education. What power do teachers hold? What power do learners hold? How can the balance of power affect what one learns or teaches? Consider the following works as inspiration for further research on this topic.

	Text Page
"Butterflies"	12
"Battle Royal"	169
"The Conversion of the Jews"	770
"Cathedral"	379
"Theme for English B"	13
"Dulce et Decorum Est"	1052
Fences	466
"Graduation in Stamps"	332

3. What role do parents, grandparents, or other relatives play in the education of young people? What role—or roles—should they play? Consider the following works as inspiration for further research on this topic.

	Text Page
"Butterflies"	12
"Battle Royal"	169
"The Conversion of the Jews"	770
Fences	466

	Text Page
"Education"	21
"Graduation in Stamps"	332

THEMATIC PHOTOGRAPH (p. 903)

Considerations

1. What has the woman in the picture learned? Think beyond the easy literal response as you answer.

2. How does the instructor respond to his student's success? What might he have learned from teaching this particular student?

3. Write a journal entry assuming the persona of either the student or the teacher. Describe a significant event that led up to the moment captured by the picture.

READINGS

Donald Barthelme, "Me and Miss Mandible" (p. 904)

I must admit, it is rather daunting to write an instructor's guide entry for a short story that so beautifully parodies the form: "Many pupils enjoy working fractions when they understand what they are doing. They have confidence in their ability to take the right steps and to obtain correct answers." The narrator, Joseph, reports reading these two sentences in Miss Mandible's textbook; the second sentence becomes a motif that appears throughout the story.

Varying this motif, I would say, "Many readers enjoy Donald Barthelme's works when they understand that they do not have to find the right steps to obtain correct answers." The nonrealistic aspects of the story may give some students difficulty, but if they can be convinced to look for the truths that flit in and out of the absurdities—and the truths that are, in fact, absurdities— they should really enjoy this story.

Miss Mandible takes her name from the anterior mouth appendages that form strong biting jaws in some insects. This formidable image does not really fit the way Joseph looks at the teacher. He does not see her as someone about to devour him but rather as an attractive woman whom he desires. Nevertheless, the sense of the menacing presence of authority is suggested by the teacher's name.

Apparently, Joseph finds himself back in grade school because he has not learned the lessons of life well enough. As an insurance adjuster, he helped an elderly woman to win a claim against his company because he believed her claim was just, and so he was "given a new role"—not just fired or demoted, but actually sent back to elementary school. Acting in an honorable way is not acceptable in the business world.

In school, life is no less absurd for Joseph than it was at work or in the army, where it took him "a fantastically long time to realize what the others grasped almost at once: that much of what we were doing was absolutely pointless, to no purpose." As he sits in Miss Mandible's class, he seems to be faced mainly with useless information, and on the playground he encounters the jockeying for power and love relationships that reminds him of his former life.

When Miss Mandible finally gets around to asking for a larger desk to accommodate Joseph's size, the custodian informs her that the state has decided the size of sixth graders and since Joseph does not fit that size, no variant desk can be provided. (For those who have struggled with various school systems for just such small, sensible changes and who have received just such absurd, stonewalling responses, Joseph's predicament will have a particular poignancy.)

In the conclusion, Joseph finally acts like an adult and carries out his fantasy of seducing Miss Mandible. If he had hoped to escape from the dull school authorities through this act, he was mistaken. Now they will charge Miss Mandible with contributing to the delinquency of a minor, ignoring Joseph's protests. Joseph will be sent to a doctor "for observation"; perhaps the only hopeful note is that Joseph's classmate Bobby Vanderbilt, in silent sympathy, gives the culprit his prized "Sounds of Sebring" recording as a farewell gift.

Toni Cade Bambara, "The Lesson" (p. 914)

In her dedication for her anthology *The Black Woman*, Bambara writes: "To the uptown mammas who nudged me to just set it down in print . . . so maybe that way we don't keep treadmilling the same old ground." This dedication suggests the reason for Miss Moore's summer lessons and field trips. Although Sylvia has a grand time describing Miss Moore in terms often reserved for the stereotyped elementary school teacher—prim, proper, and always looking "like she was going to church"—it is clear that her teaching goes way beyond ordinary classroom exercises.

When I teach this story, I continue to be amazed by many students' initial response. Over and over I hear some version of this statement as

Miss Moore's purpose for bringing the children to F.A.O. Schwartz: "She wants them to see what they can have if they work hard and get into better circumstances." Usually someone else will point to details like the shame even the ebullient, self-confident Sylvia feels as she enters F.A.O. Schwartz or Sugar's comment that she doesn't think "all of us here put together eat in a year what that sailboat costs." Surely we are meant to be sympathetic with Sylvia and Sugar—we are not to feel that Sylvia should be ashamed or that Sugar is simply envious. Finally, consider Miss Moore's comment, "Imagine for a minute what kind of society it is in which some people can spend on a toy what it would cost to feed a family of six or seven." She asks the children to think about the *society* in which they live. She knows that no matter how hard most people work—and this certainly includes middle class as well as poor people—their salaries will not buy them "their share of the pie."

Both Sylvia and Sugar are deeply affected by their trip to F.A.O. Schwartz. Sugar voices her view of the lesson, but Sylvia does not want to give Miss Moore the satisfaction of hearing her acknowledge the deeply troubling inequities she is beginning to recognize. Sugar responds to the lesson by racing swiftly away, thinking of the ice cream Sylvia has proposed. Sylvia, confident that she can run even faster, stays behind "to think this day through": to consider the endless complications and complexities of growing up in a democracy that often seems to foster inequality.

Grace Paley, "The Loudest Voice" (p. 921)

I've found that students respond more fully to this story when they all understand certain basic tenets of Judaism. For instance, many Christian students do not know that Jews do not believe in the divinity of Jesus. They need to recognize that Chanukah is not "Jewish Christmas" and to understand the relentless persecution Jews have experienced throughout their history.

Certainly Shirley's father is developed as the more sympathetic parent. He argues that being exposed to Christmas is not the worst thing that could happen to a Jewish child. He points out that "history teaches everyone. We learn from reading this is a holiday from pagan times also, candles, lights, even Chanukah. So we learn it's not altogether Christian. . . . What belongs to history, belongs to all. . . ." He sees his daughter's participation in the holiday religious pageant as "introducing us to the beliefs of a different culture." The mother, on the other hand, fears that her daughter will gradually be pulled away from Judaism if she participates in ceremonies relating to the Christian religion. It's easy to see the father as broad-minded and sensible and to stereotype the mother as narrow and whining. Still, near the end of the story, she offers an insight into her objections when she defends Mr. Hilton's failure to give major roles in the pageant to several Christian children: "They got very small voices; after all, why should they holler? The English language they know from the beginning by heart . . . the whole piece of goods . . . they own it."

With this speech, she grudgingly acknowledges the (probably inadvertent) wisdom of Mr. Hilton's choosing Jewish children to play major roles, but she also demonstrates her understanding of who holds the power both in the school her child attends and in the new country where they now live. Shirley's father may see the play as simply being introduced "to the beliefs of a different culture," but Shirley's mother understands that, in fact, they have been introduced to the beliefs of the dominant culture. Certainly the Christians in the story show no interest in or understanding of Judaism; otherwise, how could they end the play with Shirley's describing the crucifixion of Jesus by proclaiming "as everyone in this room, in this city—in this world—now knows, I shall have eternal life"? The father is apparently willing to look on this appalling ignorance as something benign; the mother is less comfortable with what she hears and sees.

Shirley herself seems entirely at ease with her experience. From her participation in the pageant, she has learned that she may be "foolish," but she is not "a fool." I take this to mean that, like her father, she takes a lighthearted, humorous approach to the troubles of the world, but like her mother she recognizes the need to face those troubles squarely. Her prayer at the end suggests that not only has she retained her own religious beliefs, but also feels sorry for the "lonesome Christians" who, in her eyes, lack the warmth and connection of community in which she lives. The final two lines indicate that while she obviously feels the deepest empathy with her father, she also understands her mother's views. She plans to keep speaking out loudly so that her voice may be heard over the "very small voices" of her fellow classmates who are "blond like angels."

Clark Blaise, "A Class of New Canadians" (p. 927)

Norman Dyer pictures himself as a god when he enters his classroom. Although he has earned the Ph.D., he rationalizes that he is willing graciously to condescend to teach an evening course in English as a second language (ESL). His only concern for his students is how they look at him. He imagines that they love him because he is bringing to them the possibility of becoming fluent in one of the languages of what he regards as the cosmopolitan city of Montreal. He also implies that one of his main reasons for teaching the class is to get more money so that he can continue to refine his lifestyle into the sophisticated ideal he desires.

Dyer holds contempt for the United States, although his reasons are not entirely clear. He seems to approve of socialistic governments more than capitalistic democracies. For instance, he disapproves of the student who questions the Swedish national housing policy. On the other hand, his own life seems devoted to conspicuous consumption. He treasures his "small but elegant" apartment and prides himself on knowing all the best restaurants. In addition, he longs for exclusive clothing that would give him "the authority of simple good taste."

Because Dyer has the luxury to live as he does, he pictures himself as superior to his students, many of whom are simply trying to find a way to better themselves according to their own definitions. Dyer seems completely unable to empathize. Several of his students complain that it's difficult to learn English in Montreal because the city is so diverse. They can get along in their own languages or in other languages they know. Dyer refuses to see the multicultural nature of the city as a possible drawback in any way.

His smallness and narrowmindedness reach a climax when Miguel Mayor (his last name means "the greater") approaches him at the end of class. Learning of Mayor's desire to move to the United States and regarding this goal, as well as Mayor's elegant wardrobe, as threatening to his own fragile self-image, Dyer makes only a minor change in Mayor's poorly written letter, which will almost certainly ensure the failure of his job application. In the final image of the story, we see Dyer standing in front of the clothing store, pondering his encounter with Mayor. Dyer fights against learning anything about himself and justifies his decision by imagining that he knows what is best for Mayor.

Danny Santiago, "Famous All Over Town" (p. 935)

Rudy imagines that what happens in school will affect his whole life, and in many ways he seems to be right. Yet the reasons for the effects are probably different from what he thinks. For example, Eddie, who pictures himself as a future CPA, is not particularly concerned with what he learns about subject matter. Instead, he's learning how to work within the system to get along, get up, and get out. When he tutors Danny, he tries to teach him strategies for getting along with teachers, for achieving high grades, and for accumulating activities that will look promising on college applications. Eddie never talks about the learning or knowledge that should be represented by the good grades; he sees them as goals in themselves. Unfortunately, Eddie's view is accepted by many today as sensible and practical. Many people are highly cynical about education, believing that educational institutions, for the most part, only teach conformity to a certain set of rules that students do not understand and do not see as connected to any learning that is meaningful for their lives.

The conclusion of the story makes painful reading for all who believe in the possibility of growth and hope within the classroom. Most poignant of all is the fact that Miss Bontempo has good intentions and understands at least the theories of involving students in their learning. However, her delight when Rudy asks a question that allows her to display her knowledge and her subsequent distress when he is able to leap ahead, building his own ideas on what he has learned from her, show her shallowness as an educator. Eddie's cynical views have proved correct, and although Rudy is seen as a hero by his buddies who think he deliberately provoked Miss Bontempo, we know that he has simply learned a new and harsh lesson about the limits of the classroom in which he is being taught.

Students, I expect, will note that Rudy and his friends are able to predict the story's outcome because of their real-life experiences. Miss Bontempo seems blissfully unaware of that possibility. In addition, I would hope that at least some students would ask, "So what if Rudy had 'read ahead' in the book?" One would hope that Miss Bontempo could have turned that possibility into a moment of praise rather than condemnation. I suspect most instructors reading this story will barely be able to stifle the urge to jump into the midst of the action and rescue Miss Bontempo, Rudy, and the rest of the class from the disastrous results of her fumbling response to this ultimate "teachable moment."

Henry Reed, "Naming of Parts" (p. 942)

This poem shows in a poignantly ironic way a breakdown in communication between student and teacher. The instructor, whose voice is heard in the first four lines of the first three stanzas, explains the parts of a rifle. He is almost certainly a military instructor, and the young trooper who hears him translates his dry lecture into a sensual reverie. As the instructor explains an instrument of death, the student imagines the life-giving flowers and bees. The "spring" of the rifle becomes in his mind the season of spring. In the final stanza, the student's vision integrates his own images with those of the instructor, showing that the "naming of parts" can mean much more than the instructor realizes.

Walt Whitman, "There Was a Child Went Forth" (p. 943)

This poem suggests that education comes not just from school but also from the events, objects, people, and places that we observe each day. The child will become a combination of these images, some of them positive, some negative.

Students will disagree about the effects of the parents on this child. Some see the father as entirely negative, yet he is described as "strong, self-sufficient, and manly." Without the details that follow, he almost certainly would be seen as a positive role model. The mother, at first, seems positive, yet on second reading, her "mild words" and clean cap seem to suggest a passive person without much to distinguish her or make her an individual personality.

Marianne Moore, "The Student" (p. 945)

The speaker suggests that the true student must learn voluntarily. Unlike sheep that can be forcibly shorn of their wool, students cannot be forced to give forth what they truly have learned. Students are like wolves—their coats (what they have come to know) are magnificent—but they must give them over voluntarily. The true student may also seem sometimes to be unmoved by significant things; but the apparent lack of response may, in fact, indicate that the student is so overwhelmed by what he or she has comprehended that no reaction is possible.

Louise Glück, "The School Children" (p. 947)

As these children go to school, it is as if they are crossing a great ocean. Teachers "on the other shore" wait behind great desks. The children are like apples offered up by the mothers to the teachers who will teach these children to be orderly and to learn in silence. The mothers, left behind, try to imagine how to escape from their homes, which are now like orchards barren of fruit.

Anna Lee Walters, "A Teacher Taught Me" (p. 948)

The short lines and recurring refrain give this poem a chant-like rhythm. Students will probably find the narrator's response to the boy with "transparent skin" readily understandable, but opinion may be divided over her reaction to the teacher. Why does she resent what seem to be sincere expressions? Students who have been in this situation themselves may see the condescension in the teacher's choice of words and in the way she makes the narrator stand apart from the other students.

Linda Paston, "Ethics" (p. 949)

The first section of the poem sets up a typical classroom situation where the teacher poses a hypothetical question that the students find tedious and distant. When the speaker, Linda, suggests an alternative possibility to the teacher's either-or dilemma, she is ridiculed. Years later, when the speaker's own visit to a museum makes the ethics teacher's query truly meaningful, she finds that none of the classroom possibilities fit. She sees that human life and fine art are intertwined; one cannot be valued above the other. And certainly very young people cannot be expected to understand fully the depth of this truth. Ethics, she suggests, cannot be learned at school but only by living life in a full and thoughtful way.

Gary Gildner, "First Practice" (p. 950)

The speaker looks back with the eyes of childhood on Clifford Hill who coached the football team. The reference to the grade school basement (where students went for atomic attack drills) suggests that the players are quite young. In addition, the speaker takes literally, as would a young child, Hill's contention that this is a dog-eat-dog world. Some students may be surprised by Hill's request that any girls leave, but others will know that this cigar-chomping coach regards the word "girl" as equivalent to coward or weakling.

Hill's approach to sports teaches team members that winning is the most important goal and that learning to hate is an essential part of becoming a successful athlete. I take his command "but I don't want to see / any marks when you're dressed" to mean that he is also calculating and sneaking, showing his players how to injure without making any bruises that parents or other authorities are apt to notice and question.

Students have very different responses to this poem. Some contend that even coaches like Clifford Hill have something valuable to teach. Others claim that few coaches share his views. Still others see Hill as typical and use his attitude as evidence that young people— particularly young men—are often harmed by what they learn when they play organized sports. (For a similar view of sports, see Paul Theroux's "Being a Man.")

Tom Romano, "The Teacher " (p. 951)

I think this is a wonderful, affirming poem with a speaker who appreciates his students as much—or even more—than his own teaching. The short opening and closing stanzas frame the longer middle stanza, which develops the delightful image of the teacher as leader who succeeds most fully when he ends up as follower. His gracious acknowledgment, in the final stanza, to the students' request that he extend to their minor errors "the same courteous understanding" he extends to his own, shows his generous and openminded vision of the teacher/student relationship.

Frances E. W. Harper, "Learning to Read" (p. 952)

Frances Watkins was orphaned at age three and was raised by her uncle, who ran a school for free black children. Through her schooling and later work as a teacher, she became passionately devoted to the abolitionist movement. Before and after marrying Fenton Harper, who was also committed to the abolitionist cause, she lectured widely for antislavery organizations. Like "Learning to Read," many of her poems suggest the importance of education as a means of liberation. A theme worth pursuing is the subversive nature of true learning. Every oppressed group has been to one degree or another denied the opportunity to study in the same way as those who hold power in society.

Antler, "Raising My Hand" (p. 953)

The first two stanzas provide images that should bring back to all who remember their grade school days the frustration of knowing the answer but not being called on to give it. In addition, the second stanza suggests that the teacher purposely calls on those who do not know the answer. Why might she/he do this? (Compare, perhaps, with the response of Miss Bontempo in "Famous All Over Town.")

The final stanza shows how the lessons learned in early school experiences can stay with us to return whenever we face similar expectations or challenges. For the speaker in the poem, his memory of not being called on in school parallels his sense of anticlimax when only "the wind" responds to his "excitement and expectancy" as he views a moving scene in nature. The classroom has become his touchstone for disappointment.

David Mamet, *Oleanna* (p. 955)

When reviewing a performance of *Oleanna*, *The Boston Globe* said, "David Mamet has raised outrage to an artform" and *The New York Times* announced, "*Oleanna* is likely to provoke more arguments than any other play this year." I agree.

The play will almost certainly prove extremely controversial to teach, and instructors may well find themselves mediating heated exchanges among students. I chose to include the play in this anthology because it seemed to me a complex treatment of a difficult theme. In the play, a male professor and his female student sit down to talk when she arrives at his office for an unscheduled meeting. As the two begin their discussion, it becomes clear almost immediately that they are on different wavelengths. Carol, a twenty-year-old student who is worried about her grades, does not understand the language of the academic world. She is confused by words and phrases like "term of art," "virtual warehousing of the young," "concept," and "precept," and begs the professor to teach her and to reassure her that she is not stupid. The student seems to want straightforward explanations and is baffled that she has tried to do everything the professor asked yet is still failing. The professor, John, who is constantly interrupted by telephone calls apparently related to the purchase of a new house, tries to reassure Carol, but it is obvious that he is primarily interested in himself and in his own stories. To comfort her, he tells an anecdote about his own school days and tries to explain the book he has written expressing his outrage at what he had experienced in school and what he has observed other students experiencing. Ironically, he does not see that in insisting on his own view of the educational experience, he is forcing Carol into a mold just as much as his teachers forced him. She resists thinking that the college experience is "prejudiced" and tries to explain that she comes from a different social and economic class from his. Throughout the discussion, Carol barely gets to finish a sentence, while the professor discourses on his educational theories as well as his concerns about his tenure. As Act I ends, Carol is about to tell John something that she says she has never told anyone, but he is interrupted by a call that is supposedly about his house but turns out to be announcing a surprise party. At this turn of events, John completely forgets the deeply emotional moment when Carol has begun to reveal herself to him. Instead, bound for his tenure announcement party, he bids her a hasty good-bye.

If the play were to end here, we would simply have had a look at yet one more struggling student looking for meaning in her education and failing to find it as she talks to her well-intentioned yet self-centered professor. However, the play does not end here, and Acts II and III show an astonishing change in the balance of power. Carol has joined a support group, which seems mainly to have taught her a series of "empowering" phrases. She does not understand the complexity behind these phrases any more than she understood the "concepts" and "precepts" John was trying to explain in Act I. Instead, recognizing that she has not gained what she needs to pursue her education, yet confused about the reasons, she seizes on the concept of sexual harassment and accuses John. While there has certainly not been any overt harassment in Act I, it's possible to see behind some of John's actions a condescension toward women. For example, it's highly unlikely that he would have patted and comforted a male student as he does Carol. Nevertheless, most audience members share John's growing sense of baffled anger as he meets with Carol in Acts II and III and listens to her reasons for pursuing her complaint against him. The final, dramatic moment in Act III, however, confirms the play's ambiguity. After one last exchange with Carol, John reverts to words commonly used to humiliate women, calling Carol a "vicious little bitch" and a "little cunt." Further, he grabs her and begins to beat her, stopping only when he catches himself in the act of raising a chair over his head to hit her. Carol's final comment, "Yes, that's right," which she repeats twice, suggests that both she and he recognize the primitive nature of the power struggle in which they have been engaged. When he cannot win with words, John turns, in the end, to his physical advantage over Carol.

When you are preparing to teach this play, you'll find interesting a series of reviews that have been collected in *Stages of Drama*, third edition, St. Martin's Press, edited by Carl H. Klaus, Miriam Gilbert, and Bradford S. Field, Jr. Here's a sample of the intriguing comments you'll find:

> David Mamet understands that envy is the gasoline on which a competitive society runs, and no modern American playwright has been bolder or more brilliant in analyzing its corrosive social effects.
>
> > John Lahr, *The New Yorker*,
> > 1992

> I found Mr. Mamet's two-character duel a welcome jolt of nervy political theater. No, he didn't get sexual harassment "right," but I gleefully appreciated his theatrical broadside against the stifling value system of "permissible" thinking.
>
> > Susan Brownmiller
> > Author of *Against Our Will:*
> > *Men, Women and Rape*

> A play isn't a prizefight. Or is it? The audience at the performance I attended was clearly for either the male or the female character; even when, after the show, some theatergoers (mostly men) strained to explain to their companions (mostly women) how they could see both sides of the story.
>
> > Enrique Fernandez
> > Editor of Spanish-language
> > magazine *Mas*

The most dangerous aspect of the play is its ending: the professor beats the young woman. . . . The evening I saw the play, the audience cheered and urged him on.

> Deborah Tannen
> Author of *You Just Don't*
> *Understand: Women and*
> *Men in Conversation*

Frederick Douglass, "Learning to Read and Write" (p. 987)

As Frederick Douglass describes his process of becoming literate, he focuses on people who helped as well as people who tried to deter him from his determination to learn. Master Hugh's wife plays both roles. At first she treats Douglass as she would any other child and instructs him in the rudiments of the alphabet. Her husband soon puts a stop to that by making clear "that education and slavery [are] incompatible with each other." Once she has been warned, she becomes almost fanatical in her attempt to keep Douglass away from books. Douglass attributes her change in heart to her husband's training, although he says, "She was not satisfied with simply doing as well as he had commended; she seemed anxious to do better."

Perhaps, as Douglass suggests, Master Hugh's wife has simply been corrupted by the institution of slavery, but his earlier description of her as "a pious, warm, and tenderhearted woman" who "had bread for the hungry, clothes for the naked, and comfort for every mourner that came within her reach" makes her striking change hard to understand as self-motivated. Being completely dependent on her husband, her changes might well reflect her fear of him and her recognition that her own survival rested on fulfilling his wishes.

Douglass describes several white people who help him learn to read. The poor children who teach him in return for the bread Douglass gives them are presented as particularly sympathetic. Douglass notes that he must withhold their names to protect them from reprisals for their kindly acts. Through telling this episode, Douglass helps gain support for his cause among the predominantly white audiences to whom he often spoke.

He also establishes common ground by describing Richard Sheridan's defense of Catholics (predominantly Irish) in England. Until 1829, Catholics were not allowed to vote in England. Douglass further suggests his sympathy for and connection with the Irish by describing his encounter with the two "good Irishmen." After helping them unload a scow, he engages them in a discussion of slavery and they encourage him to seek freedom. He implies, then, that there are many people—women, poor white children, Irish Catholics—who can understand the plight of the slave and who have themselves experienced oppression.

Throughout the essay, the primary theme is Douglass's incredible drive to become literate. He shows the painstaking means he had to follow to learn to read and write and describes how his anger against slavery increased as he was able to read the works of those who fought against all kinds of enslavement. The connection between education and freedom becomes clear. Those who remain ignorant or who, like Master Hugh's wife, turn their backs on what they know to be true can never be fully free.

Alice Walker, "In Search of Our Mothers' Gardens" (p. 992)

This memoir can be divided into two parts. The first considers the history of black women in the United States, focusing on colonial American poet Phyllis Wheatley as a central example. The second section moves the focus from Wheatley to Walker's mother. The heritage of today's black women who are writers and artists, then, is twofold: first, they gain inspiration from women like Wheatley who, under extremely trying circumstances, persisted in their art; second, they are motivated by women who created beauty from whatever they found around them. These women serve as informal yet extremely important teachers, conveying valuable lessons.

The quotation from Jean Toomer that introduces the memoir praises the strength that comes from a full-spirited life of the mind and heart, suggesting that this power allows those deprived of external freedom to thrive in spite of the repression they suffer. Toomer's quotation leads to Walker's opening paragraph, where she describes his observations about the black women he met on his trip through the South. Commenting on their intense spirituality, Toomer said that "they were themselves unaware of the richness they held." This passage opens the opportunity to discuss the relationship between the spiritual life and the life of the mind—the connection between belief and knowledge.

The rest of the memoir looks at the lives of black women and at the way they created beauty from what they saw and found around them. Walker suggests the connection between the current generation of black women who are artists, writers, and poets and their mothers and grandmothers who "handed on the creative spark, the seed of the flower they themselves never hoped to see; or like a sealed letter they could not plainly read." At the beginning of the memoir, Walker challenges Toomer's definition of Southern black women as "saint," claiming that instead they should be called "artist." She explores this theme through historical examples as well as through the example of her mother who created beauty through the flowers she cultivated around "whatever shabby house" their family was forced to live in.

Walker concludes with an analogy, showing the relationship between her forebears who, under the most disheartening conditions, found a way to express their creativity, and the women of her own generation who are now free to use whatever media they choose—words, paints, clay, and so on—to reflect their own inner visions.

CHAPTER 11
WAR AND POWER

At a conference I attended, the keynote speaker asked, "Why is it that every city and every small town has memorials to men who died in war, yet none have monuments for the women who died in childbirth?" The speaker's question made me stop and think about war and to ask whether it was, as she implied, primarily a male concern. You may want to introduce this theme by asking students to respond to this speaker's question. Consider asking them to write for five minutes or so; then ask volunteers to read their comments as a way to initiate discussion.

Certainly nearly all wars have been fought mainly by men. Even in the recent conflict in the Persian Gulf, where women troops became visible, they were not allowed in combat. Although not many women have actually fought in wars, however, they have certainly been as profoundly affected by war as have men. Their lives have been changed in ways that may be less obvious than the changes in the lives of men suffering from combat wounds or post-traumatic stress. Yet those changes are often equally profound. Consider, for example, the female characters in "On the Other Side of the War," "I'm Your Horse in the Night," and "Spoils of War," as well as the speakers in "Patterns" and in "Mother and Poet."

Most of the selections in this section ask questions about war and about traditional assumptions concerning war and duty to one's country. To introduce those traditional assumptions, you might ask students to read "Mother and Poet" or "Dulce et Decorum Est." These works suggest conventional views of war and patriotism. Thinking about these views leads to considering the following questions.

- How are those left behind affected by war? ("On the Other Side of the War," "I'm Your Horse in the Night," "Spoils of War," "Patterns," "Mother and Poet," "What Were They Like?")

- How do young people form their assumptions about war? ("Mother and Poet," "Dulce et Decorum Est," and "War Cards, Purpose, and Blame")

- How do we know "the enemy"? ("On the Other Side of the War," "Guests of the Nation," "Spoils of War," "The Man He Killed," "The Conscientious Objector," "What Were They Like?," and *Picnic on the Battlefield*.)

- What is the relationship between private and public duty? ("Guests of the Nation," "The Things They Carried," "Mother and Poet," "The Conscientious Objector," *Picnic on the Battlefield*)

ADDITIONAL SELECTIONS FOR CONSIDERATION: WAR AND POWER

Title and Author	Text Page
### Fiction	
"The Red Convertible: Lyman Lamartine," Louise Erdrich	160
"The Warriors," Anna Lee Walters	391
### Poetry	
"My Father in the Navy," Judith Ortiz Cofer	422
"Naming of Parts," Henry Reed	942
### Drama	
Hamlet, William Shakespeare	209
Fences, August Wilson	466
Antigone, Sophocles	423
### Essays	
"My People," Chief Seattle	528
"Arrival at Manzanar," Jeanne Wakatsuki Houston and James D. Houston	531

SUGGESTIONS FOR TEACHING ADDITIONAL SELECTIONS

1. How do the families of those who serve in the military respond to their close relatives' war experiences? To consider this question, read the following works that show families affected by war and military service. After reading these selections, do additional research to address the question that opens this topic. In addition to reading more fiction and nonfiction, consider interviewing people whose family members served in the military during wartime.

	Text Page
"The Red Convertible: Lyman Lamartine"	160
"My Father in the Navy"	830
Fences	466
Antigone	1077

2. Create a dialogue on the topic of honor, duty, and responsibility during wartime between the following individuals. You may imagine these people as they are at any point in the selection or as they might speak from beyond the grave, looking back at their experiences.

	Text Page
The narrator in "The Red Convertible: Lyman Lamartine"	160
Antigone	1077
Chief Seattle ("My People")	528

THEMATIC PHOTOGRAPH (p. 1005)

Considerations

1. Describe the details of this picture that you noticed first. Then look carefully for other details. Do the new details you discovered change your response to the picture? Explain.

2.   Explain how this picture relates to the theme of war. What aspect or aspects of war does it represent? Is this a picture you would have chosen to represent war? Explain.

READINGS

Elizabeth Gordon, "On the Other Side of the War: A Story" (p. 1006)

A possible summary of each section of the story:

I. *The Way We Came to America*

The narrator begins with a scene establishing that her father is an American who served in the war in Vietnam and her mother is a Vietnamese woman he met while serving his tour of duty. In addition, the speaker's paternal grandparents, who live in West Virginia, are introduced: They are "as broke, as stubborn, and as sharp as folks can be."

II. *No One Had Expected*

The second section contrasts the speaker's mother and father through describing their expectations of marriage partners and married life prior to meeting each other.

III. *Things Got Mixed Up*

The narrator describes the small mistakes and confusions her mother experienced and her father's response: "He didn't know whether to laugh or cry, but he kissed her because there was nothing he could say."

IV. *The Photograph*

The photograph, taken in 1965, shows a mother and daughter in front of a typical row of American frame houses with a typical American car parked beside one of them. Yet the narrator describes the photo as "not quite right," perhaps because the mother looks dark and somehow "different" while the daughter shows a combination of "different" and familiar features.

V. *When I Started School*

All the previous sections seem to lead to this point. The differences suggested in the small confusions of the mother and in the puzzled responses of those who look at the "not quite right" photograph are summed up in the multiple choice form the family is asked to fill out for their daughter. None of the choices under "race" fits exactly and the family seems stymied until the father comes up with the wise and gentle solution: he tells the mother to put an "h" in the blank, an "h" that stands for "human race." Readers, I think, will echo the daughter's response, "[I]t sounded like a good race to me."

While this story is not exactly about war, it reflects, as the title aptly suggests, another side of war. I liked this gentle yet not saccharine story because it offers a hopeful view of an American soldier who was profoundly affected by the war in Vietnam. Certainly the more devastating and disturbing effects of this war should not be ignored (and they are amply represented in "The Red Convertible" and in "Spoils of War"). Yet, I also enjoyed reading a piece where the soldier came back having faced his responsibilities and continued to learn and grow as he lived with and loved his "h" for "human race" wife and daughter. His response, and the warmth of the narrator's voice, suggest hope for healthy survival for those who are, in one way or another, part of a war.

Luisa Valenzuela, "I'm Your Horse in the Night" (p. 1009)

During discussion of this story, you may want to mention for students unfamiliar with Central and South American politics, the organized underground movements that exist in such countries as Argentina, Chile, and El Salvador. As background information, you may also want to mention that Portuguese is the primary language spoken in Brazil while the narrator and Beto are Spanish speakers. This accounts for her stating that she "translates" the title of the song.

After reading the first six paragraphs, most readers will infer that the speaker and the man who appears at her door are lovers who have been separated by the man's absence, apparently to fight covertly in a revolutionary action. The man cautions secrecy about his whereabouts, suggesting that he is an underground fighter rather than a soldier in a regular, government-approved army. The woman seems to think a great deal about the relationship. She wonders and worries about the past and the future, while the man seems concerned only about the present as he plays the "hot" Gal Costa recording, offers the speaker a drink of cachça, and takes her in his arms as they "continue recognizing, rediscovering each other."

While the woman and Beto make love, she claims the Gal Costa song "I'm Your Horse in the Night" refers to a woman who is in a trance and who has become the horse of the spirit who rides her. Beto jokes that the reference is simply to sexual intercourse. The woman is the horse of the man as the speaker is Beto's horse.

As the story continues, ambiguity enters. The speaker is awakened by a phone call telling her Beto is dead. She denies this, and almost immediately regrets her denial because she realizes the phone call might be a trap. When the police arrive, it's hard to tell whether the narrator is simply covering for Beto or if she herself now believes that he only visited her in a dream. She gives details of Beto's having left her months before, and these thoughts may be simply passing through her mind or they may be what she says to the police as they torture her.

The final paragraph provides no resolution. On the one hand, as the narrator languishes in jail she imagines that she's now free to be inhabited by the spirit of Beto, dead or alive, while she sleeps. She seems convinced that the interlude at her house was only a dream. Yet the final sentence suggests that somewhere in the depths of her soul the belief persists that Beto was actually with her. She still holds out the hope (or fear) that somewhere hidden in her house may be the Gal Costa record and half-empty bottle of cachça, which would prove the reality of the visit and which would provide hope for Beto's survival.

This is a story that shows the horror of terrorism and torture in a war that intrudes into people's daily lives—even, perhaps, into their dreams, which the narrator says then become nightmares.

Frank O'Connor, "Guests of the Nation" (p. 1013)

Although the setting of the story may seem obvious, I've found that many students do not recognize where it is taking place. Understanding setting is essential, so I begin teaching this story by asking for evidence suggesting the story's locale. Details include the following:

> Irish place names such as Claregalway
>
> Irish dances such as "The Seige of Ennis"
>
> Irish names such as Mary Brigid O'Connell
>
> References to the English as "the enemy"
>
> Irish dialect such as "Ah, you divil, you . . ."

Students may also need to be reminded that although Ireland was officially granted home rule by the British in 1914, hostilities continued, leading to the creation of Sinn Fein, the political group that, following the Easter Rebellion in 1916, formed a military wing called the Irish Republican Army (IRA).

Some students may find it hard to believe that prisoners could become so friendly with their guards, so you may want to mention that there are groups of German prisoners of war from World War II who have held reunions—and invited their American guards to attend. The psychology of how and why such friendships occur may prove an intriguing discussion topic.

Nobel and Hawkins both enjoy a good argument while Buonaparte and Belcher are quieter. The prisoners both seem more experienced and knowledgeable than do the guards, yet all four clearly grapple with the concept of loyalty. Buonaparte, the narrator, reflects the way each character grapples with the sense of individual loyalty in conflict with loyalty to a government or to a cause. Jeremiah Donovan's cold-hearted excitement at the thought of the execution provides a foil for the anguish Buonaparte and Belcher experience. The old woman, a magnificent minor character, is a seer who recognizes the prisoners' humanity as well as their failings and, in the end, forces both Buonaparte and Nobel to face what has happened.

The details of the execution insist that the reader recognize the terror, agony, and revolting ugliness of death in war. These are not stereotyped executions of brave prisoners smoking a final cigarette and refusing a blindfold. Instead we see the botched shooting, the pleas of the condemned, and the moral dilemma faced by the executioners.

Tim O'Brien, "The Things They Carried" (p. 1023)

To begin discussion, you might read aloud the first two paragraphs of the story, asking students to listen for details they find particularly memorable. Follow the reading by requesting a list of the "things" these troops brought with them into the jungle. As students mention items, list on the board the names of the troops and the items they carried. Then ask students to focus on one soldier and to quickly skim the story looking for other items carried by that man. Next ask for a brief written response speculating on what that soldier's choices suggest about his hopes, fears, and values. Begin discussion with several students reading aloud what they have written.

The story focuses on the letter Lt. Cross carries with him. When Ted Lavendar is killed, Cross blames himself for the incident, believing that his daydreams of home and of girls like Martha caused him to relax discipline in a way that was dangerous to his men. Yet even before Lavendar's death, Cross questions the pebble Martha sends him. He carries it, perhaps, as a last, desperate attempt to believe that, magically, he and his troops will be safe from the traps, buried bombs, and sniper's bullets that surround them. Cross's response when Lavendar dies shows grief not only for the young soldier but also for the lieutenant's own youth and past. After this he can never again be the same; he can never return in the same way to the world he once knew.

Janice Mirikitani, "Spoils of War" (p. 1038)

This disturbing story might be taught as a pair with "On the Other Side of the War." Just as Gordon's story shows a kind, honorable Vietnam veteran, Mirikitani's shows a violent, disturbed veteran. All we know of the veteran comes from the free-association lines that run through his head and are represented in poetic form in the text. The lines that open and close his imaginings indicate that he has been taught two things: to hate and kill "the enemy" and to despise yet desire the Vietnamese women. (Students may not know that "poontang" is army slang for the female sexual organ.)

The rest of the veteran's thoughts indicate that he had a lover while he was in Vietnam who both soothed and enraged him. He says that she helped him "forget my My Lais"; some students may be able to identify for the class this reference to the slaughter of Vietnamese civilians by American troops under the order of their lieutenant. As the veteran continues to think of his Vietnamese lover, her image becomes confused with violence, blood, and death, and he seems driven to rape by his unresolved anger and terror.

His crime is made particularly horrifying because we get to know the victim well. Violet is an Asian-American who wears a T-shirt bearing the inscription "Lotus Blossom doesn't live here," suggesting that she rejects the traditional stereotype of the quiet, subservient oriental woman. In addition, she is working through a series of conflicts related to her parents' expectations and, especially, to her relationship with Josh, a war protestor. As Violet considers her time with Josh, she recognizes that he admires and encourages her strengths rather than expecting her to take a secondary role as do her parents.

The ultimate irony of the story is that Violet's determination to escape the stereotypes that haunt her is cut short by the veteran's determination to play out the stereotypes of war and the warrior that haunt him. Although the term "spoils of war" generally means the booty that the winning side confiscates, here it clearly indicates the ugly consequences that continue well beyond the battlefields.

Jorge Luis Borges, "The End of the Duel" (p. 1044)

The original feud between Cardoso and Silveira was based on an incident that is now forgotten. Even those telling the story cannot remember whether it was related to a "quarrel over some unbranded cattle or a free-for-all horse race." Like many feuds, the hatred builds up over a period of time with both opponents increasing their sense of self-righteous indignation. When the gaucho militiamen come to recruit soldiers for the "whites" in the civil war, those who are impressed into service seem to have no more idea about the roots of the war than they do about the roots of Cardoso's and Silveira's feud.

Throughout the war, the two are able to set aside their differences and to kill as they are ordered without thinking. In an equally unthinking way, they agree to participate in the horrific race proposed by the commander of the "reds." Adding to the horror is the response of their fellow "whites" who beg to be allowed to bet on the race even though they know that they are next in line to be executed. The final line indicates, perhaps, the true "end of the duel": Cardoso, although his throat is cut, still struggles to beat his opponent and dies, probably never knowing "he had won." The question, of course, is what had he won? And what had, in fact, been won by any of the men involved in this civil war?

After discussing the story, students may enjoy reading the discussion that immediately follows the selection between Borges and several other writers in which he explores his process of writing and the meaning he sees in his story.

Thomas Hardy, "The Man He Killed" (p. 1051)

The speaker in the poem is almost certainly a manual laborer; perhaps, judging by the reference in line 15 to "traps," he hunts for a living. He enjoys having a drink at a local bar and has the imagination to speculate that a man he has killed in battle might also enjoy such a pursuit. The repeated word "because" in lines 9 and 10 suggests the speaker's struggle to understand why he killed the other soldier. At first he comes up with the obvious, standard answer—perhaps the one he heard from his superiors—"I shot him dead because / Because he was my foe." Yet when he thinks further and tries to discover just why this man was his enemy, he simply comes up with more examples suggesting parallels between the dead soldier and himself.

Wilfred Owen, "Dulce et Decorum Est" (p. 1052)

Because of the publicity concerning the use of chemical weapons in the Gulf War, some students may think the setting of this poem is recent. In fact, Wilfred Owen was a British soldier who fought in World War I and was killed just a few weeks before the armistice was signed. The "old beggars under sacks" are his compatriots, sick and weakened from trench warfare. Owen's diction *lame, blind, drunk, deaf, blood-shod* suggests the exhaustion and disaffection of the men— a very different picture from that offered by recruiting posters. The graphic details of the gas attack insist that the reader see and think about the ugliness and horror of war rather than the glory and honor suggested by patriotic slogans.

Karl Shapiro, "The Conscientious Objector" (p. 1055)

The final stanza suggests that the speaker is not one of the conscientious objectors, but rather an observer. Because he says, "Your conscience is / What we come back to in the armistice," he may be a soldier. Yet he also discusses how "the soldier kissing the hot beach" will feel, so I think it more likely that the speaker is instead a somewhat detached voice—perhaps a member of the press?—who comments on what he sees.

Students may not know the story of Noah, so you may want to explain the significance of the dove, the bird Noah released at the end of the flood. When the dove returned with an olive branch in its mouth, Noah knew that somewhere it had found dry land, signaling (along with the attendant rainbow) that God was now at peace with humankind. Since then, the dove has remained a symbol of peace.

Students also may not fully understand what the term "conscientious objector" signifies. This poem was first published in 1947, so Shapiro was almost certainly describing conscientious objectors from World War II, but there have been resisters to every war since then, and there were resisters to previous wars as well.

Carolyn Forché, "The Colonel" (p. 1055)

First question: Is this a poem? Certainly it does not follow any of the traditional poetic forms, yet I would call it a prose poem (rather than simply a prose paragraph). Both the staccato, insistent rhythm of the short sentences and the powerful figurative language ("The moon swung bare on its black cord over the house") place this work in the realm of poetry.

Why did Forché choose to arrange her images as a paragraph rather than in stanzas? I think a clue may come in the third-to-last sentence: "Something for your poetry, no? he said." Perhaps she chooses not to oblige in any way the unspeakably cruel and arrogant colonel. These images will not be recorded in what he would call poetry but will be set out starkly, almost in the form of a report.

Elizabeth Barrett Browning, "Mother and Poet" (p. 1056)

This poem works well to emphasize the difference between poet and speaker. While Barrett Browning may have shared the views attributed to Laura Savio, the poet is distinct from the woman she creates. It's also intriguing to speculate on the relationship between history and literature. Barrett Browning wrote the poem in 1861, immediately after the battle in which the second son is killed. Does she entirely invent Savio's response? Is this poem based on something

Savio wrote? Was Barrett Browning in communication with Savio? Here's a topic for research.

Ariel Dorfman, "Hope" (p. 1060)

This poem would work well paired with "Mother and Poet." Here the speaker, like Laura Savio, expresses her pain at facing the fate of her son during war. Unlike Savio's son, however, the son in this poem is not dead and the mother ponders the bitter irony of feeling hopeful at the news that her son is being tortured. At least receiving news of the torturing means that he is still alive.

Walt Whitman, "The Dying Veteran" (p. 1062)

The speaker in this poem says of the words he heard from the old, dying Revolutionary war veteran, most "likely 'twill offend you." This comment might make an interesting starting point for discussion or writing. How do students respond to the veteran's lyrical praise of his days in battle? He seems unable to appreciate peace and instead yearns for the time that was probably the most significant period in his life.

Denise Levertov, "What Were They Like?" (p. 1062)

Levertov, who was an active participant in protests against the Vietnam War, published this poem in a volume called *Poems 1960–1967*. These dates show that she felt deep concern for the people and culture of Vietnam even before the war escalated in 1969–1971. Knowing that the poem was written early in the war helps to explain the setting: far in the future where nothing is left of the Vietnamese culture because of the war's destruction. Whatever might have been beautiful, joyful, or treasured has been lost.

Who are the two speakers in this poem? The first may be an archaeologist, a historian, or possibly a military officer, now thinking back over his time in Vietnam. Whoever he is, the second speaker acknowledges him as an authority figure, twice addressing the first speaker as "Sir."

Randall Jarrell, "Gunner" (p. 1063)

Speaking of another poem, Jarrell said that he wrote it "acting as best friend." His view of the Gunner's description of his life and death suggests the same persona in this poem.

The speaker uses ordinary, mundane images to describe his life before the war and, rather surprisingly, also uses homely images ("like rabbits"; "like a scab") to envision what happens to him in war. In the final stanza, he imagines his medals being sent home to his cat and his pension being like "so many mice" with which his wife is rewarded.

War, then, becomes like a horrifying game of cat and mouse. This speaker refuses to glorify war or death in war.

Fernando Arrabal, *Picnic on the Battlefield* (p. 1065)

Even the opening stage directions suggest theater of the absurd. Zapo sits at his watch post listening to bombs explode, clearly terrified, then takes out a sweater he is knitting and begins to work on it, as if he were a gentle old grandmother taking her ease. When his parents, Mme. and Mons. Tépan, arrive on the scene, the situation becomes even more a dark comedy. Both parents regard war as a game, with Mons. Tépan reminiscing about his own fine uniform and comparing the hazards of war to the danger of getting off a subway car while it's still moving. Mme. Tépan, with no apparent regard for her son's situation, argues with her husband over the color of the enemy's uniforms in a past war and also admits that she engaged in trivial bets about the outcome of that war, placing her wager for the enemy. At this point, Zapo seems concerned not so much about the dangers of his parents' excursion to the battlefield as about the impropriety of their being there.

As the Tépans proceed with their picnic, the parents act as if they are visiting their son at summer camp or at a boarding school. They inquire about his hygiene habits and about his "scores" (hits of enemy soldiers) as if they are grades. When the son admits that he shoots without aiming and if he does, by chance, hit someone he prays for the enemy, his father chides him to be braver.

When Zépo arrives on the scene, his uniform, his gestures, and his name, which mirror Zapo's, all make clear that he is the double of Zapo; the same, but simply with the label "enemy." Zapo's behavior toward him emphasizes the youth and innocence of both soldiers; they see war as a game of tag (or perhaps wish that it could be so simple).

The episode of the picture-taking continues the absurdity. Zépo, apparently not at all disturbed at being taken prisoner, objects to the picture of himself as a captured trophy because it might one day disturb his fiancée. Following the picture-taking, which mimics and parodies the ceremonies accorded war heroes, Zépo is invited to join in the picnic. It is as though everything is speeded up here and, now that the enemy has been humiliated, the war can be over and Zépo can be invited to share food and to discuss the war in the same way we have so recently seen former enemies from World War II discussing their experiences in battle.

Students should enjoy the continuing absurdity of the Tépans sheltering from bombs under their umbrella as they discuss their daily life as well as the disgust of the stretcher-bearers who fault Zapo for not producing any corpses for them to take away. As their job is to find dead and wounded, they focus simply on that task and not on the obvious fact that they should be rejoicing rather than lamenting the lack of "business."

As the play progresses and Mons. Tépan struggles to understand the definition of the term "enemy," the differences between the two sides shrink until Mons. Tépan finds himself wondering if the same general might be orchestrating both sides of the war. As the play draws to a close, the four characters ponder the boredom of war as well as its apparent purposelessness. They imagine that the soldiers will return to their units to tell their friends to stop fighting because they have no clear reason. Just as they begin to celebrate what seems to be a highly logical decision, one that makes some sense of the absurdity, the battle begins again and they are all cut down by machine-gun fire. The final image cuts through all the satiric comedy and indicates that, in the end, just as the mother used to imagine, the enemy—war itself, rather than any individual soldiers—will triumph.

Sophocles, *Antigone* (p. 1077)

When I assign *Antigone,* I spend a few minutes providing the background of the play, which would have been familiar to Sophocles's audience. Ismene explains the story of her father and brothers in lines 36-42, but unless students have read *Oedipus Rex,* they often miss the significance of what happened previously. The complexities of the royal family's intrigues can be daunting.

Born to the king and queen of Thebes, Oedipus is banished from birth because an oracle had predicted he would kill his father and marry his mother. He is taken to the hills and after a series of events he is adopted by the king and queen of Corinth, who never tell their foster son about his origins. Later, after hearing the same prediction from another oracle, Oedipus leaves his foster parents, believing that he can thus prevent himself from killing the king whom he believes to be his father and marrying the queen whom he believes to be his mother.

When he flees from his foster home, he heads for Thebes where he encounters the king on the road. After a quarrel, Oedipus, not realizing the king is his birth father, kills him and in a short while marries the king's widow, Queen Jocasta. Of course, neither mother nor son recognizes the other. They have four children: Eteocles, Polyneices, Antigone, and Ismene. When Oedipus discovers that he has killed his birth father and married incestuously, he blinds himself and leaves Thebes, leaving his two sons to assume the throne. Originally, they agree to rule in alternate years, but when Eteocles's first year as king ends, he refuses to yield to his brother. Polyneices then convinces Adrastus, the king of Argus, to help him attack Thebes and overthrow

Eteocles. During the ensuing battle, Polyneices and Eteocles fight a duel
and both are killed. Creon, the brother of Jocasta (Oedipus's mother
and wife) then ascends the throne, ordering that Eteocles be buried
with full honors. Creon also decrees that Polyneices be left to die in the
field where he fell because he had attacked his native city.

Because the Greeks believed that the soul of a person who had not
been buried with proper rites could not be received into the world of the
dead, Antigone's distress is understandable. She faces not only the loss
of her brother, but also the pain of believing that his soul cannot find
rest. Creon, on the other hand, insists on the primacy of civil law. He
believes he cannot make an exception, even for his nephew, because to
deviate at all could lead to the breakdown of order.

Most readers are far more sympathetic with Antigone than with
Creon, yet the play does not present simple stereotypes. Creon endures
enormous pain and loss and, in the end, comes to see that his rigid
refusal to consider alternatives has led to a tragic outcome. Antigone, on
the other hand, may be justified in her final action, but her insistence
on the rights of the individual have caused enormous pain—to both
herself and others.

To help students see the role of the chorus and Choragos and to
understand the structure of the drama, you may want to use this guide:

Prologue:

Antigone and Ismene discuss their brothers' deaths and Antigone
urges Ismene to help her bury Polyneices, defying Creon's order and his
threat to impose the death penalty on anyone who disobeys him. In
this scene, Ismene serves as a foil to Antigone. While Antigone is
impetuous, strong willed, and convinced that justice should follow the
law of god rather than the law of man, Ismene is cautious, concerned
with civil law, and fearfully convinced that women should assume a
subservient role to men.

Párados:

The chorus and Choragos describe the battle between Eteocles,
whom they portray as a stalwart defender of Thebes, and Polyneices,
who leads an alien army against his homeland and engages in a duel
with his brother, which leads to both their deaths.

Scene I:

Creon, who has assumed the throne of Thebes, proclaims his intent
to uphold the laws of the state; he forbids the burial of Polyneices. At
that moment, a soldier who had been guarding Polyneices's body
arrives and fearfully informs the king that someone has attempted to

bury the body. Creon is outraged; completely losing control of his temper, he questions the sentry furiously and then argues bitterly with the Choragos.

Ode I:

The chorus provides philosophical observations about the wonders of the human race, noting that humans are more powerful than animals and have control over all forces except death. In addition, the chorus commends the human reason that leads to creating and observing civil law.

Scene II:

A defiant Antigone is brought before Creon. She admits burying her brother and says she is willing to die rather than to follow what she believes to be an unjust law. Creon and Antigone argue about customs, values, and laws related to honoring the dead. Ismenê now wants to defend her sister, but Antigone refuses, claiming that Ismene lacked the courage to act and cannot, therefore, take credit for what has happened.

Ode II:

The chorus reminds the audience of the tragedy of Oedipus and of the continuing curse that haunts his children. Creon is denounced as arrogant and filled with pride, and the Ode ends with a warning that "man's little pleasure is the spring of sorrow."

Scene III:

Although Haimon is betrothed to Antigone, he swears to support his father, Creon. (Students are sometimes surprised that Haimon and Antigone could be engaged as they are first cousins, but such relationships were expected among royalty in ancient Greece.) Creon praises Haimon as a worthy son and says he will be better off without Antigone. When Haimon urges his father to take a more moderate view of the civil laws and to pay attention to his advisers, Creon becomes angry. It is clear that he sees any act against the state as a personal affront. Although the Choragos urges against it, Creon orders Antigone's execution.

Ode III:

The chorus describes both the power of love and the dangers of love carried to an extreme.

Scene IV:

The chorus and Choragos pay homage to Antigone and express sorrow for her death sentence. Antigone fears that people will not understand her actions and will ridicule her while the chorus again ponders the connection between Oedipus's tragedy and Antigone's fate. Creon refuses to reconsider and, as he orders Antigone taken away, she says she looks forward to dying.

Ode IV:

The chorus recounts the tragic stories of those who have opposed the will of the gods.

Scene V:

Teiresias, an ancient blind man with a reputation for wisdom, advises Creon to look at recent strange occurrences in nature as a warning to reconsider his treatment of Antigone. Creon stubbornly refuses until the Choragos reminds him that Teiresias has never been mistaken in his pronouncements. Creon then leaves, determined to save Antigone.

Paean:

The chorus and Choragos invoke Iacchos (Bacchus or Dionysius, the god of misrule and chaos as well as of wine and revelry).

Exodus:

A messenger arrives and describes to the Choragos the dramatic change in Creon, from "happy once" to "a walking dead man." Haimon and Antigone have both committed suicide. When Eurydice, Creon's wife and Haimon's mother, learns the news from the messenger, she also commits suicide. Creon ends the play a broken old man, finally realizing that pride kept him from seeing reasonable alternatives or from taking good advice. He has learned to be wise, but only after he has lost all that he valued.

Donald Hall, "War Cards, Purpose, and Blame" (p. 1108)

Hall's introduction (paragraphs 1–3) suggests a fine way to begin discussing this essay. Ask students to list the names of any films about war they can remember seeing. Then ask them to choose one film and to write a brief response statement. (If students cannot think of a film, they might write about a television program—perhaps a series like *China Beach*.) Asking several students to read their response statements leads to discussing "War Cards, Purpose, and Blame" and to considering Hall's response to *The Last Train from Madrid*.

This essay, in a slightly different version, appeared in an anthology of Hall's work, *The Movie That Changed My Life* (New York, Viking, 1991). Students should have plenty to say about how, why, and whether this film did, in fact, change Hall's life. Some may question whether an eight-year-old could actually be so deeply moved; others may recall memories from their early lives that confirm the kind of profound insight and change that Hall describes.

Reading Robert Frost's poem "Design" aloud could lead to a discussion of one of the essay's central issues: the terrifying randomness of death, typified by the arbitrary executions in *The Last Train from Madrid*. Both Frost's poem and Hall's essay might be compared with Amy Lowell's "Patterns" to pursue this theme further.

Ernest Hemingway, "A New Kind of War" (p. 1116)

Hemingway calls the Spanish Civil War "a new kind of war." From the earlier descriptions, perhaps he uses that title because this war's vicious battles are fought while civilian lives continue nearby in some semblance of normalcy. The civilians he encounters see the reality of the war, yet seem concerned mainly with their own lives rather than with the outcome of the military encounters.

Hemingway begins this essay using second person, a technique that has at least two significant effects. First, although he is clearly talking about himself, the reader is invited to share the experience in an intimate way. Second, by saying "you" rather than "I," he establishes distance, creating himself as a character who is on the scene being observed by the writer who describes him. He becomes, then, both actor and observer, and I think this dichotomy reflects the milieu he describes. This "new kind of war" seems unreal at times because instead of fighting in it, Hemingway and the people with whom he lives are watching it.

The war becomes real, however, when the American Friends of Spanish Democracy (Americans who have volunteered to fight against the fascists) call Hemingway to the bedside of the badly wounded Raven. At that point, the narrative switches from second person to first person as Hemingway feels personal connection with the fighting that has previously existed only as distant rifle and machine-gun fire.

The conversation between Raven and Hemingway shows Raven's idealism and bravery. One of the first questions he asks Hemingway concerns not his own wounds but rather American public opinion about the war. Hemingway is sympathetic to Raven, yet he finds his quiet courage hard to believe. When Raven describes how he was wounded, Hemingway assumes that he is exaggerating.

Later, Hemingway discovers from another man who fought with Raven that he has told the truth. Hemingway implies that this is a war in which soldiers are not fighting for medals and personal glory. Unlike soldiers Hemingway knew from other wars, these "new warriors" do not stretch the truth about their encounters with the enemy. In this war, he sees "Jay Raven, the social worker from Pittsburg with no military training" fighting heroically and motivated, Hemingway suggests, strictly by idealism.

CHAPTER 12
DEATH

Although death and dying are topics currently popular, I find beginning discussion of this theme difficult. Many students are far too familiar with death. In any given class, several people will have lost close family members or friends. Especially when the death is recent, both reading and discussion may be extremely painful for such students. Keeping these students in mind, I introduce this theme by assigning Elizabeth Kübler-Ross's essay comparing modern attitudes toward death and dying with traditional views. Kübler-Ross suggests problems these modern attitudes raise both for those who are dying and for their survivors. Beginning with her essay "On the Fear of Death" provides the opportunity for students who may not have experienced the death of someone close to them to understand, to some degree, the feelings of those who have. In addition, discussing Kübler-Ross's essay allows those students who have had close experiences with death to express their own beliefs and responses. When I teach this theme, I usually begin by saying that, for most people in our society, death is a painful and difficult topic. I tell students that, as always, their observations and comments are welcome, but I remind them that they will not be forced to share any feelings or opinions they wish to keep to themselves.

"The Jilting of Granny Weatherall," "In the Cemetery Where Al Jolson Is Buried," and "I heard a Fly buzz—when I died" show the thoughts and experiences of people who know they are dying. Death comes as a shocking surprise in "A Rose for Emily" and "The Cask of Amontillado." And the two waiters in "A Clean, Well-Lighted Place" suggest the differences in the way the young and the old look at death.

"To Hell with Dying," "The Bustle in a House," "To an Athlete Dying Young," "Elegy for Jane," and *On Tidy Evenings* all focus on those who have survived the death of someone they loved, knew well, or admired. Assigning these pieces together provides the opportunity of discussing what, if anything, the survivors have gained from their loss. Do they have new insight concerning their relationship with the dead person, with others, or with themselves? What future can students project for these survivors? In connection with survivors, consider also "The American Way of Death," which calls for a critical look at American funeral practices.

Most of the selections look on death as an enemy to be fought. Consider, for example, "To Hell with Dying," "In the Cemetery Where Al Jolson Is Buried," and "Death, Be Not Proud." Yet other attitudes are also suggested. For example, Collin whose final hours are described in detail in *On Tidy Evenings* seems to accept death, and the speaker in "To an Athlete Dying Young" sees death as a preserver of the athlete's honor and glory. In "A Rose for Emily," apparently Miss Emily ironically saw death as the one way to keep Homer perpetually part of her life.

ADDITIONAL SELECTIONS FOR CONSIDERATION: DEATH

Title and Author   **Text Page**

Fiction

"The Red Convertible: Lyman Lamartine," Louise Erdrich	160
"The Warriors," Anna Lee Walters	391
"Shiloh," Bobby Ann Mason	665
"A Good Man Is Hard to Find," Flannery O'Connor	805
"Guests of the Nation," Frank O'Connor	1013
"The Things They Carried," Tim O'Brien	1023
"Spoils of War," Janice Mirikitani	1038
"The End of the Duel," Jorge Luis Borges	1044

Poetry

"Do Not Go Gentle into That Good Night," Dylan Thomas	80
"Richard Cory," Edwin Arlington Robinson	193
"Mid-Term Break," Seamus Heaney	203
"Journey of the Magi," T. S. Eliot	413
"The Country Midwife: A Day," Ai	606
"Annabel Lee," Edgar Allan Poe	695
"Lord Randal," Anonymous	833
"My Son, My Executioner," Donald Hall	836
"The Man He Killed," Thomas Hardy	1051

Title and Author	Text Page
"Patterns," Amy Lowell	689
"Dulce et Decorum Est," Wilfred Owen	1052
"Mother and Poet," Elizabeth Barrett Browning	1056
"The Dying Veteran," Walt Whitman	1062
"The Knight, Death and the Devil," Randall Jarrell	Art and Poetry Section
"Before an Old Painting of the Crucifixion," N. Scott Momaday	Art and Poetry Section
"Home Burial," Robert Frost	1213
"Out, Out—," Robert Frost	1217
"First Death in Nova Scotia," Elizabeth Bishop	1225
"the rites for Cousin Vit," Gwendolyn Brooks	1235
"To the Young Who Want to Die," Gwendolyn Brooks	1237

Drama

Hamlet, William Shakespeare	209
Antigone, Sophocles	1077
Fences, August Wilson	466
Trifles, Susan Glaspell	608
Picnic on the Battlefield, Fernando Arrabal	1065

Essays

"My People," Chief Seattle	528
"I Remember Papa," Harry Dolan	895
"War Cards, Purpose, and Blame," Donald Hall	1108

SUGGESTIONS FOR TEACHING ADDITIONAL SELECTIONS

1. Consider violent, premature death compared to death in old age. Think how you might personify death in each case. How

would Death look, talk, and act? Read the following selections as you think about this comparison.

Violent, Premature Death

	Text Page
"The Red Convertible: Lyman Lamartine"	160
"A Good Man Is Hard to Find"	805
"Guests of the Nation"	1013
"The Things They Carried"	1023
"Spoils of War"	1038
"The End of the Duel"	1044
"Richard Cory"	193
"The Country Midwife: A Day"	606
"The Man He Killed"	1051
"Patterns"	689
"Dulce et Decorum Est"	1052
"Out, Out—"	Art and Poetry Section
Hamlet	209
Antigone	1077
Picnic on the Battlefield	1065
"My People"	528

Death due to Aging and Illness

	Text Page
"The Warriors"	391
"Do Not Go Gentle"	80
"My Son, My Executioner"	836
"The Dying Veteran"	1062
"the rites for Cousin Vit"	1235
"I Remember Papa"	895

2. Consider the impact of death on those who witness it or those
    who survive the deaths of others. Use the following works to
    raise possibilities for further research on this topic.

	Text Page
"The Red Convertible: Lyman Lamartine"	160
"Shiloh"	665
"Guests of the Nation"	1013
"The Things They Carried"	1023
"Richard Cory"	193
"Mid-Term Break"	203
"The Man He Killed"	1051
"Patterns"	689
"Dulce et Decorum Est"	1052
"Mother and Poet"	1056
"Home Burial"	1213
"First Death in Nova Scotia"	1225
Hamlet	209
Fences	466
"My People"	528

3. Consider how the perception of death changes with point of
    view. For instance, choose an incident directly relating to death
    from any of the works listed under "Additional Selections" and
    describe it from a point of view different from the one provided.
    For example, describe the death of Mr. Wright in *Trifles* from
    Mrs. Wright's point of view. This writing might take the form
    of an entry in Mrs. Wright's journal, or perhaps an interview
    Mrs. Wright, during the final days of her life, grants to her
    future biographer.

THEMATIC PHOTOGRAPH (p. 1123)

Considerations

1. What is your overall impression when you first look at this picture? What one word or phrase (other than "death") would you use to describe it? Explain.

2. Contrast the photographer's view of the cemetery to the view the person driving the truck might have.

3. Describe and comment on the trees that grow among the gravestones and their significance in the photograph.

READINGS

Katherine Anne Porter, "The Jilting of Granny Weatherall" (p. 1124)

Certainly the concept of jilting is central to this story. As Granny lapses in and out of consciousness during her final hours, her mind wanders through the past and she fixes especially strongly on the day she was left at the altar by her fiancé, George. Of all the experiences of her life—including the apparent death of her daughter, Hapsy— the aborted wedding was the most profoundly disturbing and disappointing. And at the end of the story as Granny approaches death, she once again feels jilted. She has no sense that Christ, the bridegroom (a reference, probably, to the parable of the wise and foolish virgins), awaits her. This moment of emptiness, of spiritual void, far outlives any other sorrow in her life.

How are we to read the story of this jilting? Some students see Granny as a strong, independent woman, a person who has, as her name suggests, weathered all that life has brought. She deserves admiration and sympathy as her children, the doctor, and the priest hover around her, disturbing her last hours with their own concerns. For those who see her this way, the concluding image seems a cruel irony. Others, however, consider Granny self-centered and filled with unreasonable pride. No one can suit her or please her, and most of her memories involve recalling her accomplishments and the days when her children were dependent on her.

Although she does say a brief prayer acknowledging that she could not have done all she did without the help of God, in the end she turns to human comfort rather than religion. The rosary beads slip from her fingers as she grasps her son's hand. Some students see this as evidence that Granny fails to end her life with peace because she is unable to give herself over to faith.

I favor some version of the first reading. Granny seems to me a remarkable, feisty woman who banishes young Doctor Harry with sharp words even as she feels within herself the physical and emotional evidence of death: "Her bones felt loose, and floated around in her skin, and Doctor Harry floated like a balloon around the foot of the bed." She has always been able to overcome adversity, looking with scorn on the fiancé who deserted her and managing to raise her children alone after her husband's death. Now she wants to control death by denying its power, and when she cannot, she finds herself once again on her own—deserted in time of need.

William Faulkner, "A Rose for Emily" (p. 1132)

Although some of my students swear that they were not surprised by the ending of the story, I have to admit that the first time I read it, I was astonished by the final scene. The iron-grey hair on the pillow burned itself into my mind as I raced to reread what I had believed to be a rather simple character sketch of a Southern lady during her declining years.

Faulkner's chronology lulls many first-time readers into complacency and then jars them awake to confront the concluding images of Emily's bloated body, Homer's rotted skeleton, and—most of all—the indentation on the pillow next to Homer. In *William Faulkner: Toward Yoknapatawpha and Beyond* (pp. 382–384), Cleanth Brooks suggests the following chronology. Although dates are not actually given in the story, Brooks bases his reading both on internal clues and on several of Faulkner's other works also set in the fictitious Yoknapatawpha County.

> 1852: Emily Grierson born
>
> 1884: Emily's father dies
>
> 1884–1885: Homer Baron arrives
>
> 1885–1886: Townspeople note smell
>
> 1901 or 1904/05: Emily stops china painting lessons
>
> 1906 or 1907: Colonel Sartoris dies
>
> 1916: Aldermen talk to Emily about taxes
>
> 1926: Emily dies

Students are quick to notice, on a second reading, that reconstructing the chronology makes Miss Emily's story clear in a way the original chronology does not. They also see that Faulkner's decision to play fast and loose with the time frame leads readers to be as shocked as the townspeople themselves and to rethink the events of the story, trying to make sense of what has happened. In addition, one student pointed out that the narrator provides certain details while withholding others so that the unsuspecting reader leaps to fallacious conclusions. For example, the narrator describes the delegation of men who surreptitiously slink to Emily's house at night and spread lime near the foundation, hoping to speed up the decay of whatever is causing the smell. After a week or two the smell goes away, and the townspeople— like most readers—fall into *post hoc* thinking and assume that the lime has done its work.

After recovering from the shock of acknowledging Miss Emily's necrophilia, students usually wonder about Faulkner's theme. Certainly the story has to do with the consequences of denying change. From the beginning, Emily refuses to admit the passage of time. She hides her father's body for days, she lives in a house surrounded by a decaying neighborhood, she refuses to allow the post office to give her a mailbox. The townspeople both resent and admire Emily's position as a member of one of the old, antebellum grand families. She represents to them a monument to the fallen South, which they regard with a mixture of shame and nostalgia. In addition, they pity Emily as a woman who was first repressed by her father and then (they think) deserted by her lover. Both the ambivalent attitude of the townspeople and the story's evocative title reflect Faulkner's themes. Certainly, to deny the passage of time and the need for change is dangerous. On the other hand, the past is not all bad; its strengths should be recognized. Suggesting the first theme, Homer may be Emily's rose: preserved, yet dead and decayed. Suggesting the second theme, the rose may be the townspeople's regard (or the story itself) offered as a gift to the person who most clearly represented the town's own conflicted feelings about the passing of the old South.

Alice Walker, "To Hell with Dying" (p. 1142)

Some students consider Mr. Sweet Little an inappropriate companion for young children. They cite his alcoholism, his lack of ambition, and what they regard as his manipulative, phony deathbed scenes as evidence that he provided an extremely negative role model for the narrator and her siblings. On the other hand, Mr. Sweet has many supporters who note his kindness toward the children and his ability to be the perfect playmate because he regards them as his equals. The narrator also provides an explanation for Mr. Sweet's lack of enthusiasm for work, telling us that he "had been ambitious as a boy, wanted to be a doctor or lawyer or sailor, only to find that black men fare better if they are not." Some students find this reason a rationalization while others sympathize with Mr. Sweet's response; when he discovered he could not follow the careers he favored, "he turned to fishing as his only earnest career and playing the guitar as his only claim to doing anything extraordinarily well."

Although the story focuses on Mr. Sweet, the narrator is an equally important character. As she tells the story, she unfolds the discovery of Mr. Sweet's importance in her life. Just as Mr. Sweet gave unquestioning acceptance to the narrator and her family, so too did they give unquestioning support to him. Never challenging his choices or giving him lectures, they troop dutifully to his bedside each time he announces a crisis. The narrator comes to believe in the strength and importance of love and, by the time Mr. Sweet really does die, she has become a strong, caring adult capable of understanding that a literal resurrection need not take place. Mr. Sweet may not be revived in body, but he has passed his gift of love to her.

This story raises the intriguing question of distinguishing fact from fiction. In the Georgia countryside where Walker grew up, her grandparents had a neighbor named Mr. Sweet Little. Like the character in the story, Mr. Sweet was a talented guitar player who drank to excess, loved to gamble, and who, in Walker's words, "went 'crazy' several times a year." She and her brothers and sister grew to love and respect Mr. Sweet, whose music and attitude toward life made them "feel empathy for anyone in trouble." Walker says nothing about any deathbed scenes during her childhood, but when she was a student at Sarah Lawrence College, she received word that Mr. Sweet had died. Feeling isolated and depressed on a campus where "there were only three or four other black people, and no poor people at all as far as the eye could see," she had contemplated suicide. When she thought about Mr. Sweet's life and death, she wrote "To Hell with Dying" to honor his memory. She describes the experience like this:

> I was too poor even to consider making the trip home, a distance of about a thousand miles, and on the day of Mr. Sweet's burial I wrote "To Hell with Dying." If in my poverty I had no other freedom—not even to say goodbye to him in death—I still had the freedom to love him and the means to express it, if only to myself. I

wrote the story with tears pouring down my cheeks. I
was fighting for my own life. I was twenty-one.

from "The Old Artist: Notes on
Mr. Sweet" in *Living by the
Word, Selected Writings
1973–1978,* New York,
Harcourt, 1988.

Walker later showed the story to one of her professors, who, in turn,
sent it to poet Langston Hughes. Two years later, Hughes published "To
Hell with Dying." It was Walker's first publication.

"To Hell with Dying" has now been published by Harcourt Brace as
a children's book with astonishingly evocative illustrations by
Catherine Deeter.

Amy Hempel, "In the Cemetery Where Al Jolson Is Buried" (p. 1148)

The references to show business begin in the second paragraph with
Best Friend telling Patient that no one in America owned a tape
recorder before Bing Crosby did. In addition, she refers jokingly to
Tammy Wynette and Paul Anka, and both Best Friend and Patient call
the hospital "The Marcus Welby Hospital," referring to the idealized
1960s medical drama television program. The show business references
represent both the Best Friend's lack of ease with the Patient and her
desire to find light, ironic subject matter to keep the conversation off
the real subject at hand—the Patient's terminal illness. The Best
Friend has a need to distance herself from death—to orchestrate what
is happening as though it were a fictional film, a television program or
a stand-up comedy review that she could control.

Paragraphs 50–55, which discuss the earthquake, suggest that this
episode becomes a symbol for the Best Friend's futile wish to be able to
affect events outside her control. She describes herself and the Patient
trying—and failing—to stave off aftershocks by chanting "Earthquake,
earthquake, earthquake." This incident makes her wary of facing
sorrow and disaster. She recognizes that acknowledging the threat of
death will in no way make it disappear, just as "thinking about" the
earthquake did not prevent its happening. Her response to this sense of
helplessness is to avoid visiting the hospital and, when she does visit,
to be unable to connect intimately with her friend and the death she
will soon have to face.

The structure of the story reflects the Best Friend's fragmented
view of the Patient and her situation. Best Friend has no idea how to
deal with the changes in the Patient. When Best Friend leaves the
hospital, after having declared her intention to return home and after
having admitted to herself that she cannot return to the sick room, she

feels "exhilarated"—the sense of relief at being alive that most of us feel after reading an obituary or attending a funeral of someone near our own age.

The final anecdote of the mother chimp who learns human sign language and is then able to express her grief at the death of her baby suggests the pain the narrator feels at being unable to express her sorrow in any way other than joking anecdotes and memories. Unlike the mother chimp, she is not yet "fluent . . . in the language of grief."

Edgar Allan Poe, "The Cask of Amontillado" (p. 1156)

Poe's "The Cask of Amontillado" pairs well with Faulkner's "A Rose for Emily." Both stories look at warped sensibilities, at wounded pride that sees imposing death on another as the only way to maintain their own sense of self. The gothic settings in both stories carry a fine irony: Miss Emily will do anything, including facing down the board of aldermen, to keep her house; yet her house, which she sees as essential to her life, is also a tomb of death. Similarly, in "The Cask of Amontillado," the wine cellar that contains the wine that Fortunato considers the central purpose for living is also the place that seals his death.

As you teach this story, you may find that students become bogged down with the French and Latin phrases. I encourage persistence in discovering meaning through context. Very little of the story's significance rests on the reader's being able to translate exactly.

Montresor tells this story, as he says in the final paragraph, fifty years after it happened. It seems likely to me that he is telling it on his deathbed as a confession or justification of what he has done. Perhaps the listener is a priest, a friend, or a family member. Whether he truly regrets his action is a question students may enjoy discussing. The pure pleasure he takes in graphically describing his revenge makes me think he is not completely repentant, but rather savors, even after all this time, his triumph over his rival.

The question often arises as to why, exactly, Montresor avenges himself on Fortunato. It seems that Fortunato constantly taunts Montresor with one put-down after another. His remark about Montresor's not knowing the sign of the exclusive Masonic society is one example. And Montresor's ironic response—waving the trowel with which he will later build Fortunato's grave—shows just how seriously Montresor takes these comments. Montresor's family crest displays a foot crushing a serpent that is biting the foot. The snake can be seen as a symbol for Fortunato, and the family motto, "No one injures me with impunity," foreshadows his fate.

Ernest Hemingway, "A Clean, Well-Lighted Place" (p. 1162)

One of the biggest problems students relate having as they read this story is keeping straight which waiter is speaking during the extended dialogue of short sentences that begins with "He's drunk now." I recommend simply writing "o" (for older waiter) and "y" (for younger waiter) next to each line so that it's easy to see the differing philosophies emerge.

The younger waiter is impatient, eager to get home to his wife, and disgusted with the old man who has attempted suicide the previous week. The older waiter understands the old man's desire not just for alcohol but also for a warm, comforting atmosphere where he feels a bit less isolated than he does when he goes out into the dark.

As the young waiter and old waiter talk, it is clear that the young waiter correctly identifies himself as "all confidence." And when the older waiter responds, "You have youth, confidence, and a job. . . . You have everything," it is clear that he understands what the old man does not have and what he, himself, must soon face not having. Both the old man and the older waiter must soon face death, represented by the dark and chaos of the bodegas and the solitary rooms that await them when they must leave the "clean, well-lighted place." The old waiter's lack of faith and sense of loss are reflected in his repetition of the Lord's prayer, substituting the Spanish "nada" (nothing) for the words that would usually confirm belief and hope.

John Donne, "Death, Be Not Proud" (p. 1166)

The speaker sees Death as a powerful enemy, yet in line 4 this frightening force is addressed as "poor Death." The pity implied by this phrase foreshadows the paradox in the final lines. When the speaker asks death in line 12 "why swell'st thou then" (that is, why are you filled with pride?), he is preparing to deliver the *coup de grâce*. Death will "die" because it cannot keep the faithful from passing into eternal life.

e. e. cummings, "buffalo bill's defunct" (p. 1167)

Like Donne in "Death, Be Not Proud," cummings directly addresses Death, giving him the honorary title "Mister." The word choices, as well as the rhythmic patterns, establish the poem's ironic tone. The speaker describes Buffalo Bill as "defunct," which makes him sound like a species that has become extinct rather than a human being who has died. Bill's handsome appearance, his blue eyes, and his amazing feats—riding a "watersmooth-silver stallion" and shooting clay pigeons—are destroyed by death. The final question, addressed to "Mister Death," seems to ask the meaning of death and to ponder what we become after death. The capitalized "Jesus" in line 7 may suggest a possibility of salvation or may make an ironic comment on the traditional hope for salvation.

This poem provides a fine example of the visual impact poets achieve through line and word arrangement. As an experiment, ask students to write the poem in sentence form, using standard capitalization, punctuation, and the spacing between words. How does their response to the poem change with these alterations?

Ruth Whitman, "Castoff Skin" (p. 1167)

The speaker regards the elderly woman with affection, yet without mawkish sentiment. Recalling the woman's pride and sense of humor when she described herself as having a "pretty good figure / for an old lady," the speaker explains her view of the woman's death.

When the woman's spirit leaves her body, it is like a snake leaving its old skin. The body, "a tiny stretched transparence," has been outgrown and the soul now moves on to its next stage of existence.

Jane Cooper, "In the House of the Dying" (p. 1168)

I believe that the speaker in the poem is the daughter of the woman who lies dying in an upstairs bedroom. The "tired aunts," her mother's sisters, have come to help during the final illness. The speaker sees a significant division between the way she thinks about death and the way the aunts and—by extension—the dying mother think about death. To the speaker, death seems a constant, daily presence. (Has she lost many people she loved? Is she contemplating suicide? Does she think constantly about death as it comes to those she does not know, but hears and reads about?)

To the aunts, death is a solemn and momentous event, like the visit of a priest to the terminally ill. The speaker questions her feelings because, although she is able to accept death, she is uncomfortable with love and cannot make the commitment to marriage. Her mother, on the other hand, has been "washed through by the two miracles." What are these miracles? Perhaps love for husband and love for children? Or the miracle of birth and the miracle of death? (And the ability to be touched and moved by each of these miracles.)

Emily Dickinson, "Apparently with no surprise" (p. 1169)

Dickinson's poem might be compared with Donne's "Death Be Not Proud." Here the Frost, the agent of death, is personified. But unlike Donne's Death, Dickinson's Frost acts without intent, "in accidental power." After the death of the flower, the Frost ("the blonde assassin") leaves, replaced by the Sun. Note the play on the word "unmoved," meaning, I think, both that the sun continues in its usual path and that it is unaffected by the drama that has taken place. Frost and Sun are all part of the natural cycle that is approved by God. The Flower's happiness is of no concern to the Frost.

Questions to ponder: Does the phrase "an Approving God" suggest a pagan rather than Christian deity? Does the first line describe the flower or the frost? Does the poem suggest the way death may creep up on all of us?

Emily Dickinson, "I heard a Fly buzz—when I died (p. 1170)

In Jane Cooper's "In the House of the Dying," the aunts who have come to keep the death watch "buzz on like flies around a bulb." In Dickinson's poem, the dying person hears a fly. Why might flies be associated with death? Of course, flies are attracted to carrion, and yet in Cooper's poem the image suggests that they are also attracted to light. And for Dickinson's speaker, the fly seems to be the final symbol of this world, the last thing the speaker hears as she passes from this world into the next. In line 15, the "Windows" are probably the speaker's eyes (the "windows of the soul"). As the speaker's life ebbs, the light fades and she cannot "see to see": she is unable physically to see her current world or emotionally and spiritually to comprehend the next world.

Emily Dickinson, "The Bustle in a House" (p. 1170)

Whereas "I Heard a Fly Buzz" focuses on the experience of dying, "The Bustle in a House" offers images that capture the essence of grieving. In the nineteenth century, most people died at home rather than in hospitals or nursing facilities. So, as the family prepared for the funeral, there would have been literal cleaning to be done. Dickinson makes that cleaning image a metaphor, showing those who are left "Sweeping up the Heart / And putting Love away." The survivors don't stop loving the person who has died; instead, they store the love in their memories, knowing that they will be able to display that love fully only after they, too, have become part of "Eternity."

A. E. Housman, "To an Athlete Dying Young" (p. 1171)

This poem uses classical allusions to foot races, laurels, and the dead hero who visits the underworld to suggest a theme common to all times: those who die young do not have to endure aging and the gradual loss of their physical and mental powers. For those who do live, the victor's chair can become like a coffin that buries them in images of their past glory.

To begin discussion of this poem, ask students to write briefly for or against the following proposition: It is better to die during the height of one's triumph and success than to outlive fame and become forgotten.

Theodore Roethke, "Elegy for Jane" (p. 1172)

A list of images from this poem suggests the qualities the poet admired in his lost student:

> pickerel smile
>
> startled into talk
>
> A wren, happy, tail into the wind
>
> My sparrow
>
> my skittery pigeon

Jane, who "balanced in the delight of her thought," was a young woman whose every move suggested life, energy, and quickness. The "pickerel smile" flashed across her face like a slim fish darting through a stream. Her words, thoughts, and actions took her quickly in many directions as though she were a bird startled from brief repose. Death has silenced her forever, and the poet takes no comfort from what is left, "the sides of wet stones." (Her grave marker? Or simply representative elements of nature?) These stones, and the moss that surrounds them, stand still and rooted, dark contrasts to the vital student he remembers.

William Stafford, "Traveling through the Dark" (p. 1172)

The speaker travels through the dark both literally and figuratively. He drives through the night and, when he encounters the body of the pregnant doe with the still-living fetus, he must travel through the dark of his conscience and imagination to reach a decision.

The line "I thought hard for us all" suggests to me that the speaker weighs all the possibilities and probabilities. He knows he has to push the carcass into the canyon because if a car were to strike the body in the night, a bad accident could result. Yet he also has the sensitivity to acknowledge that to serve human lives, he must cut off an animal life.

I think the speaker has no other choice, but students frequently argue that he could have dragged the deer to his car and taken her to a veterinarian to see if the fawn could be delivered. Alternately, they suggest that he could have at least tried to deliver the fawn himself. I have to acknowledge these as possibilities, but I think very few people would even have the decency to stop after seeing an animal body in the road. Even fewer would hesitate while thinking about the fawn "alive, still, never to be born."

Several students have suggested a correlation between the speaker's decision and the decision to have an abortion. To me, this is a farfetched connection. Certainly the speaker does do some soul-searching, but the dilemma seems much different from that faced by a pregnant woman. (For example, the speaker could simply drive away, leaving both the danger and the decision to be faced by someone else.)

Harvey Fierstein, *On Tidy Endings* (p. 1174)

This play is certain to raise heated discussion as it deals with several controversial issues related to gay relationships and to AIDS.

When Collin dies from an AIDS-related illness, Marion, Jim, and Arthur suffer a wrenching loss. Marion loses an ex-husband whom she still loves; Jim, a father; and Arthur, a lover. The play focuses on the complex dynamics among these three people, particularly Marion and Arthur. The circumstances and the setting (the apartment Collin and Arthur shared, now neatly packed as Arthur prepares to move out) are certainly grim. Yet the tone of the play, much of the time, is light and wryly humorous. Marion and Jim argue, each using the standard clichés of mother-son disagreements. If Jim asks, "Why" too many times, Marion responds with "Because I said so." When Marion invites Jim to look around the apartment one last time, Jim tells her to "get a real life." And after Jim has left the apartment supposedly bound for his friend's apartment, he delays this last departure by hanging around in the elevator and the lobby.

When Marion's lawyer, June, arrives, they discuss the papers that delineate the division of Collin's property between Marion and Arthur in very much the same tone they use to discuss June's being double parked. June even makes jokes about using her commission from a life insurance policy to pay the bill if her illegally parked car is towed. However, the conversation between Marion and June also has serious moments, all of which indicate that Marion is a thoroughly decent person. She resists June's suggestion that they contest Collin's will and points out that Arthur deserves to have what Collin has left him as witness to their three-year relationship. And when June callously notes that "no one wants to buy an apartment when they know the person died of AIDS," Marion quickly silences her and June apologizes.

Still, Marion is not perfect. She rationalizes taking several items from the apartment by saying that then Arthur will have "one less thing to pack." In addition, she presents him with a list of friends and relatives and suggestions of items that belonged to Collin that Arthur might give them. The tension between Arthur and Marion becomes increasingly clear as Marion awkwardly tries to assure him that Jim doesn't blame him for Collin's death. Arthur confronts Marion with Jim's pain and with his own pain, demanding that she see complications he believes she has ignored. Marion, in turn, spills out her anger at having lost both a man she loved and also the dream she had for a happy family life.

From this intense scene, the play moves for a moment to sadly ironic humor as Arthur describes his weight gain following Collin's death: "I called the ambulance at five A.M., he was gone at nine, and by nine-thirty, I was on a first-name basis with Sara Lee." But, refusing the easy path of continuing with the tension-breaking humor, Arthur further expresses his anger and resentment, insisting that Marion acknowledge his place in Collin's life and the sorrow he feels at being forced to leave the apartment they shared. In the play's most powerful speech, he orders Marion to let go of Collin and to admit that Collin belongs to him: "This death does not belong to you, it's mine! Bought and paid for outright. I suffered, I bled for it . . . I paid in full for my place in his life and I will *not* share it with you."

While Marion does defend her decision to sell the apartment, she also recognizes that Arthur has been mistreated: ignored by many of Collin's friends at the funeral and omitted from the obituary notice. Yet she explains her actions and words by describing in detail Collin's decision to leave and her discovery that he had AIDS. She also admits that she was jealous of Arthur and Collin's relationship, yet she assures Arthur that he made Collin happy, as she could not, and she praises Arthur's incredible loyalty during Collin's sickness.

Arthur thinks back over the past few months, concluding by asking that he be left "an intangible place in [Collin's] history." Marion's reply, "I understand," suggests that she now sees Arthur's situation more clearly, and, in the bargain, has gained more knowledge of herself. As a gesture to confirm this new understanding, both for herself and for Arthur, she insists that Jim come to the apartment to say good-bye. Just before he arrives, Marion acknowledges that she has AIDS antibodies in her blood. The announcement suggests that she and Arthur will, in fact, continue to share Collin no matter what either of them thinks. Looking at the legal papers, Arthur says, "You know, we'll never get these done today," and Marion replies, "So, tomorrow," suggesting that they will not say "Good-bye" and neatly "tidy things up" as June, the lawyer, insisted. Their pain goes beyond any one relationship or any one death.

Jessica Mitford, "The American Way of Death" (p. 1194)

To deal with her highly emotional subject, Mitford chooses to take a breezy, ironic approach. She begins by creating the corpse as a character, Mr. Jones, who takes on an existence quite apart from the person who once occupied the body. She provides a list of the processes to which the corpse is subjected that is at once horrifying and humorous. By piling detail on detail, she suggests both the excesses of the American funeral industry and the absurdity of a society that tolerates such excesses.

According to Mitford, the practice of embalming, required neither by civil nor religious law, is not necessary because of "considerations of health, sanitation, or even of personal daintiness." She believes that the desire to make the dead person "presentable for . . . public display" motivates the family. And she strongly implies that the funeral director is motivated by greed. Rather than simply performing a necessary service, the director—according to Mitford—goes through a series of rather grotesque procedures that are costly to the survivors and serve only to render the deceased cosmetically acceptable to a death-denying public.

By quoting from the professional journals and textbooks used by funeral directors, Mitford suggests that the excesses of the funeral industry are organized and intentional. She strengthens her argument by showing that her examples are not isolated instances nor are they far-fetched projections; instead, they represent the norm.

Discussing this essay leads, as Mitford's title suggests, to considering the American way of death. Students vary greatly in their response to her challenges. Some believe that anything that provides comfort to the bereaved is well worth the money spent. Some believe that an elaborate funeral procedure represents the final gesture of love toward someone who has died. Others agree with Mitford and see the entire process as barbaric and as increasing, rather than alleviating, suffering.

Elizabeth Kübler-Ross, "On the Fear of Death" (p. 1200)

Like the poem Kübler-Ross chooses as an introduction, this essay suggests that death and dying are subjects that are meaningful and worthy of concern. Kübler-Ross contends that, with the rising cost of medical care and the increasing tendency to hospitalize or in other ways institutionalize the seriously ill and dying among us, we have come to ignore—and fear unduly—the final stage of life.

Although the essay relates to all humans, Kübler-Ross writes with counselors (such as chaplains and social workers) in mind. She believes that our society increasingly turns its back on the elderly and on those who suffer life-threatening illnesses. Doctors often look on terminal patients as failures; because the physician is pledged to protect life, death becomes the enemy who must always be fought. Friends and relatives may fear the dying person because his or her struggle reminds them of their own mortality which they want to ignore or deny.

In addition, Kübler-Ross notes the complex relationship between fear and guilt. Because nearly everyone, from every time and culture, has regarded death as negative, death has come to be "associated with a bad act, a frightening happening, something that in itself calls for retribution and punishment." People close to someone who dies may feel that somehow (perhaps through a wish, subconscious or expressed) they have caused the person's death. Children are particularly prone to these feelings and Kübler-Ross warns that pretending death has not happened, by using euphemisms such as "he's just asleep" or "she's gone on a long journey," may magnify their convictions that they are somehow guilty and that death is just too terrible to even talk about.

Through the example of the farmer, Kübler-Ross suggests what she considers a more healthy approach to death—both for the person who is dying and for those who care about that person. She argues that professionals should support the person who wants to die at home, claiming that following such "old-fashioned customs" shows that the counselor can accept "a fatal outcome." In addition, death in familiar surroundings "requires less adjustment" for the patient and helps the "family to accept the loss."

The sections describing children's reactions to death, and particularly the incident of the old farmer, might be compared with Alice Walker's "To Hell with Dying." Kübler-Ross also mentions aspects of modern funeral customs (see especially paragraphs 15–22) that might be compared with Jessica Mitford's "The American Way of Death."

CHAPTER 13
THREE AMERICAN POETS

ROBERT FROST

This collection of Frost's poetry provides an opportunity for students to look closely at several selections by the same writer and suggest aspects of subject and style that exemplify his work. In addition to the selections in this section, his poem "The Road Not Taken" appears in Chapter 1.

You might ask students to read several of these selections and then to work in groups compiling lists that suggest typical aspects of his poetry. After the groups reconvene, ask for comments on their responses to the various aspects that they have identified. After reading the selections in this text, would they choose to read more of Frost? Why or why not?

Frost had a gift for writing powerful lines that stay with readers even in this age that eschews memorization. In an interview, he once said that poetry should make the reader "remember what you didn't know you knew." Consider asking students to write in their journals several lines from Frost's poetry that they find worth remembering and to explain why they chose these lines.

Possible aspects of subject and style include these:

1. Poems tend to fall into two groups: (1) lyric poems like "Stopping by Woods on a Snowy Evening" or "Nothing Gold Can Stay" that often look at some aspect of nature as a path to a philosophical observation, stated or implied; (2) narratives like "Home Burial" and "Out, Out—" that often suggest the harshness and sorrow of rural New England life

2. Use of rhyme and other sound devices that simultaneously create the rhythms of poetry and the rhythms of human speech

3. Use of unrhymed, yet rhythmic, lines (blank verse), particularly in the longer narratives

4. Images and subjects related to nature (and to human nature)

5. Nature shown as beautiful yet untamed, full of surprise, with the potential for evil as well as good

"Mending Wall" (p. 1212)

As students read this poem, they often need help in identifying Frost's two friendly antagonists. The speaker (probably very much like Frost himself) takes an ironically humorous view of his stolid neighbor who sees routine, order, and lack of change as the essential elements of human intercourse. It is the neighbor—not the speaker—who insists that "Good fences make good neighbors." The language of the poem certainly suggests that the speaker does not "love a wall." His view, symbolized by the ripely beautiful apple trees, contrasts sharply with the neighbor's, which is represented by the unchanging, hardy pine trees. The speaker playfully hints that his neighbor may fear the apple trees' surreptitiously seeking a snack of pine cones, yet it is the neighbor who actually sneaks around in darkness (line 41). The neighbor seems limited and narrow in his thinking, insisting that his father's old saying about fences and neighbors must continue to be true, simply because he has always believed it to be true.

Although the speaker jokes about the annual spring ritual of rebuilding the wall, he does not simply oppose walls. For instance, he states that he has rebuilt his own wall when hunters have torn it down (lines 6, 7), and he seems pleased that it serves as a shelter for rabbits when they run from the hunters. Thus, while the poem seems to me to show the speaker—and his view of walls—as much more appealing than the neighbor, it does not entirely condemn the old Yankee's fortitude in the face of constant change.

"Home Burial" (p. 1213)

To introduce this poem, you might remind students that the death of children was far more common in the past (even in the early part of this century, before the discovery of antibiotics and immunizations). In addition, some students may not know that the family graveyard was common, particularly in New England. Some people were buried in the churchyard or in a community burial ground, but many, many families had their own plots.

Students find this poem powerful reading. Frost manages to take the death of a child—and his parents' subsequent anguish and loss of communication—and create a poem that is filled with honest sentiment rather than cheap sentimentality. The husband and wife seem to represent two different ways of dealing with agonizing loss. The wife, Amy, plunges into a deep depression "for which no saying is dark enough." In addition to her grief for her lost son, she also sees the absolute loneliness of the path to death: "from the time one is sick to death, / One is alone, and he dies more alone." This loss of a child has forced her to face her own mortality, and she feels herself utterly bereft, with no sense of connection to any other human being. The husband, on the other hand, seems to deal with the child's death by denying its power in his life. He never refers to the sex of the child; his son seems to remain unformed for him. Although he understands his wife's grief in his mind, he cannot fathom it in his heart. He wants her back as she was before this loss and does not seem to understand the impossibility of such a hope. He can only find his wife again by following her into the valley of the shadow, thereby risking the loss of his own tenuous barrier against overwhelming sorrow.

"Out, Out—" (p. 1217)

The boy in this poem, already expected to do "a man's work," seems a child who has been made to accept adult responsibility before his time. The speaker (perhaps a neighbor or family friend) telling the story comments that he wishes "they" (presumably the adults involved) might have said "Call it a day . . . / To please the boy by giving him the half hour / That a boy counts so much when saved from work." Yet the blame is not placed too heavily on the parents, probably farmers who have to work hard to grub a living out of the New England soil. The boy's death is a random event, with no clear cause or purpose.

Although the poem is highly accessible, you may want to read to students the passage from *Macbeth* from which the title is taken, asking them if (and how) their response changes when they recognize the allusion.

> She should have died hereafter;
> There would have been a time for such a word.
> To-morrow, and to-morrow, and to-morrow
> Creeps in this petty pace from day to day
> To the last syllable of recorded time;
> And all our yesterdays have lighted fools
> The way to dusty death. Out, out, brief candle!
> Life's but a walking shadow, a poor player,
> That struts and frets his hour upon the stage
> And then is heard no more. It is a tale
> Told by an idiot, full of sound and fury,
> Signifying nothing.
>
> > (Macbeth, on learning of Lady
> > Macbeth's death)
> > *Act V, Scene 5*

"Nothing Gold Can Stay" (p. 1217)

This poem provides a fine example of Frost's use of traditional poetic forms. Written in rhymed couplets, the poem moves incrementally from individual images to a philosophic statement. Each of the first two couplets provides an example of beauty that lasts only a moment. The third couplet with its allusion to the garden of Eden enlarges the time frame of the poem, inviting the reader to think back to the very beginning of creation. In the closing couplet, the poem comments on the significance of the first two examples and of the broadening of those examples provided by the reference to Eden in lines 5–6.

"Stopping by Woods on a Snowy Evening" (p. 1218)

I've had success teaching this poem by asking students to identify the conflict the speaker experiences and to reflect on the speaker's response to that conflict. Some students, especially those who have read this poem very early in life, may think of it simply as a beautiful New England winter scene with a man admiring the charming scenery, and then reluctantly recognizing the need to go home for the night. Other students, especially those who have had a meaning dictated to them in another class, may insist that the woods represent death. Yet Frost himself, when questioned by participants at the Bread Loaf Conference in Middlebury, Vermont, in 1960, said, "People are always trying to find a death wish in that poem. But there's a life wish there—he goes on doesn't he?" I agree with Frost; the woods may be "lovely, dark, and deep," but they are also cold and final. The speaker, I believe, values his promises to life enough to keep going toward the warmth and light of home.

"Acquainted with the Night" (p. 1218)

Unlike many of Frost's poems, this one does not have a rural setting. Frost's speaker describes a ritualistic journey, through the rain and around the lonely city. The intricate yet regular rhyme scheme suggests the complexity of this quest. Each stanza begins with a line that rhymes with the second line in the previous stanza and the poem closes with a rhymed couplet that connects, through rhyme, to the first and third lines in the first stanza and the second line in the fourth stanza. This is a variation of the villanelle and, like the villanelle, creates recursive sense through the connection of the opening and closing stanzas. Readers thus experience a sensation of repetition and doubling back that suggests the speaker's walk is not an isolated instance but rather a repeated search for meaning.

Students sometimes have trouble identifying the "luminary clock" in line 12. I believe this is a reference to the moon whose light is not bright enough to overcome the sense of depression suggested by the poem's repeated first and final lines, "I have been one acquainted with the night."

"Desert Places" (p. 1219)

Unlike most deserts, this one is not depicted as hot but rather as frozen and bitterly cold. It seems to be a metaphoric rather than an actual desert. The images in this poem might be contrasted with those in "Stopping by Woods"; in "Desert Places" the winter scene is anything but inviting. For example, the hibernating animals are not seen as safe and warm but rather as "smothered in their lairs." Yet as stark and frightening as the landscape is, the speaker suggests that it is less terrifying than the interior deserts of the mind and spirit. This vision might be compared to that of "Acquainted with the Night."

ELIZABETH BISHOP

This collection of Bishop's poetry provides an opportunity for students to look closely at several selections by the same writer and suggest aspects of subject and style that exemplify her work.

You might ask students to read several of these selections and then to work in groups compiling lists that identify typical aspects of her poetry. When the groups reconvene, ask for comments on their responses to the various aspects that they have identified. After reading the selections in this text, would they choose to read more of Bishop? Why or why not?

Bishop's poems often capture in a single image a particularly strange or powerful vision. Consider asking students to identify several images they find particularly striking and to explain (perhaps in a journal entry) why they responded strongly to the images they have chosen.

Possible aspects of subject and style include these:

1. Poems often begin with a specific, concrete image (an animal, a place, an object) and then explore its significance.

2. The poet adopts a skeptical, ironic point of view; poems often contain a poignant or bitter humor suggesting a sense of isolation in the speaker.

3. The language is clear with simple diction that also often creates a sense of the surreal, a feeling of dislocation in time and space.

4. The poet experiments with verse and line form, yet has profound understanding and respect for traditional forms (see, for example, "Sestina").

"The Man-Moth" (p. 1222)

Bishop displays her gift for flight of fancy in this poem that plays with an image created by a newspaper misprint. Seeing "man-moth" where the writer had intended "mammoth," Bishop shows her sympathy for the plight of both human and animal captured in the vision of the half-man, half-moth. The second stanza generates many possibilities for writing as it suggests the very different way the Man-Moth views what we would call reality. For instance, he believes that the moon (which most of us see as solid) to be "a small hole at the top of the sky." Students may be interested in creating their own fanciful creatures and developing their visions of the world. Or they may want to follow the Man-Moth into various other parts of the world as we know it and explain how he sees our everyday experiences.

Consider, also, the final stanza. Why might the Man-Moth want to swallow his tear? If he did hand it over to a human who then drank it, what might result? If students choose to write in response to these questions, you might suggest that they look for support for their observations in the other stanzas of the poem.

"The Fish" (p. 1223)

The speaker in the poem sees the fish in a highly complex way. He is both ugly and beautiful, both adversary and hero. Consider, for example, his "brown skin" that hangs "in strips / like ancient wallpaper" (lines 10–11). Yet contrasting with this image of ruin is the comparison of his skin to "full-blown roses" (line 14) and even the barnacles that cling to his side resemble "rosettes of line" (line 17). At first, the fish is clearly an opponent, and the speaker celebrates her victory as she hoists him high above the water. Yet as she gazes triumphantly on her catch, she begins to observe details that gradually win her admiration and respect. The five fish hooks hanging from his ancient mouth seem like the medals on the jacket of an old war hero. As she considers the fish's battles and the valor and determination he has shown in facing them, she salutes his courage by letting him go.

Students may need help with the final triumphant rainbow image. I have found that very few know the story of Noah and of the rainbow as a symbol of hope. I have also found that many students assume the speaker of the poem is male because the topic is fishing. While I can't prove that the speaker is female, I always (arbitrarily, some may think) assign the speaker in a poem the same gender as the poet unless there is obvious evidence to the contrary. In addition, since Bishop, in fact, enjoyed fishing, I see no reason not to believe that her speaker could be female.

"First Death in Nova Scotia" (p. 1225)

Nearly every image here evokes the coldness, stillness, and finality of death. The narrator is a young child; she has to be lifted up to look at Arthur. The title suggests that she has not seen death before, and certainly not the death of someone close to her own age. As she is brought to look at Arthur, she notices the stuffed loon and the photographs of royalty. Like Arthur's body, they are unmoving representations of living creatures. Arthur himself is described as an art object who has not been completed. He will not live out his life and the narrator's final question suggests her wonder, fear, and confusion as she tries to contemplate what happens to us after death.

The dominant colors in the poem are red and white. For instance, the stuffed loon, who rests on a white marble table, has a deep white breast and red glass eyes. As the child looks at her cousin Arthur, she is immediately struck by his whiteness and seems to associate him with the loon. Arthur's bright red hair contrasts with the unnatural paleness of his skin, just as the loon's red eyes contrast with his white feathers.

Point of view plays an important role in the impact of this poem. Students might write on their ideas of how the poem would be changed if the narrator were the speaker's mother or her Uncle Arthur.

"Sestina" (p. 1226)

As students approach this poem, they may want to identify the situation and to consider how the "Little Marvel Stove" and the almanac relate to the situation, as well as to identify the significance of the tears that dominate the poem both figuratively and literally. Initially, the grandmother seems to hold her tears inside, laughing and chatting to conceal her sorrow. Outside the house, the steady pelt of raindrops suggests the tears and sadness that are part of the scene inside as well as the inner landscape of the people in the poem. The stove and the almanac both serve as seers, capable of intuiting the inevitability of the grandmother's tears. Her sense of pain and loss seems infinite and is apparently linked with the child's fate. The speaker tells us, for instance, that the little drawings used in the almanac to indicate the changing of the phases of the moon seem to shed tears into the child's garden.

Students may want to reread the biographical introduction to Bishop's work before they read this poem. There's certainly room for speculation that the grandmother in the poem is Elizabeth's and that the child is Bishop herself.

"In the Waiting Room" (p. 1227)

Students may begin consideration of this poem by describing what happens to the nearly seven-year-old Elizabeth as she sits waiting for her aunt. The following lines deserve special consideration:

> . . . you are an *I*,
> you are an *Elizabeth*,
> you are one of *them*.

As Elizabeth looks at the pictures in the *National Geographic*, the people they represent initially seem far away and strange, even horrifying. She then hears, or thinks she hears, a yelp of pain from her aunt whom she quickly dismisses as "a foolish, timid woman." Almost immediately, however, Elizabeth realizes that these creatures she has seen as "other" are, in fact, human, just as she is human. This realization probably brings with it the recognition that she is also linked to her aunt and to her aunt's experiences and responses. This child now sees that she cannot escape being part of the world with all its faults, peculiarities, strangeness, and wonder.

Several students have told me that reading this poem was a powerful experience for them because they could remember a moment like this when they suddenly began to think of themselves both as a separate "I" and yet as somehow almost frighteningly linked to the adults who had previously seemed to them like another species—all-powerful and all-knowing.

"One Art" (p. 1230)

Like the speaker in the poem, Elizabeth Bishop did live in "three loved houses" (one in Key West and two in Brazil), but, as in the poem, she lost each one of them. This poem seems to me a brave and honest look at loss and at the way we respond both to small losses (door keys, family keepsakes) and to giant losses like the loss of love implied in the final stanza.

The speaker's contention that "the art of losing isn't hard to master" may mean that we are forced to face loss and, therefore, must learn how to do it in order to survive or may mean that what seems like disaster initially turns out, somehow, to be bearable. Whatever the exact meaning, the poem seems to me a courageous salute to the strength of the human spirit.

You may want to point out that in this poem Bishop uses a complicated verse form, the villanelle, with such skill readers are usually not conscious of the tightly controlled structure and rhyme scheme.

GWENDOLYN BROOKS

This collection of Brooks's poetry provides an opportunity for students to look closely at several selections by the same writer and suggest aspects of subject and style that exemplify her work.

You might ask students to read several of these selections and then to work in groups compiling lists that suggest typical aspects of her poetry. When the groups reconvene, ask for comments on their responses to the various aspects that they have identified. After reading the selections in this text, would they choose to read more of Brooks? Why or why not?

In an interview, Brooks states that "what I'm fighting for now in my work [is] an *expression* relevant to all manner of blacks, poems I could take into a tavern, into the street, into the halls of a housing project." As students read, they might consider whether they believe Brooks has fulfilled her goal. Further, they might think about the relevance of her poetry to readers other than those she describes in her statement. Are her poems significant and meaningful for readers who are not black?

Possible aspects of subject and style include the following:

1. Many poems show extraordinary verbal skill, particularly an ability in what Brooks calls "word play."

2. Intricate verse forms are both experimental and yet also use traditional devices such as rhyme.

3. Black dialect and jazz rhythms are combined with traditional poetic diction.

4. Most poems focus on ordinary people in familiar places and circumstances, often looking at the juxtaposition of pain and joy.

"kitchenette building" (p. 1233)

The central image of this poem is the dream, introduced in line 2. The speaker imagines a dream trying to survive while the dreamer is surrounded by old cooking smells and the odor of rotting garbage. The dream takes on a grand persona, becoming a beautiful being who tries to flutter like a delicate bird or butterfly and to sing an aria like a gifted opera singer. But the dreamer cannot take much time to nurture the dream because her thoughts must turn to the daily realities such as dashing into the shared bathroom before all the hot water is used up.

Students who are interested in the "dream" image may want to find a volume of Langston Hughes's poetry and read "Dream Deferred."

"The Mother" (p. 1233)

The images and language in the poem show the speaker's ambivalent feelings about abortion. She believes that her decision was right for her, given her circumstances, yet she does not deny what has been lost through making that choice. Some images suggest her own losses; for example, she has never nursed the "lost babies," and has never had the pleasure of admiring them with a "mother-eye." Other images reflect her understanding of the lives the aborted children will not be able to live. They will never know "lovely loves," "tumults," or "marriages," and they will never giggle, play, or cry. The accumulation of these details suggests that the mother has created in her mind a strong sense of these never-born children and that she holds great love and respect for their potential, never-lived lives.

from "The Womanhood" (p. 1234)

This poem, published in 1949, typifies a theme in many of Brooks's earlier poems. She herself often felt shunned because of her very dark skin, believing that many black men ("bronzy lads") preferred women who, although not white, had lighter skin ("cream-yellow shining"). The second verse suggests the beauty of the dark-skinned woman whose spirit shimmers like silver, yet notes that few prefer the treasure of stars (which show their beauty through darkness) to the more obvious power of the sun, which symbolizes the light-skinned women.

"The Bean Eaters" (p. 1235)

The description of the old couple in this poem gives us intriguing hints of their lives and their selves. Why, for example, are they described as "Mostly Good"? Why does the poet capitalize these two words? What is signified by their persistence in "putting on their clothes / And putting things away"? What are the connotations of the words "twinklings" and "twinges," and what do these two words suggest about the nature of the couple's memories? What is suggested about the couple's life by the list of possessions in the final two lines?

Students may enjoy listing the significant objects that could be found right now in their rooms and speculating on what their list says about their current life.

"the rites for Cousin Vit" (p. 1235)

Although the relationship of the speaker to the deceased may not be of great significance, I was amazed to find that of a group of approximately 100 students who wrote a placement essay on this poem, more than 70 described Vit as the speaker's aunt. A cousin is generally closer to one's own age than is an aunt, and thus the funeral takes on different overtones because the speaker is thinking back over the life of someone of her own generation rather than someone from her parents' generation. The death of a contemporary forces a more painful, direct look at one's own mortality than does the death of someone older.

I also found that many students saw Vit as a rather bad character, citing her frequenting of bars and "love-rooms" as evidence. To me, this reading overlooks the playful and loving tone of the poem as the speaker describes an imagined resurrection. For the speaker, Vit (whose name, of course, comes from the Latin for "life") was a person who was always active, always doing something. The speaker sees Cousin Vit as someone whose spirit cannot be dominated, even by death. Certainly the speaker does not seem in any way to condemn Vit but rather to celebrate the intensity and energy with which she lived her life.

"Of Robert Frost" (p. 1236)

I included this poem, published in 1963, because it relates to another of the three American poets included in this section. With the line "Some glowing in the common blood," Brooks seems to suggest a connection between her own work and Frost's. Students might be asked to identify similar themes, approaches, or philosophical views they discover in the works of the two poets.

Brooks also praises Frost by saying, "He is splendid. With a place to stand." How might students define the "place" where Frost stands? The place where Brooks stands? How are they similar or different?

"Boy Breaking Glass" (p. 1236)

Published in 1968, this poem looks at destruction as a form of creation. The stanzas in quotations seem to be spoken by the artist—the "boy breaking glass."

The final stanza is particularly intriguing. The list of things the artist does not have include two primary symbols of the United States: Congress and the Statue of Liberty, which serve as bookends to enclose a list of pleasures that include the sublime (love) and, by comparison, the ridiculous (lobster, luau, the Regency Room). It seems to me that the speaker annotates the artist's statements about creative destruction by suggesting his alienation and sense of isolation from all that makes up the country in which he lives (the "sloppy amalgamation").

"To the Young Who Want to Die" (p. 1237)

This is one of Brooks's more recent poems, published in 1981. Nearly all students, especially those of traditional college age, find this poem moving and affirming. While the speaker acknowledges the seductive powers of death, she argues passionately for life. She invites those who feel unable to go on to "See what the news is going to be tomorrow." She provides hope and ends with a moving image that urges the young to see green—the symbol of new growth—as their color, and she emphasizes that they must not think of themselves as grass growing on graves, but rather as the renewing green grass of spring.

CONNECTIONS:
ART AND POETRY

As students consider these works, you might ask them first to look at the art that inspired (or was inspired by) the accompanying poem. Ask them to list the details they notice and to make inferences based on what they see. Then ask them to read the poems, noticing new details or different inferences that come to mind. They might keep in mind, also, the list of questions that precedes the Art and Literature section.

Knight, Death, and the Devil, Albrecht Dürer (1471–1528)
"The Knight, Death, and the Devil," Randall Jarrell (1914–1965)

Jarrell provides a twentieth-century look at Dürer's medieval engraving. Dürer shows Death taunting the knight who rides stolidly along, refusing to acknowledge either his own mortality or the ever-present evil that lurks in the form of the Devil.

Jarrell sees Dürer's Death as a "teetotum" (a child's toy) who seems far less menacing than his companion, the Devil. Students may see more threat in death and may also be less apt than Jarrell to interpret the knight's expression as "folds of smiling." Does the knight's persistence in the face of the inevitable represent the strength and conscious resolution suggested by Jarrell's poem? Or does it indicate the human resistance to acknowledging danger and the potential for threat and change? The knight may be intent on reaching the safety of his castle; perhaps he does not even see the strange figures, or perhaps he refuses to admit they are there.

Two Girls, Henri Matisse (1869–1954)
"Matisse: Two Girls," Molly Peacock (1947–)

Peacock's speaker suggests the connection between art and the viewer when she describes the trees as "the tops of old maples," but then quickly adds that in Matisse's painting "They are not maples . . . they are green clouds slashed with brown stripes." Then she asks this significant question: "but don't you like to look / at the places and faces in pictures to find out / where and which you are?"

The speaker at first identifies herself as "the frightened one in blue" and the figure in the yellow dress as the person to whom she addresses the poem. Yet later, as she notices the lack of wine and cigarettes, she says, "it is not us." Continuing her speculations, the speaker ponders her mother's role in the scene she imagines. Perhaps the single place set at the table is for the mother who has not yet had breakfast. She does not hesitate, then, to introduce figures, events, and objects that exist outside the painting to which she is responding.

Details like the exact match between the colors in the window scene and the colors of hair and dress of the woman in blue become the basis for inferences: "Her hair . . . / is the color of the antlered branches / behind her, and her dress matches the sky. What a burden she has to distinguish herself!" Perhaps most memorable in Peacock's poem is the way the speaker moves through various interpretations and possibilities. She does not seek a single correct way of seeing Matisse's work but rather immerses herself in its infinite possibilities. In addition, she sees the painting in personal terms. She does not wonder who Matisse had in mind as he worked but instead considers what she can learn about herself as she responds to his *Two Girls, Red and Green Background*.

The Starry Night, Vincent van Gogh (1853–1890)
"The Starry Night," Anne Sexton (1928–1975)

Sexton chooses as an epigraph for her poem a line from one of van Gogh's letters. In it, he suggests that, for him, going out into the night to paint the stars is comparable to a religious experience. Sexton's poem reflects the sense of spiritual exaltation suggested by van Gogh's painting. She sees the night sky as overwhelming, awesome, and yet also offering deliverance. Her poem is filled with female images (a tree looks like a "drowned woman" and the moon seems about to give birth). Sexton sees the magnificent swirling star masses as a serpent or a "great dragon" that she may regard with fear but also sees as a glorious means to leave her earthly life.

The Lady of Shalott, William Holman Hunt (1827–1910)
"The Lady of Shalott," Alfred, Lord Tennyson (1809–1892)

Painting in response to Tennyson's poem, Hunt envisions the lady turning from her mirror and struggling to free herself from the threads of her weaving. While the poem does not show her physically caught by the weaving, certainly Tennyson's images suggest that she is mystically held back by her lonely occupation. Hunt also suggests the forces that may pull at the lady. On one side is an image of the virgin, kneeling in devoted prayer, while on the other a male figure stands waiting as he plucks fruit from a tree. The lady, then, hears the call of the contemplative, spiritual life but also longs for the world of humans and, perhaps, for romantic connection with the brave and handsome Lancelot.

The Kermess, **Pieter Brueghel, the Elder (1520–1569)**
"The Dance," William Carlos Williams (1883–1963)

Brueghel's painting captures a group of lively, lusty peasants dancing the Kermess at a country fair. Participants in this dance join hands and form an ever-expanding circle as they weave in and out, welcoming new participants. Students will be quick to notice the marvelous rhythm of the poem, which captures the energy and joy conveyed in Brueghel's painting. The enjambed lines and, particularly, the repetition in the final line suggest the movement of the dancers as they "go round and / around."

This poem must be read aloud!

I Saw the Figure 5 in Gold, **Charles Henry Demuth (1883–1935)**
"The Great Figure," William Carlos Williams (1883–1963)

Williams's poem inspired *I Saw the Figure 5 in Gold* which Demuth completed in 1928 as a symbolic portrait of the poet. Students enjoy finding the clues Demuth provided, including the initials "W.C.W," and the names "Carlos" and "Bill." Demuth uses lettering reminiscent of advertising billboards to create this painting, which is one of his "poster portraits." The figure 5 dominates the painting as well as the poem; Demuth's repetition of the 5 echoes Williams's "gong clangs" and "siren howls" and, in addition, suggests the staccato rhythm of the poem. The squared-off red forms in the painting bring to mind the fire truck while the white circles remind the viewer of the lights (perhaps street lights?) of the poem's second line.

Landscape with the Fall of Icarus, **Pieter Brueghel, the Elder (1520–1569)**
"Musée des Beaux Arts," W. H. Auden (1907–1973)

Because the reproduced painting is so small, students may have trouble seeing the small, struggling figure of Icarus in the corner of the painting, just below the ship. Of course, Icarus's smallness is significant. Auden's poem introduces Icarus only at the beginning of the second stanza, suggesting that Brueghel's Icarus serves as a symbol representing the theme of the first stanza: the Old Master painters truly understood suffering. In the second stanza, Auden explains what he believes Brueghel's painting tells us about suffering. We all must somehow bear our troubles and tragedies alone. The world goes on—the plowman plows and the ship sails away—even as Icarus experiences both loss of pride and loss of life.

It may be interesting for students to speculate on the reason Auden titles his poem with the name of a museum rather than the name of Brueghel's painting. (Possibly he did it to emphasize that he sees this painting as representative of the vision of the Old Masters—not just of Brueghel.)

Two Chained Monkeys, Pieter Brueghel, the Elder (1520–1569)
"Brueghel's Two Monkeys" Wislawa Szymborska (1923–)

Szymborska's poem evokes the common dream of taking an exam for which one is not prepared. In his dream, the two monkeys of Brueghel's painting seem to be both the subject of the exam and the professor. As the speaker tries desperately to find an answer for the test in the course, "History of Mankind," one of the monkeys provides a hint "with a gentle / clinking of his chain." Perhaps the monkey suggests both the origin of humankind and the lack of freedom most humans experience.

The Love Letter, Jan Vermeer (1632–1675)
"When a Woman Holds a Letter," Sandra Nelson (1951–)

You may want to point out that the title of the poem is also its first line. Students should enjoy speculating on the sender of the letter and on the recipient's response. Nelson's poem suggests that the woman may have received a note from a lover—possibly a secret lover, since she looks "up to heaven to see / if anyone is watching." After offering this observation, however, Nelson introduces another possibility. Perhaps instead of looking (with guilt?) toward God, the woman gazes toward her female servant. Might she be a confidant? Even a go-between? Or does the letter recipient simply seek the comfort of sharing her secret with another woman?

The Breakfast Room, Pierre Bonnard (1867–1947)
"Breakfast Room," Eamon Grennan (1941–)

I think the phrase "the words" in the first line refers to "breakfast room." Grennan suggests with the first stanza's images of delicious intimacy that the idea of a breakfast room has always evoked for him a warm and familiar, yet somehow sensual, space. Here the ritual of eating the first meal of the day together both restores lovers to their everyday world and reassures them of the privacy of their connection with each other.

In the second stanza, Grennan lists the details of Bonnard's breakfast room, creating with words the color and light of the painting. He sees in the half-hidden female figure someone who is both somewhat disillusioned (asking "You think this / changes anything?") yet also hopeful (preserving the "sense that things / are about to achieve / illumination"). The rest of the poem suggests a feeling I often have about paintings—that they remain forever wonderfully ambiguous, giving me the impression that, as I look at the details and figures, I am "on the brink of something / always edging / into shape, about to happen."

The Nighthawks, Edward Hopper (1882–1967)
"A Midnight Diner by Edward Hopper," David Ray
"Nighthawks," Samuel Yellen (1906–   )

Reading both Ray's and Yellen's poems provides students with the opportunity to compare the different responses works of art can evoke. Seeing the distinct vision and power of each poem should underline the point that there is no single "correct" response to art.

The point of view in each poem is startlingly different. Yellen's poem describes the diner, places the viewer/reader in the scene itself, peering through the glass. Then the speaker speculates about the dark and lonely lives of each nighthawk, ending with the concluding paragraph that sees the viewer/reader as taking pleasure from the nighthawks' pain. He proposes that we are satisfied with the painting because we see our own lives to be so much better than those depicted.

Ray, on the other hand, describes a museum-goer (the "Madman" of line 12) who seeks out the paintings of classical beauty yet on leaving the museum purchases only a postcard reproducing Hopper's Nighthawks. Rather than envisioning the viewer as taking pleasure from invidious comparison of his own life with the life of Hopper's people, the speaker suggests that the "Madman" identifies with the "man trapped at midnight underneath the El." Here the viewer is fascinated by likeness rather than by difference.

Bowling Match at Castlemary, Cloyne, 1847, Daniel MacDonald (1821–1853)
"After Viewing The Bowling Match at Castlemary, Cloyne," Greg Delanty

Students should enjoy speculating about the speaker's relationship with the person who viewed the painting with him. I think the speaker is male and his companion a woman—perhaps his wife or lover. He indicates a joking rivalry with the bowler whose shirt is open and whose trousers are "as indecently tight as a baseballer's." The speaker compares the response of the crowd to MacDonald's bowler with the response he imagines in himself and his companion. If they should go out into the countryside to watch Sunday bowlers, they would be able to put aside for the moment the cares and worries of their lives. The spectators in the painting (which was completed in 1847) lived in a country beset with famine and with the massive emigration of many, especially young men and women. Yet caught at this moment, the bowler suggests a sense of strength and power that no doubt evoked pride and hope in those who watched him.

Crucifixion, Jacopo Tintoretto (1518–1594)
"Before an Old Painting of the Crucifixion," N. Scott Momaday
   (1934–   )

Momaday's view of this painting of the crucifixion should evoke
great controversy in discussion. The painting shows Christ at the center,
surrounded by both his enemies and those who mourn him. Momaday's
response suggests a view of hopelessness and despair. The speaker
claims "The Passion wanes into oblivion," yet simply by the existence
of the painting and of this poem, that line seems to be contradicted. In
the final stanza, the speaker says, "the human act / Outrageous is in
vain." I am not entirely sure to what "human act" he refers. Is it the act
of the Roman soldiers who have crucified Christ? Or is it the "human
act" of Christ (in corporeal form) accepting his
fate?

Walking Man, Alberto Giacometti (1901–1966)
Giacometti, Richard Wilbur (1921–   )

You may need to help students see the way this poem falls into two
sections: lines 1–29, which describe the speaker's discomfort with
statues of humans that are sculpted from rock; and lines 30–60, which
contrast the speaker's response to Giacometti's bronze sculpture,
Walking Man. The speaker sees the tall, thin figure as capturing
perfectly the sense he has to being "unspeakably alone." Particularly
powerful is the speaker's description of Giacometti's man as an
anonymous figure who can hide nothing; his "fullness is escaped/Like a
burst balloon's: no nakedness so bare/As flesh gone inquiring of the
bone."

The Old Guitarist, **Pablo Picasso (1881–1973)**
Blue Air, **Robert Motherwell (1915– 1991)**
"The Man with the Blue Guitar," Wallace Stevens (1879–1955)

Stevens's poem must be read aloud. The rhythms, rhymes,
assonance, onomatopoeia, and alliteration provide a sound track that
brings a new dimension to Picasso's guitarist.
   The first stanza of the poem puzzles me. The guitar player is
described as "A shearsman of sorts." Is he someone who shears sheep?
Or do the angles of his body suggest the shearing breakage of surfaces
that move away from one another? Or does the somewhat mystical
guitarist who does not "play things as they are" shear the listeners
away from the world as they expect it to be?
   You may want to mention to students that only the first four stanzas
of Stevens's very long poem are reprinted here. Some may wish to read
the entire work.

Robert Motherwell's painting responds both to Picasso's work and to Stevens's poem. His composition seems to be based on the human figure, but it has been transformed into geometric shapes, suggesting, as does Stevens's poem, the disjunction from what we call "reality" that Picasso's guitarist evokes.